D1761374

9510000137237

Night Fighter Navigator

Night Fighter Navigator

Beaufighters and Mosquitos

in World War II

Dennis Gosling DFC

Pen & Sword
AVIATION

First published in Great Britain in 2010 by
Pen & Sword Aviation
An imprint of
Pen & Sword Books Ltd
47 Church Street
Barnsley
South Yorkshire
S70 2AS

ISBN 978 184884 1888

A CIP catalogue record for this book is
available from the British Library

Printed and bound in England
By CPI UK

Pen & Sword Books Ltd incorporates the Imprints of Pen & Sword Aviation,
Pen & Sword Family History, Pen & Sword Maritime, Pen & Sword Military,
Wharncliffe Local History, Pen & Sword Select, Pen & Sword Military Classics,
Leo Cooper, Seaforth Publishing and Frontline Publishing

For a complete list of Pen & Sword titles please contact
PEN & SWORD BOOKS LIMITED
47 Church Street, Barnsley, South Yorkshire, S70 2AS, England
E-mail: enquiries@pen-and-sword.co.uk
Website: www.pen-and-sword.co.uk

Gray's Elegy brought the poet Thomas Gray (1716–1771) worldwide acclaim. Less well known was this short but prophetic poem he wrote in 1737, which became uncannily accurate in the Second World War over two centuries later.

The day will come when thou shalt lift thine eye

To watch a long-drawn battle of the skies.

Aged peasants, too amazed for words, stare at the flying fleets

Of wondrous birds.

And England, so long mistress of the sea

Where wind and waves confess her sovereignty

Her ancient triumphs yet on high shall bear

And reign the sovereign of the conquered air.

Acknowledgements

To Maxine Downes who was the saviour of my sanity when my malevolent computer was playing games with me, sent emails for me, printed dozens of manuscripts and was always at my beck and call.

To Jane Hutchings, the first to make me realise that my tome could have a wider appeal than the circle of relatives and friends for whom I had originally intended it.

To Graham Woodford, my friend who helped me in so many ways.

To Barry Crabtree, my son-in-law, whose journalistic experience and contacts were invaluable to me in a field into which I had never before ventured.

To Pen & Sword who dared to publish a war book that was different from the norm and led me through the intricacies of a literary contract.

To all those good people I had carefully selected to give me a cross section of the public who read and reported their opinion of each chapter as I completed it.

Last, but by no means least to my beloved late wife and Mum and Dad, of whose presence at my side I was always keenly aware. Their love gave 'Our Dennis' strength to carry on when I sometimes flagged.

My grateful thanks to you all.

Contents

Dedication

To my dear Mum and Dad who unstintingly gave me their all, loved me so much and strived so hard to make me what I am. I shall never be able to repay them. I can only say 'I tried'.

Dennis Gosling

Foreword

So many people have urged me to put my wartime memories on paper. They say that later generations should know what war meant to an ordinary young man from a working class background. For you to understand and appreciate that our life and times – indeed the world's – were so different from today I must, as they say, 'set the scene'.

I shall try to tell it just as it was, 'warts 'n' all' – how it seemed to me as it happened. I promise every word is true – I will not change anything for dramatic effect. My aim is for you to walk with me through those fateful days – to share my life as I lived it. To laugh with me and perhaps cry with me.

The only exception is that I have altered some names – not many but a few – so that I do not embarrass them or more likely their families. After all these years most have passed on.

So that is it! My hope is to bring those long gone days back to life. If I do I know you will enjoy this read.

CHAPTER ONE

Ah Yes, I Remember it Well!

I was born on Friday 13 May 1921, the son of Grace and William Gosling at 8.00 am. There was great rejoicing as I was the only child amongst the three Ogley sisters. Ethel (always known as Polly) was the eldest Ogley sister and Grandma Ogley lived with her and her husband Uncle Tom. Grace and Elsie were always together and known as 'the twins' although there was eighteen months between them. Of course, I was undoubtedly spoiled!

Dad had served in the Great War with the King's Own Yorkshire Light Infantry in France and Italy as a machine-gunner. He never spoke of the war but was always ready to tell of his visits to foreign parts, particularly Venice. Folks just did not go abroad in those days! Their lives revolved around their families, their jobs and their hometown.

Mum was a truly amazing woman. She was born with a dislocated hip but she never complained. She always said 'can't' was not a word – if you were determined nothing was impossible and of that belief she was the living proof. She was the epitome of thrift – a word now sadly lost it seems! On a bus driver's wages of £2 a week, she bought a new house and was berated by her mother as the first in their family to go into debt – with the Halifax. When Dad went to war she went back to work at the Co-op Tailoring Department. She rarely spoke of the war, but when she did it was of her sadness that a young man from work had been conscripted and later shot as a deserter. She said 'We never thought the army would take him, he was too small to carry a backpack poor lad.' She spoke of many friends who had received the dreaded telegram informing them that their husband, son or brother was killed or missing in action, or of the Zeppelin raids or the drastic food rationing. But she laughed that she could not stop her legs going from hours of foot treadling the sewing machine at work even when in bed – dislocated hip and all!

Dad was a tram driver and then a bus driver and later a trolley bus driver. He was teetotal, a non-smoker and was proud that he always handed Mum his wage packet unopened. When he came back from the war he wanted to start a family. Mum's disability was clearly a problem – she was up against all the odds – but as ever she duly delivered (this time literally).

I am told I was a sweet child, well behaved, polite, with fair, blond, curly hair. My mother's friend Nellie French, a well known local artist and photographer, painted a picture of me as 'Bubbles' complete with a clay pipe and soap suds, which was exhibited for years in the Doncaster Art Gallery. When I started school at the infants in Wood Street I was unmercifully teased about it by my classmates!

We then moved from Ravensworth Road to Catherine Street, which was also a terraced house but had no steps for Mum's hip and was also on the Hyde Park tram route.

I vividly recall the joys of potty training and Mum's efforts to get me to have an afternoon nap so that Dad could see more of me. She tried everything, reading to me, cuddling me on the settee but best of all she would play hymns on the upright piano in the front room. She was a Wesleyan and I can remember those hymns to this day – eighty years on. I loved them all and she would tell me about God's goodness and his love for everyone in the world. It was my grounding in religion and I have tried to live my life by her tenets ever since.

When Dad was on 'split duty' he had to get up at 4 am to take the miners to work to the various coal mining villages around Doncaster. He then came home and took me in my pushchair round Elmfield Park before returning to fetch them back. Once he did not report for duty and it was 11.00 am before they found him at the bottom of one of the massive pits under the buses at the depot where he had fallen in the dark!

Mum decided that gas light was not good for my eyes and so we became the first household in the street to have electric lights. Neighbours and friends came to see and 'wonder at it!' They all wanted to know how costly it would be to install and run but Mum said money didn't count – it was for 'Our Dennis'.

Christmas was a magical time for much longer than it is now. Those beautiful illusions of childhood were protected assiduously by the grown ups who would shush anyone who looked like 'giving the game away'.

I remember trying to stay awake to see Santa but waking up to find he had been and there was the familiar pillowcase hung up at the foot of the bed. I was a lucky boy for in it was my main present – a clockwork Hornby train set or a small Meccano set. Then came a colourful musical top, a sugar mouse, biscuits in a tin box, a pop-up book, a colouring book, a bag of chocolate gold foil-covered coins and an apple and orange. After breakfast I had to visit all our relatives who gave me an apple and orange, perhaps more chocolate coins or cigars and a sixpenny piece. It was all breathtakingly wonderful.

Then the Gosling boys gathered at Grandma and Grandad Goslings for Christmas dinner. Uncle Percy always came up from London. He was my hero because as a Grenadier Guardsman he had brought the first Uhlan (Cavalry) helmet back from the war. He was a Police Sergeant and played piccolo in the Metropolitan Police Band. He looked most incongruous with his size and waxed moustache and the tiny instrument. There was Dad and Uncle Harry, who played clarinet, and finally there was Charlie who was a baritone of some note and his wife Auntie May who was an ALCM, LRAM and a wonderful pianist.

After dinner we all repaired to the front room and spent the evening laughing and singing together. Everyone did their bit. We had carols, hymns, popular songs of the times and tunes from light operas. We walked home at midnight, hoarse with singing but utterly content. I had to be carried half asleep and after being undressed Mum would make sure that when I said my prayers I remembered those not as fortunate as we were. With all the expensive 'must have' gizmos kids demand for Christmas now I suspect these prayers are just as relevant today – but rarely, if ever, said.

So life meandered along at an almost bucolic pace. I had left the infants school in Wood Street and I was now at the British (Beechfield School) with the 'big' boys. It was a big brick Victorian building in Chequer Road. I remember my teacher – a certain Miss Todd (who I liked so much that I remembered her in my nightly prayers) reading Rudyard Kipling's *Jungle Book* whilst another class in the Hall practised singing 'Green Sleeves'. Although worlds apart (Mowgli was obviously Indian and the song redolent of rustic England) they seemed somehow right together – quintessentially, well, British! The Empire and all that! I suppose in a way we were being indoctrinated.

At playtime we were let out into the school yard. In summer we played with homemade marble sallies and snobs. In autumn we played conkers. In winter we snowballed and made slides. The biggest was frightening as it ended against the perimeter wall. What would the Health & Safety idiots have made of that today? Even the conkers would be banned. Yet we survived.

Then into my childhood idyll came tragedy. Auntie Polly collapsed and died visiting Grandpa Ogley's grave. Then Auntie Elsie and Uncle Ted adopted a boy called Peter and thereafter we were brought up like brothers. Then barely a year later Grandma Ogley passed away – they said she died of broken heart. The idyll was suddenly over and I became aware that life could be cruel. No one or nothing had ever been cruel to me before. I felt I was growing up. When I won a scholarship to the Grammar School I knew the old life was gone for ever.

CHAPTER TWO

Gathering Clouds

I had been born into the post-war depression when life was hard for everyone. The pit communities were the longest and hardest hit. It was a time of grinding poverty and the end of all illusions of a better world for returning heroes. Was this how the country rewarded the appalling sacrifices that had touched virtually every family in the land – sometimes twice, thrice or more times? Fathers and mothers often gave their starving children what little food they had and went without themselves. No wonder men lost their self respect and dignity. When the miners from Jarrow marched to London to lobby parliament the whole working classes supported them. The Government belatedly offered some help but it was via the demeaning and hated 'means test'.

Working on the buses, Dad was on short time because the pits were shut but he was never on strike. He helped Uncle Ted who was a miner at Brodsworth to get Saturday work as a conductor. This at least meant Auntie Elsie never had to pick coal off the pit tip as hundreds of other wives did using the babies' prams as barrows. Mum felt deep compassion for them and prayed that God would bring happiness to all who were suffering such injustices.

Eventually the Depression began to recede and the working classes unsurprisingly turned to pacifism and dubious political parties like Sir Oswald Mosley's Blackshirts. Strangely, few turned to Communism (except perhaps in academia). Mainly there came a 'them and us' attitude of deep resentment. 'They' had not suffered the same deprivation because 'they' were well to do. I remember pressing my nose against posh hotel windows to marvel at what the other half were eating whilst we were lucky to be in back street 'digs' for a precious and I may say very happy week! 'They' were seen in the movies immaculately dressed, doing the 'Charleston' and 'Black Bottom', drinking wine and driving Rolls-Royces. The working class identified themselves more with 'All Quiet on the Western Front' and its tragic German anti-hero. We escaped our humdrum existence by watching glitzy Hollywood musical extravaganzas not knowing they too were a travesty of American real life.

Some of these feelings rubbed off on me of course. True I was young but I was at a formative age and I had heard and seen it all happening around me. For example, I remember the Christmas assembly at school when the poorest boy was given a pair of boots donated by some unnamed benefactor. I felt so sorry for the lad because he had ringworm and was the 'Nit Nurse's' best customer. Mum was terrified I might be sat next to him in class! Some of Mum's compassion must have rubbed off on me too.

I passed the exam for Grammar School in 1932, which meant staying on till sixteen instead of fourteen. Mum and Dad did not know if they could afford such a luxury. Mum, once again, decided that nothing was too good for 'Our Dennis'. Bless her, the cost of uniform (including a straw boater for summer term), gym kit, football togs, cricket whites, satchel and all my scholastic accoutrements must have taxed her budget of £3 a week to the limit.

Recently I was touched to find a letter from my headmaster they had kept in their old tin top hat box thanking them for the interest they had shown in my education and wishing 'a dear little boy who I shall miss' further success in the future. This was long before Parent/Teacher Associations began!

Doncaster Grammar School was in transition from having live-in boarders to ordinary day pupils. It was an old school with a splendid assembly hall over old stone-floored open cloisters and was extremely proud of its illustrious past. Four of the masters retained their WWI ranks.

The day began with assembly in the Great Hall with its choir gallery and stage. We sang patriotic songs like 'I vow to thee my country' as the Head Master led the procession of Masters in their mortar boards and multi-coloured gowns onto the stage. After prayers and notices we went to our various classrooms. Physics, science, art, Latin, geography, French and history were taught in brick buildings. Biology, English, maths and divinity were taught in wooden WWI huts. Gym was in the assembly hall.

The impact of such a diverse new curriculum in my first year bewildered me and I excelled only in art and English. However, on Tuesday and Thursday afternoons we played football or cricket or cross-country running. We had school on Saturday morning and in the afternoon inter-school games. Although I was small I always made the school teams. The drawback was I couldn't watch Donny Rovers. From a tot Dad had carried me down to Belle Vue on his shoulders. Spectators then passed you over their heads to the front so that you missed none of the action.

Best of all when on the playing fields (which only recently were known as the Corn Fields and actually grew corn) was watching the bi-plane Handley Page Heyfords, the new monoplane Wellesley based at RAF Finningley and various other types visiting this new Expansion Scheme Aerodrome.

There was also much activity at Doncaster Civil Airport from privately owned Swifts, Gulls, Moths and the local taxi hire firm to the daily visit of the two or three-engined KLM Fokkers on their scheduled airline flights from the continent to Leeds. Once a year Sir Alan Cobham brought his famous Flying Circus of stunt flyers and wing walkers. For a week Doncastrians had a permanent crick in their necks looking up to identify and/or wonder at Auto Gyros or Flying Fleas, Monospars or DH Dragons, or the re-enactment of WWI aerial battles using obsolescent military types like Bristol Fighters, DH9as (Nineacks) or Avro 504s – and of course the Auxiliary Squadron came in eventually. I think it fair to say that the most avid sky watchers were we Danensians on our playing field.

My school results improved somewhat as I adapted to the variety and complexity of the subjects. Latin was definitely a 'no-no'. I really could not see the point outside of its derivational uses. Trigonometry was not much better. Geometry made some sense but its uses seemed minimal. However, I did manage to scrape together a sufficient basis for me somewhat reluctantly to set my sights on becoming a doctor but only after my parents dissuaded me from more colourful callings like the Merchant Navy and the Hong Kong police force. It was the only one that would accept five foot four inch recruits.

Meanwhile, the outlook in Europe was bleak. Germany was clearly becoming a problem again. Hitler showed two fingers of derision to the United Nations in Geneva and the Versailles Treaty. Once again it had a large new Air Force and Army and their new pocket battleships became a credible threat to European navies. Some people began to feel that British determination never to go to war again was destined to prove as illusory as all the other post-war hopes and dreams. There was still a hard core of pacifists and appeasers. Anything but war! Surely the Germans would not want that either. Meanwhile, rearmament slowly began to spread to the rest of Europe.

In my last year at Grammar School I suffered a terrible blow. I got Nephritis and passed pints of blood through my kidneys. I not only missed my Matriculation Exams but for the foreseeable future we were told studying was out. Mum and Dad must have been devastated; all their sacrifice for nothing!

After the initial shock I went into a period that I find difficult to describe. My first reaction was anger – fate had conspired to rob me. This was followed by excesses of the emotions that are common to all teenagers, surging wildly from one extreme to the other. There were no greys in between, black to white, right to wrong, astronomical highs to the blackest depressions. Mum and Dad could not understand how their angelic child had somehow become a rebellious mixed up – well, let's face it – pain in the backside. Yet deep down there was so much insecurity. I tried to hide it by assuming the mantle of an extrovert. Even to this day I still fear someone or something will take away all that I hold dear and I would be unable to do a damn thing about it.

CHAPTER THREE

The Impending Storm

I became an Old Danensian (former pupil of the Grammar School) in 1937, not long after being medically disbarred from attaining my goal. Nevertheless, it was a fine school and its educational excellences have stood me in good stead throughout my life. For now, however, I perceived myself as a failure. Perversely this made me even more determined to prove to myself and my parents that I was capable of achieving distinction in some other way.

I had obtained work at the Co-op Tailoring Department in Station Road. My aim was to become a cutter and buyer and to this end the Co-op financed two half days at the Technical College, which at that time was quite exceptional. I flung myself into my studies – this could be my opportunity. By 1939 the Co-op was negotiating a scholarship for me at the London School of Economics. It was almost finalised when my jinx struck again – with the outbreak of war.

This time it really came as no surprise. Hitler had gone on his wilful way annexing land and breaking treaties regardless of the possible consequences. The newsreels were full of him ranting and raving at vast military gatherings – which I had to admit were most impressive. The supposed intelligentsia of our country were even more impressed it seemed. Some openly averred that we would inevitably lose if a war came. Some openly praised Nazi principles and how Hitler had resurrected Germany. Almost all overtly or covertly, favoured appeasement.

To a naïve youth from the sticks their views were appalling, even traitorous. I had been brought up to believe in honesty and decency, truth and an almost reverential pride in my country and the Empire. We had sung 'Fight the good fight with all thy might' at school and it looked as if we would be called upon to do just that. To do less would be shameful – unthinkable.

Poor hapless Mr Chamberlain flew to Munich to speak directly to Hitler but few believed he could achieve a just settlement. On his return he brandished a piece of paper declaring 'Peace in our time'. The country's reaction can be best summed up in two words – 'Oh yeah?' True it was an Americanism but nothing could be more apt.

So we carried on with our lives as best we could trying desperately to maintain some semblance of normality. I joined 'The Greyfriars' amateur theatricals and

Uncle Charlie and Auntie May's Concert Party. But it all seemed inconsequential. Indeed, everything seemed pointless. We were simply passing time waiting for the big event. It came as not so much as a blow – more as a relief. Now at last we could hold our heads high.

We had good reason to be cynical, for the last four years we had betrayed country after country starting with Sudetenland followed by Austria and most disgracefully of all poor, hapless Czechoslovakia. We had sacrificed them trying to appease Hitler, hoping that by satisfying him we might avoid becoming embroiled in another world conflict ourselves. Our politicians had lost all sense of decency, justice, honour, dignity and pride in their desperation. To be honest they were only reflecting the mood of the generation who knew the tragic sacrifice of their men folk had been for nothing – for them the 1920s and 1930s were convincing proof of the futility of war. Britain was exhausted, not cowardly, not gutless, just plain tired.

There was also the other tyrant, Mussolini. Italy had been our ally in WWI but it was patently obvious that the peacock of Rome was an ardent admirer of Hitler. He aped his gesturing and showmanship and even outdid him with his flamboyancy and braggadocio. Worse still he emulated his idol and mentor by invading Abyssinia and Rumania – bare faced lying and deviousness was endemic in his way of life.

The Spanish Civil War offered Germany a golden opportunity to evolve new techniques, blood their pilots and evaluate the capabilities of their aircraft. It foretold the forthcoming horrors of aerial destruction with the razing of the defenceless Guernica. It also brought a third dictator into the equation – General Franco. This posed another problem, would he feel obliged to reward his erstwhile allies by blockading Gibraltar? Mussolini had already claimed the Med as his sea, his Mare Nostrum, so our routes through the Suez Canal to India, Australia and New Zealand would be much longer if we had to go via the Cape of South Africa.

Imagine if you can, the strain of living through the stress of such threatening times. Each day seemed to bring another blow not least to our pride. Here we were, the head of the world's greatest empire yet cringing before these tyrants. To the young folk it was humiliating but our elders lived in dread and fear. We carried on our lives as best we could with the Sword of Damocles hanging over us. I joined Uncle Charlie and Auntie May's concert party and the Greyfriars Amateur Dramatic Society where I first became aware of girls and there were some crackers in the troupe. It all seemed inconsequential and pointless.

We were simply passing the time away waiting for the big event, which came more as a relief than a blow. At last the nightmare was over and we had a chance to fight these evils. At last we could hold up our heads!

CHAPTER FOUR

'The Day War Broke Out' – Rob Wilton (popular wartime comedian)

I lay snuggled in my warm and cosy bed. To my mind nothing comes close to a feather bed for sheer indulgence. I had enjoyed a lovely evening at the Gaumont Cinema with a girl friend, walked her back to her home in Hexthorpe as a gentleman did in those days, then walked to my home in Carr House Road. I was not too upset that I had missed the last trolley bus as the evening had already cost me two shillings and sixpence including the quarter-pound Dairy Box and that was a third of my weekly spending money. I went to the larder where I knew Mum would have left me the rest of the rice pudding from lunch as I had to work through on Saturdays. It was ice cold and delicious, especially the brown skin she knew was my favourite.

So I lay abed in a state of blissful content. Something, however, was niggling me. I could not think what it was so I nestled deeper into my cocoon. But the feeling of unease persisted like before an exam or waiting to go on stage in a play. Then Mum came in with a cup of tea and some toast. She opened the curtains and let the bright autumn sun flood in. I blinked, rubbed my eyes and sat up. 'Chamberlain is coming on the wireless soon', she said. So *that* was what was unsettling me. Of course we had given the Germans a twenty-four-hour ultimatum to get out of Poland or we would honour our treaty with them and declare war. At last the worm was threatening to turn.

I was out of bed like a shot. This was going to be *it*! At long last the truth had dawned on our Government. In ten fateful minutes it was over. God alone knew what atrocities the Germans had committed against the populations of the states they had overrun and now they had chosen the time to suit their own vicious vile ends.

You could not help but feel for our Prime Minister. He was a decent, honourable man, but he was also a politician. In pandering to the voluble millions who wanted peace he failed to understand that did not mean at *any* price. This became evident by the way they responded when the chips were down. He had been weak and gullible. Clearly he had been a disaster diplomatically – Hitler had run rings round him!

Worse still he had neglected our Armed Forces so badly that only time would tell if we would be able to defend ourselves. Sorry for him or not he was plainly not the man whom we could trust to inspire and mobilise the nation. What was needed now was a leader with a strong will and iron resolve. At this moment no one knew where he would come from. But cometh the day cometh the man so the old adage goes and so it would prove to be – but not for sometime yet.

When the broadcast ended Mum was in tears. She knew that I would be caught up in the coming maelstrom. On the other hand I was almost jubilant. This was typical of the difference between those who remembered the carnage of the last war and those who with all the naivety of youth were excited by the prospect of a great adventure. But everyone was apprehensive about the future. They recalled those H.G. Wells dramatic films depicting massed bomber raids paralysing whole cities with lethal gas bombs. Food rationing, blackouts, gas masks, air raid shelters, Identity Cards, petrol rationing and dozens of other unfamiliar things were already upon us.

However, there was universal relief that the ignominies that had been heaped upon us were now over. No longer would Hitler be allowed to humiliate us before the whole world – the Great British Empire – the greatest Empire ever – could once more hold up its head that had so long hung in shame. We had no doubt that the Empire and the Colonies would stand with us. And they did – *magnificently.*

I had my Sunday lunch and then went outside to black the headlights on Dad's Ford Popular car to make them comply with the new regulations and took it to Archie Griggs who worked with me at the Co-op but had been appointed an Air Raid Warden. This entitled him to a certain amount of deference from lesser mortals. I was surprised to find he knew little more than I did but 'guessed' it would be OK.

After Sunday high tea I went to the Baptist Church where I sang in the choir and later went to meet another workmate, my best pal Fred Hardy. We went to the Hyde Park Tavern and ordered two halves of bitter, which scarcely qualified us as seasoned topers but made us seem more mature – we hoped! He was four years older than me and reputed to be the best dancer at Buller's Dance Hall, which made him attractive to the girls. As my own feet seemed out of my control when I took to the floor I envied him but he was limited by his handicaps – he had carrot-coloured hair and glasses as thick as the bottom of a jam jar.

Naturally we talked of the war – everyone in the pub was probably doing the same. To my surprise I found Fred in no way shared my enthusiasm. He was of a timid nature and viewed the future with great trepidation. He realised that his eyesight would exclude him from active service – he would have no adventures like his mates to impress the girls. For once I was no longer envious – I had never considered that the war might bring parity in the romantic stakes. What a bonus!

And so to bed, where derring deeds of do predominated. Suffice it to say that in my dreams I outdid any comic strip heroes I had read about so avidly as a teenager!

CHAPTER FIVE

The Phoney War

The day after the declaration of hostilities was marked by a complete lack of any sign of hostile intent. True our friend in Birmingham had caused some hilarity when she told how her husband on retiring had opened the bedroom curtains and shouted 'They are here, thousands of them and they have all got their lights on'. She rushed to the window. 'Don't be so daft,' she said 'those are the stars!' There is a tragic postscript to the tale. A WWI comrade of Dad's, he worked as a night sorter and later in the war he saw there was an air raid on the part of the city where they lived. The trams stopped in an air raid so fearing for his wife's safety he ran all the way home where he collapsed and died of a heart attack. His last words were 'Thank God you are all right Nellie.'

In Doncaster in those days everyone greeted you with a cheery word or a wave. We pretty well knew all who worked in the town centre. It was our 'village'. Donny was known as 'Poor, Proud and Pretty' and we were inordinately proud of its reputation. We made the world's fastest steam engines, we made confectionery with a countrywide reputation and there was our famous racecourse – home of the St Leger Classic. Of course we had other attributes too numerous to mention. All in all it was a good place to live in and we were generally content with our lot, except we young ones felt we were stuck in a rut. Sons followed their fathers into the plant works or some other old established firm or predominantly into the pits. Boring, boring!

Well all that would obviously change now. No one knew what fate had in store and that was exciting! The Army was already in France together with a strong RAF contingent and it looked set to become a static trench war like the first. There were some significant differences however – notably the mobility of armoured forces and the effect of modern air power, although we were out-numbered and inferior to the Germans according to the press. We held a significant superiority at sea despite the new German so-called 'Pocket' battleships but U-boats and air power might change the balance.

That the Italians did not declare war rather took us by surprise, but their demeanour was belligerent and far from reassuring and no amount of propaganda could disguise our unpreparedness or their thirst for territorial expansion.

Under our declaration of solidarity with the Poles we had been forced into war by the German invasion when patently we were unable to assist them in any way because of our geographic position and with the Russian pact with Germany over the carve-up of Poland all hope of any meaningful intervention finally disappeared. However, it unmistakably declared to the world that we were still the champions of the underdog and prepared to fight for a just cause.

The Germans, meanwhile, were busy overrunning Poland. Despite their enormous numerical superiority on the ground and in the air they used all the stratagems they had honed in the Spanish Civil War.

Defenceless Warsaw was mercilessly bombed as Guernica had been for frightfulness was part of their strategy. Old men, women and children were slaughtered as part of their pitiless design. This was the new face of war, total, cynical, brutal and cruel but Teutonically efficient. When the strains of The Warsaw Concerto finally died from their defiant radio station we knew their gallant struggle was lost.

So now we knew that Hitler would turn his attention to us. We had not totally wasted this respite; Anderson Air Raid Shelters had been distributed on a priority basis. These were curved corrugated sheets you buried half into the ground and then put the displaced soil on top and they proved effective against all but direct hits.

We were also exhorted to 'Dig for Victory!' Our lovely lawns were to become vegetable patches and the wireless gave copious recipes for housewives to prepare or preserve our crops – remember that in those days there were no fridges. Some ideas were good but others ranged from the bizarre to the downright hilarious. There was no denying that food was becoming a worry for during the Polish campaign the U-boats had been taking a dreadful toll on our shipping. We had insufficient forces to protect our convoys, especially in mid-Atlantic and there was a real danger that starvation might become our Achilles' heel.

The RAF was even more ill prepared for not only were we at a numerical disadvantage but new types were coming into service too slowly and none had been tested on operations. When Lord Rothermere (of the *Daily Mail*) had donated his privately commissioned civil aircraft to the RAF he really put the cat among the pigeons for it was faster than our fighters. In the Commons the RAF had gone cap in hand begging for funding and now Parliament's parsimony was exposed for all to see. So Rothermere's Britain First had forced the Government to fund monoplane fighters like the Hurricane and the Spitfire to replace the much vaunted, but totally inadequate, old biplanes. But was it too little too late?

Life went on and unbeknown to Mum and Dad I joined the RAF Volunteer Reserve. Half of my contemporaries at school joined the Yorkshire Dragoons. Riding horses was fun, much better than squatting in a waterlogged trench and as I dreamed of becoming a latter day Biggles doubtless they fancied themselves in dashing cavalry charges with sabres flashing. In the event they went to Palestine where they were remounted on Bren gun carriers for the rest of the War.

My day release was discontinued, which was just as well as one by one the lads at work were getting called up. I was bored and frustrated, longing for my own call to arms but it did not come and I wondered if the RAF really wanted me.

CHAPTER SIX

The Day of Reckoning

The Polish campaign duly came to its inevitable conclusion and we all expected that the war would now involve the same combatants as in WWI except Germany would now be able to concentrate on the Western Front. This time there would be no Russian or Italian Fronts to dilute their military strength.

The prospect did not seem to daunt the Allies. The French had put its faith and all its resources into a massive system of connected forts they called the Maginot Line and they claimed it was impregnable. It was undoubtedly an impressive state of the art achievement but it was purely defensive and symbolised their war weariness. The Germans had encouraged this philosophy by building their own fortification called the Siegfried Line. Unfortunately, the French belief was so strong they had little left in the kitty to fund their Air Force, which mirrored the dire straights of our own air arm. Worse still, French politics were in a parlous state and there was no stomach for a fight, especially amongst the old brigade of WWI veterans.

That the expected German onslaught failed to materialise seemed to vindicate the strategists' theories and as an apparent stalemate set in the newsreels, having nothing else to report, regaled us with endless trips into the bowels of the Maginot Line and RAF aircraft lined up as for an air show, setting off to drop not bombs but leaflets over Germany so as not to provoke the enemy. It seemed the scene was set again for static trench warfare.

There were certain obvious flaws in the typically Gallic thinking – crucially the Maginot Line did not extend to the Channel in the north and terminated at the Ardennes in the south. The French relied on the Ardennes being impassable to a mass attack in the south and the Germans respecting the neutrality of the Low Countries in the north, which was surely beyond any one's belief!

In November Russia invaded Finland and despite a spirited defence the tiny state was overrun. In April 1940 the Germans, not to be outdone, invaded Norway, stealing a march on us who had respected their neutrality. By the time we could respond it was too late and we had to withdraw, which cost us dearly including an aircraft carrier and a considerable loss of face. Once more too little too late! It seemed the Germans were invincible.

The Day of Reckoning started suddenly and violently on 10 May. It came with the same swiftness and audacity so well rehearsed in previous invasions as the Germans violated the declared neutrality of the Low Countries. Using paratroops not just to fight but to spread confusion, jamming the roads with fleeing refugees to hinder enemy reinforcements, bombing towns and cities, they swept all before them. They strafed aerodromes, destroying planes on the ground, and their overwhelming numbers swiftly gave them air superiority. They pitilessly attacked the endless columns of fleeing refugees – terrorising was a calculated method of the new concept of war soon to be universally known – and loathed – as *Blitzkrieg*. Meanwhile the Germans broke through the supposedly impenetrable Ardennes. The vaunted Maginot Line was bypassed and by the end of May it was virtually over. France had capitulated and Britain was striving to bring the remnants of the British Expeditionary Force out of Dunkirk. Incredibly by dint of hastily improvised methods using every civilian craft and crew that could be mustered 140,000, including some French as well as the remnants of the British Expeditionary Force, were rescued – albeit with nothing more than their personal weapons.

Jackal-like Mussolini – or '*Il Duce*' as he preferred to be called – threw in his lot with the Axis powers hoping to profit from Hitler's success by declaring war on what he confidently concluded were the defeated Allies. This freed him to pursue his grand design of creating an Italian Empire in North Africa, expecting that while Britain was fighting for her very existence he could realise his dream of making the Mediterranean his '*Mare Nostrum*' as he had so often boasted, puffing out his chest until it almost rivalled his ample girth. The threat to our Suez Canal was obvious. He had amassed a sizeable fleet of modern warships – but we had a strong naval presence. With our Empire in mind the Navy had been spared the stringent cuts applied to the RAF – and frankly we doubted Italian morale matched their resources. We remembered how in WWI much-needed troops had to be sent to stiffen their resolve – including my father – when they were near to collapse. It was regarded as an irritant rather than another worry for us. During the Battle of Britain Mussolini tried to show his admiration for Hitler and establish himself as a full-blown partner by sending squadrons of his Air Force to help the *Luftwaffe*. The RAF saw them off in short order and they were hurriedly withdrawn, which confirmed our assessment of their calibre.

At home the Government fell and a new Coalition of all Parties was formed led by Churchill – a defining moment in our history.

I had followed the progress of the battlefront and was staggered at its speed of movement. In WWI thousands of men had died to wrest a paltry few yards of cloying mud from the enemy but in a matter of days whole countries had fallen. So much for the French vision of another trench war! So much for our own locust years of false economy and the ignominy of grovelling appeasement.

Now the pigeons had come home to roost with a vengeance and we were staring at imminent defeat. Whilst we could not forget the past this was no time for recriminations. We must now gird our loins and remember the song we so often sang at school – Elgar's immortal Pomp and Circumstance 'Britons never never never shall be slaves', which would be the fate of France and the other vanquished nations. A wave of patriotism swept the country – not the euphoric ardour of WWI but a calculated resolve and a clear understanding that the road ahead would be hard and rocky. Although Churchill's superb oratory was inspiring we had already determined to resist come what may. To our infinite delight and relief he had won the nation's heart by showing he had his finger firmly on its pulse. He had done no more than exactly articulate our response yet we knew this was the man we had so long waited for. The old adage 'Cometh the hour cometh the man' was never truer than right now. We knew that it would be far from easy, and that some, perhaps many, would pay the ultimate price but the alternative was unthinkable.

CHAPTER SEVEN

The Awakening

The aftershock of the amazing debacle of the invasion of the continent was comparable to an earthquake. True, it had been achieved by warfare that did not conform to the League of Nations' so-called Geneva Convention. This was a code of conduct that was supposed to define what was morally acceptable in killing your enemy. It fell short of chivalry but was as nearly humane as was possible in war. By any standards it was a tenuous concept and one that did not in any way benefit the victim (when you are dead you are dead) but the manner of your demise should be as decent as possible in an inherently violent profession. When Germany withdrew from the League alarm bells should have rung and the Polish campaign left no room for doubt but in their smug complacency our leaders believed it could never happen to us – and even if it did we would be able to deal with it.

We had lost virtually all the aircraft we had sent to France, which would have been even more if Dowding had not protested violently that sending more would threaten our ability to defend our homeland. However, nothing could disguise the fact that our aircraft had proved easy meat for the *Luftwaffe*, a situation that the 'alarmists' had warned of for years. Even the new Defiants (a fighter with a gun turret) introduced at Dunkirk had proved an unmitigated disaster once the German pilots realised that they were not traditional fighters with only forward-firing guns.

The design of our aircraft was at least five years behind Germany's and it would take our aircraft industry time to catch up but when it did it would reflect the advances made in aeronautical technology over those years. Germany's aircraft were already developed to their limit whilst ours would be capable of more development and refinement. Paradoxically the year Chamberlain had inadvertently won for us and the length of the Phony War might have given us just enough time. Already, new aircraft were coming from the factories, albeit slowly, but now there was a massive sense of urgency. We were urged to buy War Bonds and donate our pots, pans and garden railings to help build Spitfires, which cost £5,000 – half the price of a modest family car these days. The scrap was needed to relieve the strain on our shipping, which was suffering such severe losses from the U-boat campaign that feeding the population was becoming a real problem and the weekly rations were cut further. We relied on imports for most of our raw materials and food supplies and the sea lanes, which were our vital supply lines, were being strangled.

Britain had been lulled into complacency by assurances of our military capabilities, our aircraft's excellence, the way the Commonwealth rallied to our side and a touching belief that Right would always prevail and this time there was no doubting the justness of our cause. The Government had used the wireless and the newsreels to spread this spurious propaganda and the nation found it much more palatable than the truth. Throughout the war propaganda was increasingly used by both sides. Surprisingly the Allies became better at it than the enemy who had so often used it to deceive, confuse and intimidate. Nightly Britons tuned into the *Reichsenders* Bremen and Hamburg. Occasionally they caused consternation by breaking bad news that had been censored for security reasons but mostly their claims were so outrageous that they gave Britons their best laughs for some long time.

All road signs were taken down, which it was hoped would confuse the enemy. It certainly confused us! Perhaps it was hoped that they would have no maps but to overlook such a fundamental necessity was not typical of Teutonic thoroughness. Barbed wire was used liberally and the Home Guard mounted roadblocks, protected vital installations and practised tactics that varied from the improbable to the downright suicidal but at least they now had rifles instead of the original issue of broomsticks. Give them credit for their zeal and dedication!

The South Coast was declared a No Go Zone and access was restricted to military personnel only. Beaches were mined and fortified and whatever heavy weapons could be scraped together were sited at locations deemed to be most at risk. Petrol pipelines were laid under the sea at especially strategically vulnerable beaches to ensure that erstwhile invaders got a warm welcome when ignited. Dunkirk survivors were reorganised into new formations and were re-equipped with whatever was available but we were desperately in need of larger than rifle calibre guns.

Factories were now working round the clock trying to make good the equipment we had lost in the headlong rush to escape entrapment in France. No one spoke of their fatigue – only of how they had exceeded their targeted output. Everyone was wholeheartedly behind Churchill and they accepted his so clearly honest offer of 'Only blood, sweat and tears' – stoically not knowing nor caring what that could (and probably would) entail. He had rightly judged the mood of the people. Tell them the truth and they would respond like no other nation – the British way. Hitler and all that he stood for had to be stopped and we were the people to do it.

Technical delegations were sent hot foot to America to try to divert munitions ordered by now occupied nations to us. Not everything – because some did not meet our specifications. But we desperately needed to avail ourselves of America's massive industrial capacity. In President Roosevelt we found an ally bound only by the opposition of the Isolationists who were determined that America would never become embroiled in another European war. They thought this was not their cause so why should their young men die for it. It would not be long before events would show how wrong they were – but meanwhile Britain would stand alone.

Along with everything else the pace of call-up quickened and now the Co-op Men's Department was staffed almost exclusively by women. Our boss and a couple of other elderly men remained. One of these went twice daily to the Guild Hall to report suspicious characters hanging around the town centre – it was called Fifth Column mania. A fear of spies in our midst!

Daily, folks said 'Cheerio' to fathers, husbands and sons, trying to put on a brave face and hide the anxiety that gnawed them inside. The nation sang 'We're gonna hang out the washing on the Seigfried Line' with gusto but never far from their minds was the safe return of their loved ones.

Britain had awakened from her nightmare and was at last going to fight for her life and the liberty of the free world. And I wanted to do my bit in this noble cause.

I wangled a day off to go to the Recruiting Centre in the Cutlers' Hall in Sheffield where I took a medical test and as I passed I had an interview for aircrew. I told them I wanted to be a pilot, which I assumed was everybody's dream, but I was informed that there was a long waiting list. However, there were vacancies for wireless operator/ air gunners and in my desperation to get into this war I accepted – after all it was flying and that was what I had dreamed of since those long gone summer days on the cricket field.

I had followed the war intently – I understood the significance of every move and the consequences not apparent to lesser pundits, I had studied every book on flying I could lay my hands on to prepare myself for when the call came. Except that it didn't! I was distraught and fumed and fretted – what was wrong? I began to think it might be something to do with the London School of Economics, which pre-war was allegedly a hotbed of communism, but I never got there in the end. There was nothing to do but wait and patience was never my long suit.

And then at last my call-up came. Oh boy! What a furore it created! Words that spring readily to mind like heated or furious would be totally inadequate. In fact, I can think of nothing that would convey its impact – it provoked the mother and father of confrontations. As I said earlier I had not told my parents that I had joined the RAF Volunteer Reserve so it was a double shock for them. Of course they had realised that I would eventually be called up but my duplicity shocked them. I had read the letter unbelievingly – I was being offered a ground gunner's posting! I was disgusted – did they not know that I only wanted to fly! I defused my parent's wrath by assuring them I would turn the offer down but I neglected to tell them why. I would stoop to any depth to achieve my goal.

Just three weeks later came a letter asking me to report to the Air Crew Reception Centre at Padgate on 24 May 1940. The alacrity of my response was almost obscene!

CHAPTER EIGHT

Padlocked

My feet never touched the ground whilst I was waiting for a further letter from the RAF but it arrived a few days later saying I was to report to Padgate in a week and enclosed was a train warrant. I gathered the bits and pieces I thought I would need and put them in a small attaché case. I spent my last two evenings going round on my bicycle visiting my relatives to make my farewells. On the final evening I was waving to a friend forgetting I had changed to fixed wheel as I had not had time to adjust my brakes, so instead of whizzing past him I whizzed over my handlebars. Oh calamity! I hoped that my injuries would not affect my aspirations if I had to take another medical.

The fateful day came and off I went to the railway station where I was informed that Padgate was in Wigan (of mythical Pier fame) and was duly directed to the appropriate platform. As the train drew out a wave of nostalgia for dear old Donny engulfed me. My thoughts went back to my family and my childhood. They were such good times – why ever did I want to leave? It was but a passing phase and soon I was looking forward to the Great Adventure that lay ahead!

When I arrived at Wigan there was an RAF Corporal who was collecting other recruits and what a motley bunch they were! There were caps and trilby hats and a wide variety of haircuts, spivvy oxblood suits with pleated backs and white 'pearl' buttons, thirty bob tailors' suits and sports coats and flannels. Outside we were packed together in lorries and driven to the camp gates and on unloading we were treated to the sight of expensive cars decanting sartorially elegant types with blazers, hacking jackets, expensive suits with diamond pinned cravats and long cigarette holders! Our lot burst into gales of laughter, liberally sprinkled with ribald comments. I cannot repeat but I do remember 'nancies' figured largely! Uncouth or not I must say I enjoyed their taunts.

Once inside no time was lost in forming us into groups that were 'processed' by obviously bored staff who had seen it all before. They asked for our details and their first question was 'who is your next of kin', which was routine to them but sounded downright ominous to us. All this took until dinner time when we were taken to a canteen which they called a 'Mess', a word that was also descriptive of the cook's endeavours.

After dinner we had a routine health check and were issued with our knife, fork and spoon called our 'irons', reflecting the metal they were made of. We were then issued with a pair of black leather boots and a brass button rack and advised to buy tins of Brasso and boot polish to enable us to clean them. These we soon discovered were indispensible as failure to bring these items to a mirror brightness was a sin akin to treason! There followed two cotton sheets, two rough blankets, and three 'biscuits'. They were not at all like any biscuit I had ever tasted; in fact they were not biscuits at all but three mattresses that you placed on the iron bed you were allocated in a wooden hut.

A Corporal came to show us how beds were made in the RAF and how to use a heavy moplike device known as a 'bumper 'to polish the lino-covered floor. After talking a while we turned in early to get a good night's sleep to face what new delights the RAF had in store for the morrow. But sleep we could not – those biscuits were so rock hard they must have been named after the hard tack that had been the staple diet of the Navy in bygone days. Endlessly I tossed and turned but I never got a wink all night. How I longed for my lovely feather bed at home!

We were awakened bright and early by the Corporal who came to see how if we had absorbed his overnight instructions. Woe betide us if the floor failed his inspection for then we had to do it again and if a bed did not meet with his approval the miscreant was subjected to torrents of abuse that went on so long we were sometimes too late for breakfast. But today we were ushered into a large room where we swore our allegiance to King and Country and were given our Service number – mine was 999332 so I was in the first million in the RAF since it was formed in 1917, a feat I was very proud of. Later we were given our uniforms, which were approximately our shape and size. Anyone who dared to complain of the fit was reminded that we were Aircraftsmen 2nd Class, commonly known as 'Erks', and as the lowest form of life in the RAF Erks were not supposed to complain. It was amusing to see how this deflated the nobs who clearly felt violated by their sudden sartorial transformation and mortified by their loss of status.

They now called our hut a squad and the rest of our time at Padgate was devoted to drill practice where it became apparent that some recruits had difficulty in differentiating their right foot from their left. The results were hilarious to us but infuriated our tutors who left us in doubt of our parentage and assured us we were the worst squad they had ever attempted to make into real airmen.

We were not permitted to leave the camp in the evenings and renamed it 'Padlock' as once you were in you never got out and we were too tired to even think of what pleasures Wigan might have to offer. When we were at last adjudged fit to be seen in public we were told we were going to Blackpool and the following day we proudly marched through the streets to the railway station. At first we thought they were joking but really we did not care for any place had to be better than Padgate.

CHAPTER NINE

Blackpool – The Halfway House

We arrived at the station not knowing where we were as the station boards had been removed to confuse the enemy, formed up in squads on the platform and marched outside into the street. In no time it became apparent that we were indeed in Blackpool – so the rumours had been correct and our spirits rose at once that we should be so lucky! We were marched to a former entertainment complex called Olympia where we were formed into a new squad of fifty, assigned to various billets and acquired a new Corporal. The old one presumably returned to Padlock to torment the next intake of recruits. Good luck to them, we were certainly glad to see the back of him!

Our new Corporal marched us to our billets with orders to assemble outside the Metropole on the esplanade at 08.00 hours the next day. Our billets ranged from back street 'digs' to seafront guest houses and I was fortunate to be in the latter but a sea view was reserved for the paying guests who still occupied half the premises. There were about seven other RAF lads and I and our beds were in the attics at the top of house. The lady owner was a well preserved fiftyish dragon who ruled everyone, staff and guests included, with the proverbial rod of iron. She held her own parade for us where she arbitrarily laid down our Rules of Engagement! We were to take our meals after the paying guests had finished their dinner and adjourned to the lounge, divided from us by sliding decorated doors so that they would not be embarrassed by seeing our meagre fare. She hastened to explain this was not her fault but due to the pitiful allowance she received from the RAF for our rations, which we felt had some verity! Less convincing was her edict that after dinner we would go into the kitchen to do all the washing up, peel the potatoes and prepare the vegetables for tomorrow. But ever magnanimous, in return for this she would have her chambermaids make our beds, an accomplishment we had painfully perfected at Padlock. Desperate not to do anything that might adversely affect our progress in the RAF we meekly accepted – put more succinctly we were as green as grass!

We met at the Metropole at 08.00 hours, although some were a tad late. But every excuse offered was summarily dismissed. When our new Corporal said 08.00 he meant exactly 08.00 and nothing short of the unfortunate offender's demise would constitute a sufficient excuse. Our initial impression of him as a rather timid nonentity, even a nice bloke, clearly had to be revised now that he was exhibiting Padlockish tendencies! Worse was to follow when he marched us off to be vaccinated and injected against what disease that was rampant in Blackpool we knew not – but we did know that it hurt!

Back on parade on the seafront we marched and marched back and forth and even sideways time after time, sometimes pretending not to hear the order to 'About Turn' and going straight on until corralled by a livid Corporal. It was all good clean fun until a big man collapsed and would not get up when our Corporal ordered. The stricken man was on the ground being threatened with the consequences of disobeying an order by a knot of NCOs who gathered over him when it was noticed that three more large men were similarly afflicted. Suddenly the truth dawned – the after effects of the injections had affected the big men only so we smaller men puffed out our chests in pride. Right little tough eggs we were!

We were having a reasonably good time in our billet thanks largely to the generosity of the guests who were grateful to these young boys who were about to risk their lives for them and knew our pay of one shilling and sixpence a day did not go far in Blackpool. The manager of the Halifax Building Society in Donny who lived a few doors from our house in Carr House Road was on holiday when he spotted me on parade and gave me a pound afterwards to the envy of my mates. More and more chores were being piled upon us by 'Milady' and by the time Mum and Dad came to stay for a week things were decidedly strained. Mum and Dad took me to a theatre every night to see Arthur Askey, Webster Booth and Anne Ziegler or some other star who was doing a summer season at one of the piers or in the town.

Over the next week or so we honed our drilling to perfection punctuated by instruction on how to salute officers (long way up and short way down and the reverse for officers who had less time to respond) and the occasional route march in those boots whose constant burnishings had done nothing to make them more comfortable. My feet were raw and it came as a great relief when we completed our 'square bashing' and only assembled on the seafront to be marched to Olympia for Morse code training. I found this comparatively easy, which the instructor attributed to my musical training giving me a sense of rhythm that is so distinctive that it is as good as a signature to another operator. I passed the course end test of four words a minute with ease almost a week before the others.

Our feud with our landlady was resolved in an unexpected fashion when one of the lads came back after a convivial evening and threw up on every landing right up to our attic. If he had had the good sense to desist lower down we might have got away with it but the evidence was damning and an outraged landlady declared that our 'understanding' was ended and all our 'privileges' were withdrawn, which left us well ahead on the deal!

I had profited greatly from the course but the possible usefulness of the drills and route marches escaped me. However, some of the lads in the smaller billets were made so much at home they ensured a secure future by making themselves useful in the business even to the extent of marrying the daughter, which was a profit considerably greater than mine but not worth marrying 'Milady' for!

Despite the sometimes atrocious weather when it was almost impossible to stand up against the wind on the seafront and the fracas with our landlady I had really enjoyed my time at No. 10 Signals School Blackpool but I had completed my course and I was anxious to move on to be a part of the titanic struggle that was raging down South. I still had a long way to go but I was getting ever nearer so I welcomed the news that we were to proceed to Yatesbury in Wiltshire to complete our wireless course. I say 'we' but of the fifty strong squad only twenty-six opted for flying duties and sadly only one year later I learned that most had 'bought it' on Bomber Command.

CHAPTER TEN

The Battle of Britain

The next morning we said goodbye to the lads staying on to take the Ground Operators' course who wished us luck, although we felt we were the lucky ones for we were going to fly! Our happy band of embryonic aircrew was marched to the railway station and met by a Mongolian-looking Corporal who was apparently sent to ensure we did not defect en route – they had to be joking as we were keener than he was to get to Yatesbury! After changing to a rural line we eventually arrived at a small station, again without a signboard, to be taken to the camp in a lorry and issued with blankets and those biscuit mattresses that we had thought were a torture specially patented by Padlock. Our journey had taken so long that by the time we got to the Mess it was closed but prompted by our new Corporal they soon provided a tasty supper of sausages and mash and then we were shown our billet. Having enjoyed civilian beds in Blackpool we did not expect to sleep much on our biscuits and one glance at the floor told us that morning inspections were also back with us! But we knew we were progressing when on entering we spotted an aircraft on the airfield – albeit only a de Havilland Dominie trainer – and that meant we were a step nearer the Dream for which we would endure anything!

So began our life at No. 2 Signals School and though we immersed ourselves in our studies we, like everyone in the land, watched breathlessly as the battle waging in the South ebbed to and fro, and so I must digress from our fortunes and concentrate on the far more important fortunes of the whole nation.

It was as well that the pace of repair of our grievous losses had quickened for it seemed no time at all had elapsed since Dunkirk yet we now knew without doubt that it was Germany's intention to invade. The phase of attacks on the Channel shipping was over and now the battle was joined in earnest. The *Luftwaffe* sent formations of bombers escorted by hordes of fighters to attack targets in southern England and our defending force of Hurricanes and Spitfires engaged them in combats that filled the sky with a maze of vapour trails. Watchers on the ground craned their necks and gazed in wonderment trying to make sense of the rather pretty convoluted patterns they drew. Only when an aircraft trailing smoke and flames came plummeting to earth to explode in an all too familiar mushroom of smoke did they understand what a deadly encounter they were witnessing. If the crash was close by they rushed to render aid to a downed RAF pilot or to capture an enemy pilot and maybe 'come across' a souvenir they could treasure or sell. If no parachute had been seen there was little likelihood that the unfortunate crews had survived.

Mum wrote to say that in the North they had seen a few isolated intruders but like us had heard of it all on the wireless and seen it in the newsreels at the cinemas. Daily, the newspapers published the tally of the losses on both sides, which were possibly overstated. The true figures were difficult to assess when a split second could decide your fate in the whirling maelstrom of battle 20,000 feet in the sky. Sometimes a damaged aircraft would escape from one pursuer only to be finished off by another and both would claim a 'kill'. What was undeniable was that the RAF was giving the enemy a beating they had never experienced before – they had expected to sweep a weak opposition easily from the sky. Now they were encountering determined and skilful defenders equipped with aircraft comparable with or even better than their own. Thank God for Air Marshal Dowding whose insistence had saved more Spitfires and Hurricanes from being sent to try to save an already defeated France. Even so aircraft to replace losses were nearly as desperately needed as pilots to fly them.

The Germans had rehearsed their tactics in the Spanish War and honed their skills in Poland and France. They had thought they were invincible but early on their terror-inducing *Stuka* dive-bombers had been mauled so badly by the RAF that they never dared to use them again. Now they tried sending fewer bombers escorted by more fighters but still the Hurricanes sliced into the bombers whilst the Spits tackled the fighters flying top cover.

They then turned to a new strategy – if they could not overcome the enemy in the skies they would destroy the airfields he flew from. Every RAF station in the south-east was severely bombed and unbeknown to them many were nearly unusable. Ground staff worked furiously and tirelessly to repair the damage and the enemy was bewildered to be met by the same number of defenders the next day. This tactic was repeated until they finally gave up and turned their attention to London instead. They never knew how close they came to succeeding for plans were being made to use bases north of London like Duxford where Douglas Bader was trying to sell the idea of his Big Wing to Dowding who turned it down because it could not be assembled in the air in time to defend the Capital. It was a close run thing and probably the nearest the *Luftwaffe* came to fulfilling the boasts Goering made to Hitler that his Air Force would bring Britain to its knees in a week.

The gallant few who were always outnumbered performed miracles daily, never being found wanting in courage or dedication. In some cases young – and most of them were young – handsome men were grotesquely disfigured by fire and some made the supreme sacrifice. We may never see their like again.

At the end of the war it was revealed that the RAF had three big advantages in the battle. Firstly, the Germans were operating at the limit of the range of their fighters, which allowed them to spend only twenty minutes over this country. Secondly, if they got shot down they became prisoners of war whereas British pilots could bale out and be flying again the next day. Some flew three or more times a day because of a shortage of replacements and many were exhausted long before the battle ended. But most importantly, they did not know of our radar chain that enabled our Ground Controllers to detect the hostile armadas forming up over their newly acquired French bases. Our fighter stations were immediately informed to stand by and scrambled just in time to meet the heaviest concentrations of incoming raiders thereby giving them maximum endurance. The enemy had failed to appreciate the significance of the distinctive radar masts and although a few were bombed all bar one were operating the next morning. If the radar had been knocked out our fighters would have had to rely on visual sightings made by the Observer Corps and their ability to be vectored to the right place at the right height at the right time would have been lost. This might have been sufficient to tip the scales against us.

London now became the prime focus of the Nazi bombers who had failed by day and turned to night attacks but they also targeted industrial centres and ports. Night after night they came striving to make the civilian population break and demand an end to the war – it was a tactic at which the Nazis excelled. Alas we had no credible night fighters. The Blenheim had proved to be unable to fulfil its intended role as a day bomber and had been wiped out in France so it was now pressed into service as a night fighter. It was so slow it could not catch the raiders even when its fledgling radar worked. The RAF also tried using Defiants but having no radar it was limited to trying to catch raiders caught in searchlights but only if they were outside the gun defended zones. Our major cities had to rely on AA (anti-aircraft) guns, searchlights and barrage balloons for their defence as the Government had spent nothing on dedicated night fighters between the wars.

To try to pacify the population's demand for retribution Whitley, Hampden and Wellington bombers were ordered to attack Berlin. These were the new breed of RAF bombers. The Wellington became the most well known of them all and served through the war with distinction. It was the brainchild of Barnes Wallace whose fertile brain later spawned the bouncing bomb used in the Ruhr Dam raid, the grand slam bomb for piercing U-boat pens and swingwing aircraft. The Berlin raids were a flea bite compared with the pounding London was taking but they were excellent propaganda and made a mockery of another of Goering's boasts – that no one would ever violate Germany's airspace.

All winter long the Blenheims in their new role as night bombers attacked the thousands of barges in the French harbours along the Channel Coast. They had been assembled ready for an invasion of Britain but without air supremacy over the Channel that was impossible. Gradually it became apparent that they were dwindling in numbers as they returned to their Homeland and that could mean only one thing – the invasion was off – at least for the time being. It also presented the RAF with a juicy target. If they could breach the Dortmund-Emms Canal they would bottle up the barges in Germany and put a stranglehold on a vital supply line. However, being inland it was further afield than the easily identifiable Channel ports and consequently harder to find with the navigational equipment available at that time. Nevertheless they had some successes, which disrupted the waterway temporarily and proved another boost to the morale of a nation already exulted and relieved by victory of the Battle of Britain.

We at Yatesbury were jubilant and relieved that the victory had won us time to complete our courses and do our bit to save our country and our British way of life!

CHAPTER ELEVEN

No. 2 Signals School
Yatesbury

The skill and the sacrifices of RAF pilots in the heroic struggle being fought were a spur to us at Yatesbury and inspired in us an even greater determination to qualify as WOP/AGs (wireless operator/air gunners) and we longed to join the illustrious Few, as they were to become known. But we knew there were many pitfalls ahead like this Signals course, which was not proving easy, and there was still the Gunnery to come.

Throughout the battle our instruction proceeded as usual and we applied ourselves to what often seemed beyond our comprehension but gradually we began to make sense of it all. The main aim was to up our Morse speed from the four words per minute we had attained at Blackpool to 18 WPM. This daunting task was complicated by having to achieve the speed in four categories – namely Plain Language, Psycho (a mixture of letters and figures), Figures only and Cipher (a mixture of unrelated figures and words). To this end we spent hours and hours receiving and sending Morse to and from our civilian instructors who were mostly ex-Merchant Navy and were red hot being accustomed to working at 50 WPM using a Side to Side Morse Key. We viewed them with awe and respect as they told us how they could identify fellow operators just by listening to the rhythm of their transmissions, which were so distinctive that they were as good as any signature. Keen as mustard a small group of about six of us tried developing our own rhythms and in a short time found to our surprise that our speeds had risen to 25 WPM and suddenly the pressure was off us. We had found out that we all had music somewhere in our backgrounds so our instructor in Blackpool had been right – a sense of rhythm did help and we really began to enjoy our work even though certain categories still needed intense concentration. In a phrase 'we had cracked it!'

The need for Morse we could understand as voice radio had a limited range and the sets were often unreliable but although reliable the wireless sets we were being trained on were antiquated and cumbersome. They required ten or more toilet-roll sized coils, which weighed a ton in their stout wooden box and had to be changed to cover different frequencies. We were told new sets were belatedly reaching the fighter squadrons but their range was still insufficient to meet Bomber Command's needs, which clearly foretold our eventual destination. It was to be Bomber Command for us! Our young hearts had hoped for fighters of course but, no matter, we would still be flying!

Harder to understand was their insistence on teaching us heliography (using the sun's rays to flash messages), semaphore and signalling by flags. What puzzled us was that it seemed unlikely there would be sun at night when we would be operating and attempting to hang out of an aircraft trying to wave a flag against the slipstream we dismissed as damned near impossible and potentially dangerous. So, stationed 100 yards or more apart we concentrated on practising the Aldis lamp, which was clearly a more viable proposition – except that we had to pass on every type of communications and it would be a shame to lose out on one of these futile subjects!

We had endless training on those venerable sets, fault finding, dismantling and reassembling till we could have done it in our sleep and sometimes we did in a nightmare! Much more interesting was tuition in radio direction finding using a loop aerial like the one we saw on the Dominie on the airfield. We took bearings from various known radio beacons and located ourselves at – Yatesbury! But maybe it was getting us a step nearer our goal. And sure enough came the moment we had worked so hard for – we were issued our flying gear, which we had expected to be the greatest experience of our lives but instead had us in fits of laughter. We were ushered into a shed whose interior reminded me of a ship's chandlers with a long counter onto which a vast assortment of strange items were placed before each man. An ageing Sergeant WOP/AG shouted to us to 'About face' and called to us to 'copy me'. He proceeded to demonstrate by donning these strange items one by one in their proper order and emerged as a properly dressed airman of the time – but *we* didn't. You have never seen a more glorious cock-up in your life with some men half dressed, others unable to walk, whilst others could do nothing for laughing with straps that should have been between their legs around their heads! The trouble (or at least part of it) was that the Sergeant had got ahead of us and in the rush to catch up things had sort of got out of hand. The Sergeant, instead of losing his cool as we had come to expect of NCOs-in-Charge, was in stitches himself but he religiously went to every man in turn to put him right, which we greatly appreciated.

There was more hilarity to come for an enterprising civilian photographer was waiting for us when we went outside to take pictures of these intrepid fliers to send home to mothers, wives and girl friends and he did a roaring trade believe you me! But the best was yet to come – a great pudding of a lad from Cheshire was about to take his turn when someone said 'Put your helmet on' so he did. Then someone else said 'Fasten your oxygen mask up' and he did. Entering into the spirit of the thing another shouted 'Fasten your oxygen mask across!' and again he obliged. The result was the photo he sent home was of himself swathed from head to foot in helmet with his oxygen mask obscuring his face, wearing a one-piece flying suit and Eskimo-like boots. It could have been, well, anybody! It was not typical of the camaraderie within the squad but this lad's clumsiness and sloth had resulted many times in Ivan (as we had named our Mongol-faced Corporal) ordering us all 'Jankers' – a punishment of having to report to the Guardroom hourly with full pack until 23.00 hours. What was worse the muppet was unrepentant about it so not unnaturally the other lads relished the opportunity to gain a sweet revenge but he was too dim to realise!

Ivan enjoyed his reputation for bullying to the point of being a full-blown psychopath revelling in his authority by meting out severe and degrading punishments liberally often with little or no justification. But Ivan was soon to get his comeuppance when he ordered 'Jankers' for an inoffensive man who was a solicitor in Civvy Street and a hopelessly unfit and overweight thirty-year-old. He reported in full kit and Ivan made him run round the Barrack Square until he collapsed and had to be rushed to Chippenham Hospital with a heart attack and Ivan mysteriously was gone from us. On my way back from Malta I lighted upon him in a Canadian transit camp where he greeted me like a long lost friend and endlessly moaned that an ungrateful RAF had posted him to Jamaica. Far from being sympathetic I took great pleasure in telling him that if they had consulted me I would have strongly recommended that he be posted to Shibah where temperatures were so fierce they nearly fried you!

News of this unfortunate incident spread rapidly and added to a feeling that we had been pushed too far, and together with the conditions we had to endure in general created a discontent that manifested itself in an unexpected manner. The camp was in dire straights with many suffering from tinea as often there was no water in the taps. We shaved in tea on more than one occasion and I had to resort to sending my laundry home by post for Mum to wash. The food was not only poor but there was no variety and it consisted predominantly of the sausages we were given on our arrival – sausages, sausages meal after meal. They were said to be pulled into the camp by yard lengths directly from the factory in Calne and payment was made by yardage not weight. When the Orderly Officer asked if there were any complaints one dinner time he was told by several brave souls that we were heartily sick and tired of sausages and he promised to get us something different for supper. He was as good as his word for we were given a nice meat pie with gravy and mash but all hell broke loose when it was discovered that inside the pie were three sausages! The plates were dumped onto the floor and pandemonium broke out. The Orderly Officer narrowly escaped and summoned the RAF Police who eventually restored some semblance of order and the mob retired supperless to their huts. It was the nearest I ever got to a mutiny! There were no reprisals or punitive measures taken against us, which despite the insurgency suggested that we had a legitimate case.

As I was the baby of the squad and obviously not worldly wise I was soon 'adopted' by two mates in particular who took me under their wing to make sure I was not put upon or taken advantage of. One was a mountain of a man called Archer who was thirty-something and the other was called Bert Izzard who was about twenty-five and had worked as a butcher in Tunbridge Wells. He was dark, handsome and fit as the proverbial butcher's dog and became my first friend in the service. He had not had the happiest of upbringings but had finally found happiness, security and the prospect of a comfortable life living in his boss's house and courting his attractive daughter, all of which was put in jeopardy by his call-up papers. A cruel hand fate had dealt him but he was always cheerful and protective towards me.

One eventful day we were marched onto the airfield and six at a time loaded into one of the Dominies piloted by a civilian pilot who had the honour of becoming the first entry in my newly issued logbook. Mr Emerson sat alone up front at the controls whilst we sat in pairs behind and having a window each gave us a lovely view of the Wiltshire countryside with its many white horses cut into the hillside chalk, some of which we had seen from the train. It was glorious and confirmed what I had known for so long – I was born to fly. This was my element, my destiny and I wished this flight would never end. Two days later we were up again and once more I felt an empathy with this environment like this was where I belonged and my ardour was not diminished when two of the lads were sick.

We were nearing the end of the course and revision became the priority in every facet of our training. It had become apparent for some time that the older men were not doing as well as the younger ones – just as today the young find information technology so much easier to assimilate than the elderly. I knew Bert had been worried that he was not going to make the grade and I tried to help him as I had been fairly comfortable on the course.

He had struggled from the outset and lost confidence so when the test came he was a bag of nerves and never gave himself a chance and some of it rubbed off on me for I spent a sleepless night in doubt and turmoil. Came the morning and the officer who was going to announce the results fiddled with his papers as if he was enjoying his power to make us sweat and sweat we did – copiously! At last he was ready and in a few minutes we knew our fates. I had passed first time and Bert had done better than he had expected. He had not been outed but recommended for four further weeks training, which was a lifeline of which he took advantage. Archer was similarly given further training so Bert would have a staunch pal whilst I would be very much alone but both of them were proud that they had 'fostered' a whiz kid and I had learned a great deal from them. I had mixed emotions – on one hand I was delighted with my result but also sad at being parted from my good friend Bert who was there to see me off to pastures new. We wished each other the best of luck. We did not know what was in store for us but in a short – a terribly short – time our future would be decided by the cards we were dealt. More of that later.

I had delightedly sewn the symbol of a wireless operator (a hand gripping six electric flashes) on to my uniform sleeve as soon as my success was confirmed and preened myself in front of the first mirror I passed. 'AC 2 Gosling,' I said to myself, 'you are definitely going places!'

The next morning all the first-time passers were paraded and marched to the railway station en route for the Gunnery Course, the last hurdle in our quest to qualify as WOP/AGs. We were told that our destination was a place called RAF Penrhos somewhere in deepest Wales but no one told us that it was in a strongly Welsh Nationalist part where just pre-war a local doctor had been jailed for trying to burn down a hangar there! But we were soon to learn.

CHAPTER TWELVE

No. 9 Bombing and Gunnery School, Penrhos

When we were on the train en route to our new station we remarked how lovely the countryside was and it grew more and more beautiful the nearer we got to our destination. When we arrived at the railway station a couple of RAF buses were waiting to take us to the airfield and again the scenery enchanted us with its rolling hills and pasture land with cows grazing peacefully. It was idyllic! On arrival at the airfield we were told that we were to be billeted out in Pwhelli in civilian quarters and would be bussed to the camp for our meals. It was good news that we would not be sleeping on those awful biscuits but after our experience of camp food at Yatesbury we wondered about eating on the camp. We were then given the address of our new accommodation and were told to kill time until supper at 19.00 hours.

We decided to watch the aircraft on the aerodrome and as we wandered past the Guardroom we saw a map on the wall and discovered that Pwllheli was a small coastal town about three miles to the east on the Lleyn Peninsula facing Cardigan Bay. It all sounded too good to be true.

We then got to the airfield where rather decrepit Whitley Mk 1 bombers and Fairey Battles were landing and taking off and eventually we worked out their routine. It seemed each Whitley worked with two Battles and they were away about an hour before returning when the Battles dropped a target drogue some twenty feet long before landing. So they had obviously been doing air-to-air firing. We were excited that it would soon be our turn.

When it was time for our supper we were pleasantly surprised for it was tasty beef stew and dumplings and a sweet to follow, which exceeded our wildest expectations. We were then bussed to our new digs and to my delight we found that it was a guest house in a Georgian terrace facing the sea on the promenade run by two elderly ladies from Yorkshire. They turned out to be real darlings who nightly offered the four of us a glass of milk and two biscuits for sixpence, which was a bit steep but we never refused lest we offended them!

Others who were billeted further along the terrace were not so lucky for they encountered Welsh Nationalism for the first time. When they knocked at the door a surly landlady took them to the bottom of her garden and put them into uninsulated, unheated wooden chalets. They were intended for summertime holidaymakers but she would not have RAF lads in her house even when it snowed. The RAF tried to do something about it but found that because their agreement did not specify that the accommodation was to be in the house proper but only at that address they were powerless. So our lads continued to freeze in one of the worst winters for years. All of us suffered this kind of treatment at some time during our stay in Wales and their bigotry and open hatred disgraced the principality. Decent Welsh folk were as offended as we were at the treatment we were daily subjected to by these people simply because we were English. Not unnaturally we took a dim view of all Welsh people but now years later I am proud to count many Welsh folk among my best friends. I encountered this nonsense for the first time in the town centre when I asked a timid-looking young lady if she could direct me to Woolworths and she answered 'Why should I help you, English pig?' I was so taken aback that I could only stare at her in disbelief. Every day the buses came to take us to the camp for a substantial breakfast and then we began our instruction, which to start with was learning to strip and reassemble the two main machine-guns in use at that time – the Browning and the Vickers 'K' gun. The 'K' gun was a relic of near prehistoric vintage, and as it was gas operated (that is, the breech was returned by the gases of the previous round fired) it was too slow at 700 rounds per minute and because it was pan fed it could not be used in a turret. In short it was obsolete and another example of the pre-war underfunding. It should have been replaced long ago but was still thought to be adequate, a fallacy that cost many a WOP/AG his life as in contrast the Germans had faster guns and 20 mm cannon with telescopic sights. The Browning was in another league, however, as it was faster firing and being belt fed could be used in two- or four-gun configurations in powered turrets, which were essential because of the speed of modern aircraft.

We also had tuition in aircraft recognition, at first in daylight and as we improved in a darkened room to simulate as nearly as was possible the operational conditions we would be working in. We had to identify our own as well as enemy types and even the different exhaust patterns of the various engines in use had to be recognised as this might well be useful in hazy weather.

Before being allowed to get airborne we were taught the principles of deflection shooting to compensate for the angle of attack and speed of the target. You did not sight directly at the enemy but had to estimate where he would be when your rounds reached him, usually in front of him. To demonstrate we were taken to a firing range and put into a turret to fire at a target model aircraft moving across much like in a fairground and it wasn't easy. Few of us would have won a Kewpie Doll the first time we tried but with practice we began to get the hang of it and eventually satisfied our mentors. We were also made familiar with the many different sorts of electric or hydraulic turrets, which were later standardised on two basic types.

When we were considered proficient we began air-to-air firing from either the Whitley or Battle aircraft and found our previous impressions of the procedure were pretty accurate. The Whitley had three twin Browning turrets, front, rear and dustbin, which was retractable and situated halfway down the underside of the fuselage. It was difficult to get into and even worse to get out of! The sensation when firing from it was terrifying especially as you thought it was going to drop off all the time but each of us had to take our turn. Some of the boys were sick every time they flew and one lad was pleased to be in the rear turret when nausea overtook him for he figured that he could raise the clear view shutter in front of him and throw up out of it. Alas he had not reckoned with the slipstream, which carried it straight back to him, and having taken off his helmet and opened his collar in the hope of staving off the attack he well and truly got his own back – in his hair and face. But none of them withdrew from the course because of the nausea. One thing I found fascinating about the Whitley was that when flying it sounded as if the Halle and Mantovani orchestras had combined to play glorious soaring strains of some celestial concerto. I have never since heard the like and I wondered if it was due to the vibration of the aircraft's metal skin – whatever it was I loved it.

We had to fire a test burst as soon as we got over the sea and then we fired at the drogues pulled by the Battles making sure we fired out to sea and the hits were counted when they were dropped at base. Once we got back to our billets to find our landladies awaiting us with arms akimbo concealing the rolling pins they were carrying. It turned out that someone had fired with the targets on the landward side and shattered every pane of glass on the terrace. Whether this was a genuine mistake or retribution for some sectarian insult we never discovered – we were too busy trying to persuade our particular landladies that 'It wasn't me, honest'!

Firing from the Battles soon disclosed the deficiencies of the type for the single Vickers gun was mounted on a stalk so that all the Me 109 pilots had to do was to watch the poor gunner through their telescopic sights until he leaned inside to put on a new pan and then attack unopposed. It was adequate when it was built but long ago had become obsolete and yet another reminder of the legacy of underfunding the RAF suffered in the 1930s. To ask airmen to go to war in it was little short of a crime. They had been just so much cannon fodder (literally). No wonder the RAF needed more WOP/AGs.

Our course was coming to its end but unlike Yatesbury there were no results to be read out, simply a totting up of our proficiency ratings in the various tasks we had undertaken. We were called into a classroom and handed our logbooks and there was the news we wanted. I was ecstatic to see that not only had I passed but my assessment read 'Should be an asset to any squadron', which was praise indeed! We were told that we would be leaving on a special train at 23.00 hours that very day. We were to have our suppers and then go back to our billets to collect our kit and assemble at the railway station at 22.30 hours.

But we had one thing to do before we left. About six of us had found that after eating we had time before the bus left to grab a quick pint at a nearby pub that we called 'The Merry Widow' since we could not translate its Welsh spelling. *Mein host* would serve our drinks without speaking and then go into another room and the few locals who were in would quickly sup their beer and leave, again without a word to us. No need to ask where their allegiance lay and we noted it for future reference. This night, knowing we were leaving, we entered the pub as usual. He with a face that would sour any beer took our money without a word and disappeared as usual. The locals were leaving together as usual when we flung our six pints at their necks! They ran off like scalded cats and we ran to our bus and told the driver to hot foot it to our digs. We arrived at the railway station half expecting to be arrested by the RAF Police but not a one was in sight and we left the 'Land of Song' singing ribald farewells to Wales and everything Welsh with gusto!

Our destination was Uxbridge, a transit camp as old as the RAF itself, to await our postings to an operational squadron, which we expected to be in Bomber Command maybe to fly the singing Whitleys or maybe Wellingtons. But we hoped it would be one of the new types just entering service.

CHAPTER THIRTEEN

Uxbridge and a False Start

It was just as well that our train had been specially requisitioned for us because when we got to Uxbridge railway station at 07.00 hours I had to be shaken awake or I would have gone right to the end of the line. I had spent half the journey sewing on the stripes we had been given for lads who had tried but failed to sew on their own and caused much hilarity by getting them too low or high or somewhere under their armpits! I could have made a packet if I had charged them a bob a time. So, bleary eyed, we were loaded into a fleet of lorries sent to meet us, arrived at No. 1 Depot and were given breakfast. The camp, which dated back to the separation of the RAF from the Army in WWI, was still its major transit centre and the permanent staff were skilled in handling the endless flow of migrants. After breakfast we were assembled outside the Mess and the air gunners and bomb aimers who had travelled down with us were marched off, leaving us WOP/AGs with the Station Warrant Officer (SWO). Giving some of his minions a list apiece he ordered them to take the appropriate number of men to where there were vacant spaces in various wooden huts that formed the camp – very slick indeed! This left him with three of us and he sent the other two off with a Corporals and then took me to a hut himself and told me he was going to put me in charge of it! The hut had beds for about forty men and I had a room of my own at one end so I unpacked my kit and had a nap before taking my dinner in the Sergeants' Mess where I was waited on by Mess orderlies, a novelty I had not experienced before. After supper I went to the bar. (Glory be! What a difference a few stripes make!) I had a couple of pints and then, still tired by the long journey and the adrenalin rush of our departing escapade, I retired to the luxury of having my own room for the first time since leaving home. I scarcely noticed that I was on those damned biscuits again before I was deep in the arms of Morpheus.

My slumbers were rudely shattered by a loud hammering on my door. I leapt out of bed and opened the door to be confronted by an agitated airman who almost shouted 'Sergeant, come and look at this!' He led me into the hut and pointed to several beds with pools of fluid round them. He said 'This ain't on yer know – they've been coughing all night. Couldn't get a wink of sleep!' The awful truth dawned on me. This was not the result of a drunken night out – this was the dreaded tuberculosis or 'consumption' as it was commonly known in those days. It was reputed to be highly contagious so I quickly dressed and hurried to see the SWO. I told him of the situation and suggested the unfortunate victims be put into a spare hut but he said the camp was so full he simply did not have a hut to spare. I persisted that something *had* to be done and we eventually agreed the only solution was to put their beds together at one end of the hut instead of being dispersed among the others. He was a decent sort of chap and warned me not to be too sympathetic towards the other airmen in the hut as they were awaiting posting after coming out of the glasshouse (prison).

So back I went and explained the problem to the men who were waiting disgruntedly outside and as they could see there was no alternative I soon had them rearranging the beds. The tragic victims of this fatal disease were apologetic they had caused so much trouble and offered to assist but their offer was equally apologetically refused as the former jailbirds tried to explain their fears. I decided to install a screen to complete the segregation and went back to the SWO to beg half a dozen blankets, which were nailed to the beams.

When it was all finished I made a point of going to talk to these poor unfortunate souls and it nearly broke my heart. They were all so young and although they had an air of resignation they seemed bewildered that this was to be their fate. Some were emaciated whilst others looked quite normal except for a waxen pallor. But then you looked into their eyes. Oh dear God! Those sad, hopeless, desperate eyes told the truth. They knew their end was inevitable and they were scared – oh so terribly frightened.

Every three days one or two pairs of men dressed somewhat like Special Constables came and each pair took three or four of them away. They told me that they would take these poor doomed souls safely to their homes where, because there was no cure at that time, they would die. A railway compartment was reserved for them and fumigated before being returned to public use. They told me they had been doing this for years even though they knew the dangers they were exposing themselves to but they said 'Well somebody has to help the poor sods!' They not only deserved a medal, they deserved a chestful of medals.

Their departures made me think deeply about the frailty of life in general and about my own in particular. I recalled that rainy night in Blackpool when I was taking a solitary walk on the seafront thinking how alone I was when it suddenly struck me that I was indeed, for the first time, on my own with no one to run to for advice or support. I must rely on myself and be answerable to myself and I believed my upbringing in a loving family would see me through save for the odd occasion when someone tried to take advantage of my naivety. But now I was no longer able to think only of myself for my promotion had forced me to be responsible for others and I determined that I could not fail them. It was a massive decision for a lad of just eighteen and nine months to take but I never regretted my resolve.

I had also talked to the other lads and I could best describe it as 'enlightening'. They had been incarcerated for a wide variety of misdemeanours ranging from GBH to being AWOL and according to them it was never their fault. You had to laugh when one said he went AWOL to be with his girlfriend when she was delivering his child but he was reported to the SPs who duly arrested him. Her husband had come home from the Middle East on compassionate leave after neighbours had alerted him about his wife's carrying on in his absence. Unrepentant he said 'Sergeant, that's what you get for doing the decent thing!' Several had struck an NCO only because he had done them some dire injustice and one considered himself superior because he had floored a full blown Flight Lieutenant. One had been arrested for flogging Merlin engines to the Arabs as he said 'to make a bit on the side' and claimed he knew for certain that his officers were making much more than he had.

Every night I went into London to walk round and see the sights and many times I got into a sweat fearing I had lost my way back to the Tube station to catch a late train back to camp. As a jazz fan I loved to get a late train as then I travelled with the session men who were such superb musicians they could fit into any band and so were employed on a nightly basis to augment big bands on special occasions or for broadcasting. It was fascinating to listen to them telling each other where they had been playing that night with Geraldo, Carol Gibbons, Joe Loss or some other popular band of the day at one of London's swish ballrooms or night clubs.

However, I was restless and anxious to get to a squadron when one day the SWO called to tell me my posting had arrived and he gave me a train warrant for the journey on the morrow. The posting was not as I had expected to Bomber Command but to an Army Cooperation Squadron at Andover on the edge of Salisbury Plain.

I had enjoyed my time at No. 1 Depot Uxbridge and even the trauma of the sad episode had led me to reassess my life. So I said goodbye to the SWO, packed my kit overnight and bright and early I set off unaccompanied (being now a Sergeant and thus supposedly trustworthy) on my way to my new station.

When I got off the train at Andover I was the only RAF man amongst a number of Army types, and outside the station I found an RAF lorry driver loading stores with whom I cadged a lift to the camp.

I reported at the Guard Room and was directed to the SWO who kindly took me to draw my blankets etc from the Stores and then showed me my 'billet'. To my astonishment my 'billet' was one of a hundred or so beds in a large aircraft hangar and when I asked him if this was a temporary arrangement he sort of grinned and said 'I don't know – this lot have been here for months!' It was February and there was three inches of snow on the ground and as the massive doors were kept open a yard or so for access it was as cold inside as outside. There was no form of heating – to heat such a vast space was impossible – so the only way to get warm was to put on extra clothes and go to bed!

I soon learned from other WOP/AGs in the Sergeants' Mess that they had been in this predicament for months and had given up hope of any improvement in their lot.

Fortunately the town offered some light relief with female company, a cinema, and several pubs, which offered weekend entertainment in the form of regular fights over which was the best Service. As I was only 5 foot 5 inches tall (stretching) and weighed only 7 stone 12 lbs (wet through) I did not feel this was a sport at which I would excel and so I spent my Saturday nights at the camp cinema where the films were old but free, which on our two shillings and sixpence (twelve and a half new pence) a day was good housekeeping!

We complained bitterly about our duties as daily we had to lug a heavy box of those wretched coils through now even deeper snow, which soaked us in sweat. When we got to the aircraft we had to remove the covers from each one, showering us in snow, lug the heavy box into the cockpit and after fitting the right coil call up the various Sector Stations to report that we were at 'readiness' when in fact the aircraft had been snowbound for days! We eventually got back to our 'billets' with teeth chattering, took off our sodden greatcoats and jumped into bed. Oh! It was so nice to get warm again!

The aircraft were a mix of Mk 1 Blenheims, Lysanders and ancient biplane Audaxes with a long retractable hook underneath to pick up messages from a string suspended between two poles on the ground. We laughed about this Heath Robinson gadget as it was a relic from WWI before there was any wireless and together with the weighted message pouches (which were still in the cockpits) to drop back to tell them where to direct the fire of their gun batteries! They were all clearly obsolete and I really did not fancy flying any of them.

One day five of us who had a 'recommend' on our wireless course were summoned to the Adjutant's office where we were interviewed by a Squadron Leader who called back two of us to enquire if we wanted to volunteer for a special job and like a shot I accepted. There was an unwritten law in the RAF 'never volunteer' so the other lad turned it down but I thought 'anything to get away from here'. When I got back to the Sergeants' Mess I found the 'scuttlebutt' already had it that I was going to be sent on a suicide mission, or worse still, sent overseas – probably to some hell hole like Shibah!

Two words you quickly learned in the RAF were 'scuttlebutt' and 'gen'. Scuttlebutt I think was American in origin and was really just rumour given verity by supposedly coming from a (usually undisclosed) reliable source. On the other hand 'gen' (which I took to be a contraction of 'genuine') could be relied upon as the truth and 'pukka gen' was a stone certainty. Often it proved otherwise but I cared not I was ready for a new challenge and anyway it meant that I was going to get out of this icebox!

When I got my travel warrant the next day I was delighted to see it was for 54 Operational Training Unit stationed at Church Fenton just twenty-five miles up the Great North Road from – wait for it – Doncaster! I could scarcely believe my luck. Who said 'never volunteer'?

No one at the camp seemed to know anything about 54 OTU, not even what Command it was in, which was strange, maybe even ominous, but I knew it would do for me. Shibah indeed! To me this would be Shangri-La!

CHAPTER FOURTEEN

Church Fenton and a Fresh Start

As I knew I was leaving in the morning, my mates and I had quite a session in the Sergeants' Mess and consumed as much beer as we could afford and probably more than was good for us. The 'scuttlebutt' devotees had honed their forebodings to include new and evermore outrageous scenarios and I was impressed, nay amazed, by their inventiveness and imagination. The lack of information about 54 OTU was especially singled out as being proof that there was something fishy afoot but many were envious that I had somehow devised a way of escaping the tribulations that beset us and the thought of proper billets was uppermost in their minds.

It was 02.00 hours before I got to bed, but I was packed and ready for an early start as the warrant had specified a 10.00 hours train from Andover and I had been informed that no transport was going in that day so I should have to travel to the railway station by bus. I had accumulated extra clothing needed to survive in our 'billets' and I also had my flying gear, which was bulky and included some excellent vests and underpants to be worn under the all-in-one flying suits to keep you warm in unheated aircraft. These I had never used at Andover as their unheated aircraft had been grounded by the snow. But now they were packed into three heavy kit bags that I should have to hump around on my journey. But thereby hangs a tale – from an early age I had hated wearing underpants and I told Mum they strangled me. She tried buying me the best South Sea Island cotton ones but I rejected everything so the underpants I was issued with I gave to Dad as the electric trolley bus he drove had no combustion engine to warm him and he found these long johns ideal. I must admit that I was grateful for the vests in my constant battle to keep warm in our frozen 'billets' as they were made of a mixture of wool and cotton of a quality you could not buy in the shops. Mum, however, caused me a problem as she could not understand that I had difficulty with the Store Keeper when I went to exchange a worn pair of my (well Dad's) underpants, explaining why they had been *darned*!

I caused so much mayhem with my three kit bags on the bus that I only just made the train despite my early start and on the train I almost needed a carriage to myself.

I felt elated and excited about the new, unknown, venture that lay ahead and the thought of going back to my beloved Yorkshire. It took seven hours to reach Church Fenton and as it was almost dark by then I was surprised and pleased to find transport had been sent for me. I was assigned a billet in a hut and the Mess rustled up a bacon and egg supper for me but I was still in the dark as to what was going on in this place. I could hear that there was considerable flying in progress and this might explain why there was no one in the Mess, which only added to the mystery. It was 22.00 hours by now and I was tired from the journey so I went to my bed in the glorious warmth of a proper hut hoping I would be told in the morning.

I had breakfast in the Mess, which I again found was almost deserted. What *was* going on in this place? I then presented myself to the Adjutant who at last enlightened me. He told me that 54 OTU was for the training of night fighter crews on the new secret equipment called Aircraft Interception (AI) or radar as it later became known. I was delighted I was going to be in Fighter Command just as I had always secretly wanted. I had achieved my goal and I still was not yet twenty years old. Fabulous! Unbelievable!

The Adjutant told me I had been posted to 'D' Flight and after pointing out the way he told me that I should report to the Flight Commander. So off I went, treading on air, and on my way I took a good look at the aircraft on the airfield. There were Blenheims, Airspeed Oxfords (five-seat wooden passenger planes now adapted to RAF service and produced in their hundreds) and Defiants (now being used on second line duties after their Dunkirk debacle). True, they were all obsolescent but they were certainly an improvement on those ancient Andover relics and as this was only a training unit what could I look forward to flying when I got to a squadron? It did not matter, I had not flown for weeks and I just couldn't wait to get airborne again so anything would do!

When I got to 'D' Flight I noted that it was surrounded by several Blenheims, an Oxford and a Tiger Moth and that the Defiants were dispersed at the other side of the airfield. I went inside the dispersal hut and in an office at the end of the Crew Room was a Squadron Leader seated at a desk and I rightly assumed that he was the Flight Commander. I introduced myself and he asked to see my logbook containing the details of my proudly accumulated total of twenty-five hours flying. He did not seem impressed but with a smile he congratulated me on my course ending assessment. 'Your training does not start until Monday,' he said, 'have you anywhere to go if I give you four days' leave?' Giving him my widest, most disarming grin I replied 'Yes sir! I only live in Doncaster!' and I emerged minutes later with a pass. 'Seems like a nice bloke' I thought. Within the hour I boarded a bus and arrived home unannounced at 16.00 hours to an ecstatic welcome from Mum who told me that one night she came downstairs wondering why Dad had not come to bed and caught him crying about me. 'He's only a boy!' he had said.

The following day I went back to my old workplace to do a little showing off in my uniform with my Air Gunner's half wing on my chest and my 'sparks' and Sergeant's stripes on my sleeve. I hardly recognised the place for all the 'lads' had been replaced by women who were indifferent to my peacock display as most had boyfriends at Finningley or Lindholme and so they had seen it all before. Only the boss, the Cutters, and my old mate Fred Hardy (he of the thick glasses) remained and he was openly envious. After badgering the local Recruitment Office he had finally talked his way into the Pioneer Corps and was waiting for his call-up. My unexpected appearance only made him more impatient to get into the war as soon as possible. Poor lad, he did eventually get in and spent his whole war shovelling coal into the boilers of a hospital in Manchester but it ended happily as he met and married the daughter of the landlady he was billeted with and never came back to Doncaster. In Donny I noticed that two shops and three big commercial firms of German or French origin had changed, or Anglicised, their names and two Italian restaurants had been trashed by an enraged mob. A mob in Donny? Things surely *had* changed!

I went back to Church Fenton on Sunday refreshed by my unexpected break and raring to get started on my new challenge. In the Mess I at last met my fellow trainees and some of the instructors and soon warmed to them as they seemed to be a happy bunch just as keen as myself. Some already had experience on the equipment having been air gunners pressed into service at various squadrons without any proper training. Wanting to find out all we could about this new AI we others questioned them about their experiences and they said they were unhappy because they had to struggle to get their Blenheims up to their alleged ceiling of about 22,000 feet, gasping for oxygen in the freezing cold. If they were lucky enough to make 'contact' on their sets they had to dive to increase their speed but if they did not catch the enemy in that dive it had been frustrating to watch their quarry pull away as their speed fell off. They then had to climb up again and do this time after time for about three hours before landing, frozen stiff and thoroughly 'brassed off', but looking forward to a smashing 'flying supper' of bacon and eggs, as had become the custom, and a long lie abed in the morning. So that was why the Mess had been deserted and also explained the tasty supper I had been given – they thought I had been flying! These first-hand accounts were not encouraging, but the instructors said we would be trained on the new Mk IV equipment and the sets the air gunners had talked of were the old Mk IIIs or perhaps just prototypes. But was that 'gen' or 'scuttlebutt'?

We reported to 'D' Flight in the morning where we were joined by an equal number of pilots of different ranks, including one with a Victoria Cross, and formally welcomed by the Flight Commander who told us we were lucky to be in at the beginning of something sensational. He said that the equipment we were going to use was vital to the defence of the country – a breakthrough in technology – and impressed on us the need for complete and utter secrecy. He also disclosed that there was an Anti Submarine version known as Any Surface Vessel (ASV), which explained why the interviewing officer at Andover had enquired if I would be prepared to fly over the sea. I cringed when I recalled my reply. 'Yes sir, I flew over the sea on my Gunnery Course.' Indeed I had, but only up to three miles out, not the hundreds of miles he was thinking of. I bet he raised some laughs when he told them in his Mess! I realised that I could easily have finished up in Coastal Command and I became more than ever convinced that Fighter Command had been pre-ordained for me.

We were told that if we passed the course we would be awarded a new brevet with

'RO' (Radio Operator) on it, which news got a mixed reception as some valued the 'AG' (Air Gunner) brevets they already wore more highly. It was soon changed to 'NR' (Navigator Radio) but as I later took a Navigation Course I wore a full 'N' (Navigator) brevet. If I had worn them all I might have been mistaken for an American!

The pilots went off to dispersal to familiarise themselves with the Mk 1 short-nosed Blenheims and we were introduced to our AI sets and the principles of the system were explained to us. There was an arrow-shaped aerial on the aircraft's nose, which sent out a pulse that was reflected off any object and was received back by two dipole aerials on the wings. These 'returns' were called 'blips' and were displayed on two circular cathode-ray tubes, the one on the left showed whether the object was to the left or right and the one on the right showed if it was above or below you. Unfortunately the ground below sent 'returns' so strong they blotted out the much smaller ones from things like enemy aircraft thereby limiting the range of the set to the height you were above ground. These displays looked like Xmas trees with the left hand one upright and the right hand one laid on its side and the blips were shown like twigs sticking out of the trunk. The potential was obvious – it would enable us to find an enemy aircraft in pitch blackness and shoot it down without the crew even knowing we were behind them! As there were no navigational aids in our aircraft we had to learn to find our way back to base by using a coded pulsating beacon incorporated in the system, which was fine providing the set did not pack up. If it did we would be well and truly 'in it' unless we were near enough to base for them to get a 'fix' on our radio transmissions. The 'scuttlebutt' devotees were already at work. 'These rays make you infertile' they said, which was considered an unexpected bonus by some of the lads!

We practised in the most bizarre manner by riding round a darkened hangar on genuine 'Stop Me and Buy One' ice cream tricycles fitted with specially modified sets, trying to get behind another trike and 'shoot it down'! We were fed carrots endlessly and there were even buckets of water full of them in the Mess corridors trying to fool the Germans that our successes were due to our fantastic eyesight. We were also taught how best to look at anything in the dark by not looking directly at it but slightly to one side. We had competitions in aircraft recognition in the dark and we had to be able to distinguish friend from foe when a light was shone on a model for exactly two seconds. We even were shown the exhaust patterns of their engines as this might be all we could see on a very dark night.

Flying had begun from the outset and my logbook shows that at 14.35 hours I made a 1 hour 10 minute flight with a certain F/Lt Pain to familiarise me with the local terrain and at 04.50 hours the next morning (20 March 1941) we were up again for 1 hour 35 minutes – my first night flight! My feelings on landing were like I had never had before, perhaps exultation comes nearest to describing them, but there was satisfaction, pride, fulfilment and goodness knows what else in there too. I had loved every minute and I knew this was it for me. My night flying supper was nectar, ambrosia, or whatever the Gods were supposed to eat, my sleep was blissful, my lie in on waking was luxurious and life had never been so good! When I got up I was still in a state of euphoria. I wanted to tell someone what I had done and I knew straight away who would be interested – my old mate Bert Izzard. So I wrote him a letter asking how he was, where he was and what was he doing as I had not heard from him since leaving Yatesbury. Then I told him of my escapades and sent it to his home at Cross in Hand, East Sussex, to make sure it got to him.

On 27 March we were all called into the Crew Room and the Chief Instructor said: 'Today you are going to "crew up". I am going to lock the door when I leave and when I come back in exactly one hour you will have decided who will be your oppo when you go to a squadron! Pick someone you like because you have to weld into an equal team who have faith and implicit trust in each other. Good luck.' And out of the door he went!

We knew this was coming and had been eyeing up prospects for some days. Some wanted to team up with a Sergeant as they were unlikely to 'pull rank' on them whilst others thought they might benefit from crewing up with the highest ranking officer they could get. I was undecided. I could see that having an NCO pilot had its attractions, but I had my eye on a certain Pilot Officer who seemed to be a nice chap and was about my age. I looked around the room for him and there he was, walking right up to me! We laughed and without a word the deal was done, this was to be my oppo and I knew I had chosen well. When the Chief Instructor came back it was all cut and dried, we had all teamed up for better or for worse as the marriage ceremony says, except that we could never get divorced. From now on we flew with the same pilot doing all the exercises, day and night interceptions, beacon homings, map reading, and testing the sets every afternoon to ensure their serviceability for the night flying – everything, always together.

My pilot, Teddy Daniel, or Danny as everyone called him, was about my height, twenty-one years old, a deal plumper than me, with a rotund face, and was always smiling. His father, a retired Army officer, was Master of Foxhounds at Curry Rivel in Somerset and had sent Danny to boarding school before getting him an engineering apprenticeship at Holman's, a large West Country firm, and he had worked at their branch in Peterborough before joining up. Long after the war I met our old Flying Instructor at his shop in Falmouth where he ran shark fishing trips and he said Danny was the best pupil he ever had. I can testify to that from the many times his ability got us out of sticky situations whilst he would tell everyone I was the best navigator in the squadron.

Together we learned the art of night interception, which was simple in theory but difficult to perfect in practice. First I had to get a good contact and then do my best to ensure I did not lose it by closing the range so that the 'blip' was not overwhelmed by the ground returns (or clutter as we called it) as we turned if we were following a weaving target. I had to be careful not to approach too rapidly or we might overshoot and get in front of it where we would be seen and get us shot down. Nor could we try to avoid overshooting by suddenly throttling back for the flames from our exhausts would disclose our presence. The proper way was to slow up gradually as we neared the target, approaching slowly until we were slightly below and 200 yards or so astern and sit there until we had made a positive identification before closing to attack. If we were above the target we would be more visible against the sky than against the darker background of the earth below and it was not always easy to do so if the target was taking evasive action, which was the norm. Fine judgment of relative speed by the navigator and perfect understanding with the pilot was the key to success and that only came with hours of practice.

Although we were doing only flying training we suffered several losses, some of which were due to pilot error as about half the pilots were straight out of Flying Training School (FTS) where they had been flying twin-engined machines, which were much less powerful and lighter than the 820 horse powered Mercury-engined Blenheim, and some were finding them quite a handful. I had made friends with a young Sergeant Pilot called Phillip, and my own pilot not being in the Sergeants' Mess, he and his oppo invited me to go to Leeds with them on one of the nights we were not due to fly. We went together many times, and one Tuesday night, when his oppo was confined to camp doing Orderly Sergeant duties, Phillip and I went into a pub in Leeds and there met two girls who seemed very sociable. We bought them a drink and were enjoying their company when they said they were going to the toilet. When they went out a couple on a nearby table asked if we knew the girls were prostitutes so we supped up sharpish and high-tailed it into the blackout – we had never encountered the species before! We had a laugh trying to imagine their faces when they saw we had disappeared! The following day Phillip was doing some local flying when for a bit of fun he decided to 'beat up' a derelict windmill and he and his two passengers were killed when he dived straight into it. He had been taught that an aircraft continued to 'sink' at the bottom of a dive, even though it was in a nose-up attitude, but he had not realised how much more the heavier Blenheim would sink than the lighter trainers he had flown before – hence the crash.

Mainly the losses were because the Blenheims were simply 'clapped out', and when considered no longer fit for operations, they were sent to training establishments. Once, when taking off, an engine cowling came loose at the front, stood up in the slipstream and the aircraft rolled over and crashed. But engine fires took the greatest toll and we had plenty of them, which even involved aircraft just out of a major overhaul where they were practically rebuilt. No matter how hard the ground staff worked they just could not keep pace with the endless problems. My pilot and I were up one night in the Oxford when the port engine started to give out long trails of sparks and the Flight Commander was seen on his knees outside dispersal, hands clasped together, praying that this was not going to be another disaster. We managed to land OK but it was a close call!

Sometimes we got an enemy intruder in the circuit. On one occasion he shot down two of our aircraft and caused a panic on the ground as well as in the air. All the lights on the airfield were put out and we were told to douse our navigation lights, stack up at different heights and circle the AI beacon until it was thought he had gone away. One night our illustrious VC was at the bottom of the stack when he said to his oppo 'I can see the green light on the airfield, I am going to land'. Over-ruling his oppo's advice that it wasn't the airfield because it was on the wrong heading for the runway he went ahead – and landed at a green signal light on the main Leeds to York railway line! They both survived but at the inquiry into the crash his oppo refused to fly with 'His Eminence' again and was told he must! In vain the man pleaded that the pilot, far from having 'implicit trust' in him (which we had been told was the first requirement for a successful partnership) he instead had ignored his advice completely. The Court of Inquiry would have none of it so he resigned from the course and returned to his squadron. We all thought this was a grave miscarriage of justice, especially as the scuttlebutt had it that the pilot was not even reprimanded.

On Friday that week I got a letter from Bert's girlfriend thanking me for my letter but saying she was sorry to tell me that her darling Bert was dead. Apparently, after extra tuition at Yatesbury, he had passed his test and had been posted to Penrhos just after I had left. He was doing his air-to-air gunnery in a Whitley off Pwllheli when its engines failed and they ditched in the sea. The aircraft floated and the crew were stood on the wing except Bert, who must have been firing from the rear turret. He was stood on the tail plane when a motor boat came up, presumably a safety boat on stand-by in case of such an accident. It took all the crew from the wing on board, which would have included Bert had he been in any other turret, and then its engine packed up and it started to drift away. The boatmen could not get it started again and desperately shouted to Bert to swim to them as the aircraft was beginning to sink. At that time of year the sea would have been freezing cold and he had already died of hypothermia when they finally got to him. His girlfriend went with his parents to identify his body and she said he looked 'so peaceful'. I was gutted – my dear, sweet, caring, Bert was dead! He had looked after me like a mother and now he was gone. It seemed that fate had been against him all his life and had he passed his test first time he might have been flying safely with me as we were always together. If I had failed as he did, I would likely have been there with him, but either way, he might still have been the one to be dealt the fatal card. You never knew how the 'cookie would crumble'. I wrote a letter of condolence to Bert's girlfriend, which was totally inadequate but heartfelt and I shall remember Bert to the end of my days. I had lost two pals in a week.

Our forays into Leeds continued whenever duty allowed, and our response to the losses we were suffering was typically RAF – we got a 'skin full'! No, we were not callous, just self-protective. We all knew that we were taking a gamble when we volunteered for aircrew, and our unfortunate mates had lost their gamble, but we had to go on! There was no point in letting it 'get to us', it would only destroy our confidence, and we needed all of that for our own survival. Whenever there were lessons to be learnt from a crash, however, we certainly took heed for future reference, so they had not died in vain. But those consumption victims had taken no gamble. They had been plucked willy nilly it seemed from thousands in the RAF, and that was why their plight had affected me so.

Walking back to the camp from the railway station one night we saw red and green navigation lights turning over and over in the sky. 'Ah yes', said some of the permanent staff 'that will be Batchy rolling a Blenheim.' Batchy was one of the two Atcherly brothers who had become legendary in the RAF for their madcap antics, like landing a Tiger Moth on an aircraft carrier despite a barrage of warning red Very lights and disappearing down the lowered plane lift! A pilot less well connected would have been drummed out of the Service, but both of them were now Group Captains and this one was our Station Commander. Their antics were so widely known in the RAF that anyone a little odd was always referred to as being 'Batchy' – a most dubious accolade!

I mentioned earlier that I had seen some Defiants across the airfield and I knew they were flown by Polish crews. How did I know? Well as Orderly Sergeant one day I was in charge of a pay parade and had to call out their names along with our own lads. At the end there were fifteen or so still waiting to be paid as they had not recognised their names when I pronounced them in English – well, Yorkshire anyway! I had to take my list to each one to have them point out their entry. There was also one Englishman who had so much deducted in 'Barrack Damages' that he had only two shillings and sixpence to come. He saluted the Paying Officer, took his pittance, and was walking past the adjacent savings table when the Station Warrant Officer (SWO) called loudly 'Remember National Savings!' The lad flung his pay on to the table declaring 'You might as well have the b—y lot!' So they got his pay and he got seven days' jankers!

The Defiant had been fitted with AI but was not a success as a night fighter as having only one engine its exhausts were directly in front of the pilot, which virtually blinded him. One night a Defiant ran out of fuel causing the engine to cut and the navigator was told to bale out. He struggled to get out of his turret when suddenly the engine burst into life again and it landed with him outside hanging on to the turret's guns for dear life! The pilot had at last remembered to switch over to his spare tank!

I was once Station Duty Sergeant and went with the SWO as my officer to inspect the Poles' billets where corsets were hung alongside many beds and perfume bottles littered their locker tops. The SWO was apoplectic, he almost choked, and I got an education in RAF expletives! They had quite a reputation with the ladies as being seen out with an airman in an unusual uniform made them quite a catch but did little to endear them to us. When we were at Blackpool a Pole bit a local lass's breasts. Had we been at Yatesbury we might have thought he was hungry, but we figured he had overdone the passion! We made the episode into a bawdy ditty that we sang with gusto. I could tell you a lot of lewd tales about the Poles but I fear the Censor would be offended!

Our course was nearing its close when we were told which squadron we would be going to and Danny and I had hit the jackpot. Our destination was to be 219 Squadron at Tangmere near Chichester, the traditional home of No. 1 Squadron, and the Spitfires from its two satellite airfields at Merston and Westhampnett were flying sweeps over Northern France under the famous 'Legless' Bader. It really was a plum posting!

We had enjoyed our stay at Church Fenton but the loss of so many friends (probably about 40 per cent of the course) had saddened us and it was time to move on.

CHAPTER FIFTEEN

Tangmere and 219 Squadron

The last week at Church Fenton was somewhat of an anti-climax. I was sorry that on our last night flight we had not achieved the 22,000 feet maximum ceiling of the Blenheim for we were recalled at 16,400 feet as an intruder had been detected and no one wanted to risk another landing on the Leeds/York railway line! But I consoled myself that, although I had failed to attain the highest I had ever flown to date, at least I now knew what the lads had told us of their experiences on operations had been true. It was a bind – cold, draughty, and uncomfortable, and from 15,000 feet upwards it had definitely been a struggle to coax the clapped out thing any higher. On the other hand Danny and I had heard that 219 Squadron was equipped with the new sensational Beaufighter that presently was the last word in aviation according to the national press, so the short-comings of our Blenheim were irrelevant and we just could not wait to get our hands on one. Then I was told that I had been given a week's leave, whereas Danny was going straight to Tangmere, which I could not understand. Normally I would have been delighted but now I was full of envy and would gladly have swapped places with him.

It was the first and last time in my RAF career that I did not want to go on leave even though it meant I should be home for my twentieth birthday on 13 May. Mum and Dad were delighted to have me home and we had a lovely family get together when I suspect their meagre rations were seriously depleted. As ever, nothing was too good for 'Our Dennis'! Dear old Donny was, well, dear old Donny, except that it seemed all my friends were 'at the War'. In our block of a dozen semi-detached houses on Carr House Road, just beyond Elmfield Park, there were four of us about the same age. George Young had been with me at Doncaster Grammar School, Dennis Potter was my best mate, and both were away in the Services. A lad I will call Bob was still at home in a reserved occupation at a local garage machining intricate parts for aero engines, but he had never been a chum. Of course I did not know then, but George was to go missing flying over the Burmese jungle, Dennis was to be lost in a submarine in the Med, and stay-at-home Bob was to go to prison for greedily fiddling time sheets to get unwarranted extra pay. What price fair reward or justice? Like I said before 'Who deals the cards?'

So I spent my leave visiting aunts and uncles, lying comfy and warm in my feather bed, and visiting my old workplace, which was a disaster as I felt I did not belong there anymore. But I revelled in being cosseted by Mum, who now knew that I was going to fly Beaufighters and, having read how potent they were in the press, feared for me – as every family did for their loved ones in those days. I was itching to get away to start the next adventure and even dragging those confounded kit bags did not deter me, as I joyfully made my way to Doncaster railway station. I took a taxi across London and Danny was on the platform at Chichester to greet me with a Hillman pick up truck and a WAAF driver waiting to take me to Tangmere.

18 May was one of the momentous days of my life. It began after breakfast when I had to report to the Stores where my old all-in-one flying suit and helmet were replaced with a sumptuous fur lined leather zip jacket and trousers and the latest lightweight helmet with all its attachments. After dinner I joined Danny and the crews in the "B" Flight truck going to prepare for the nights operations. They were a lively lot, full of fun, good natured backchat, jokes and horseplay. When we arrived at the Flight Hut I was introduced to Squadron Leader Dottridge, the Flight Commander, who had earned his right to his trademark RAF moustache thanks to his exploits in the Battle of Britain. 'Dot', as he was affectionately known by all the crews, was a jewel of a man who owned a beautiful four-litre Bentley, which sat outside the Flight going 'big bugger, little bugger' as it ticked over. It was in British racing green, had a canvas top, brass headlights and a torpedo-shaped supercharger at the front and he used it to take the lads out to various hostelries on our nights off. One of these was near Selsey Bill where he was wont to drive it down the six steps on to the patio of the pub and after getting well and truly 'refreshed' would reverse it up the said steps and on to the next port of call leaving the bystanders agape muttering about 'those fighter types'!

But I digress. Danny took me to a dispersal, showed me a Beau and proudly announced that, like all newcomers, we were to get the oldest aircraft on the Flight and this was to be *our* Beau! After those Blenheims at Church Fenton it looked absolutely *pristine*. I was totally gobsmacked. It looked so enormous, twice the size of a Blenheim, with massive 1,600 hp Hercules radial engines and it weighed over 10 tons. Its short nose with four 20 mm cannon clearly visible beneath it towered above me and it also had six .303 calibre machine-guns set into the wings. Its top speed enabled it to catch any German aircraft of that time (without diving). It looked what it was – fast, aggressive, powerful, awesome, brutal, and painted in its overall black paint scheme it appeared even more deadly. Some would have called it ugly, but I was captivated by it. To me it was *beautiful*. I spent more than an hour just walking round it, inspecting the Ki-Gas pump inside the engine wells, which I would have to operate if no electric trolley was available to start the engines, noting anything and everything a navigator should know about his aircraft. I sat in the swivel seat in my 'office' with all its gadgets halfway down the fuselage under a large Perspex blister canopy, and saw a snag at once. Although I had a marvellous view astern and to the sides, I had no view forwards, and obviously a navigator wants to see where he is going – not where he has just been! With practice I adapted to this back to front navigating, but it was never easy.

Still looking astern I saw the oxygen and compressed air bottles and other bits and bobs and was pleased to see how safe and easy it would be to 'bale out' in an emergency through the ample hatch at my feet. I swung my executive-style chair round to face forward where the rubber eyepiece of the Mk 4 set was ideally sited at eye level. Beyond it, on the floor, were four foot pedals that hydraulically 'cocked' the four cannon that lay in the belly, each with a hefty drum in its breech block. There were four of these drums hung up in each side of the roof secured by pegs to stop them coming adrift in violent combat manoeuvres. However, having to wrestle an empty ammunition pan off, replace it with a full one weighing God knows how much and the size of a washing machine drum, in a bucking aircraft with 'G' forces making it even heavier or alternatively weightless, was something I did not care to think of! Scuttlebutt had it that someone had tried to loop a Beau and at the top of the loop the drums, inexplicably unpegged, had gone through the roof, breaking its back, killing the crew, which was why they were hastily replaced with a belt feed. Luckily I had to do it only once on a test firing in ideal conditions and even that left me drenched in sweat but at least I managed not to get my fingers trapped. Nevertheless it was just wonderful and I would not have changed it for anything. It was almost unbelievable that with a miserly seventy-one hours flying to my credit and at just twenty years and five days of age I was going to be entrusted with the latest, fastest, most heavily armed, twin-seat twin-engined fighter, not only in the RAF, but in the world!

The best was yet to come. Danny said 'While you were on leave I have been learning to fly these monsters and this afternoon we are going to fly in our very own Beaufighter!' Never had a leave been better spent! At 16.05 hours, my logbook tells me, we spent 1 hour 35 minutes doing a low-flying practice with the local Chain Home Low Ground Control, newly designed to detect enemy aircraft trying to get below the radar screen. To celebrate our good fortune and full of youthful exuberance, we really did get *low*.

Next day, as a matter of unfinished business, we climbed to 26,500 feet in a heated aircraft in complete comfort with no draughts – so unlike our attempt in the old Blenheim. For a couple of weeks we flew daily, honing our skills and familiarising ourselves with the local terrain, until on 4 June Danny was tested by Dot and I was tested by Wing Commander Tommy Pike, the Squadron Commander, and his Navigator Sergeant 'Bunny' Austin to assess my proficiency in Aircraft Interception. Later Pike was to become Marshal of the Royal Force Sir Tom Pike GCB, CBE, DFC and Bar, Chief of Air Staff, and so I can truthfully 'shoot the line' that '*He* used to take orders from *me*!' We must have done well for on 11 June we undertook our first dusk patrol. This was quite a compliment as dusk patrols were usually carried out by experienced crews because sometimes enterprising German pilots would try to 'bounce' the unwary whilst there was still enough daylight for them to see us. Interestingly, it was still light when we took off at 23.25 hours because Double Summer Time had been brought in for the duration of the War!

From then on we took our place on the 'B' Flight crew roster, flying two nights and having two nights off, rotating with 'A' Flight. All night fighter squadrons did this, for it had been found that this was the best way to maintain the crews' efficiency and avoid them becoming overstressed and hence more accident prone. We soon fell into the routine. When 'B' Flight was on 'readiness' we got up in time to have a leisurely dinner and were taken to the Flight by the Commer truck, for it was a considerable distance from the Mess. Then we took off to test our aircraft and the radar installation, sometimes doing an exercise with a Ground Controller wanting to check his equipment's height and azimuth calibration. We got to know the ops personnel, even their Christian names. Once we took two WAAF officers from the ops room for a trip in our Beau, one behind Danny and the other with me in the back. Having got nicely airborne I beckoned to my passenger to take my seat so that she would get a better view whilst I went to step into the escape hatch well. All at once she flung her arms round my neck. 'This is so sudden,' I thought, 'I didn't even know she fancied me.' Then I felt the slipstream tearing at my legs. The escape hatch had not been properly shut and was slowly opening against its pneumatic rams. I was stepping out into space without my parachute! It could not be closed in the air so we had to land, close it properly and take off again but this time I didn't get a hug and I did not feel *too* sorry! If all went well with our tests we went back to the Mess and had tea, but if we had a problem we had to stay until it was rectified. We went back to the Flight an hour or so before the dusk patrol took off, which varied according to the time of sunset. We took off in pairs and a normal patrol lasted around three hours but we never left until the next pair arrived to take over our patrol line some thirty miles out to sea. When we landed the Commer took us to the Mess for a slap up night flying supper of eggs and bacon and then we walked back to our billets. The following morning we rose about 11.00 hours and repeated the routine. The next two days 'A' Flight took over but we still went to the Flight and sorted out any 'bugs' that had shown up or just had a flip to keep our 'hand in'.

Meanwhile we were finding our way about the camp, which had suffered badly from bombing. Most of the accommodation and all the hangars were unusable but the Sergeants' Mess dining room was still intact and that was where we were fed. A civilian bus ran through the camp but no one was allowed to board or leave it between the two Guard Houses. There was also a civilian café near the gate with walls adorned with the signatures of legendary Battle of Britain pilots and our fond hope was that one day we would be famous enough to be asked to add our own names to this illustrious band. As the camp had been targeted so often by enemy bombers, it had been decided to disperse the aircrews as well as their aircraft. The officers had taken over a very large country house set in a leafy estate and the NCOs were billeted in 'Oving Manor', a Victorian house some two miles almost due south of the airfield. This was an advantage as it was also two miles nearer to

Chichester, which we frequented on our nights off. Often we had to walk back having missed the last bus thanks to some pubs having a relaxed attitude to the licensing laws or if we had been dallying with some local wench!

'Oving' was an eerie place, devoid of furnishings, next to the graveyard and we suspected it had once been the vicarage. It was downright spooky, especially when we walked in at three or four o'clock in the morning after we had been flying. All the rooms downstairs were filled with beds as well as the upstairs bedrooms and with its stone floors and emptiness the echoes rivalled the sound track of any horror film. In the entrance hall you could have easily built a modern detached house and the plumbing had to be seen to be believed. I had made a mate of another navigator called David Hendry, a Scotsman whose father was a river pilot on the Clyde, and he got me a bed in his room, which was next to the room of Sergeant Dye, a Sheffield lad, and his Pilot Sergeant Hodgekinson. These two were high among the top scorers in the trade, long before 'Cats Eyes' Cunningham became well known, and two of the nicest lads you would ever meet. Both were courting waitresses from the Odeon Cinema Café in 'Chi' as we now familiarly called it, where Welsh rarebit figured largely, and sometimes exclusively, on the 'Menu'.

Outside 'Oving' one of the navigators parked his lovely big Austin car, which he had used in Civvy Street to carry his wares to high class ladies' gown shops in his trade as a dress salesman. Needless to say he was popular amongst the ladies who hoped he still had a few designer frocks in stock. Late one night we came in to find his pilot sleeping on the floor in the corridor having been locked out by his navigator who had considerately put his blankets outside too, and was now 'entertaining' a popsy within.

Sadly accidents still happened and we had two in quick succession. First, one of our crews had an engine fire when on patrol some twenty miles out to sea and had to 'bale out'. The pilot was spotted in his dinghy at first light and rescued but no trace was found of his navigator. A few nights later I was walking through Chichester with David when we heard a loud bang and saw a fire reflecting on the clouds some distance away. It was a sight I had become all too familiar with at Church Fenton and I rushed to the nearest telephone box and called our Ops Room. 'Yes,' they said, 'it seems to be one of our aircraft somewhere near Merston Crossroads'.

We continued our night out, naturally very subdued, and caught the last bus back to 'Oving Manor' from where we telephoned the Ops Room to find out who had 'bought it'. In our aircraft we sat on top of our dinghies and it transpired that the CO_2 bottle that inflated the dinghy on 'ditching' had ruptured on take-off, causing the dinghy to bubble out between the pilot's legs, pushing his stick forward. The pilot could do nothing to prevent them crashing into the ground where it burst into the inferno we had seen. It was past midnight but we decided to go up to their room and get their personal belongings together. We switched on the light and started this gruesome task when suddenly the mournful strains of Handel's Largo began to fill the room sending a chill down our spines. The explanation was simple, the radio had taken time to warm up when we switched on the light, to which it was also connected, but it was enough to spook us and we retired to our beds somewhat shaken. It was a freak accident and thereafter we all carried a dagger down our flying boots to puncture any repeat of the tragic occurrence. True to our code we joked about it, 'Be careful where you stab,' we said, 'or you might as well *be* dead!' Who was it? Well just say we watched his father collect the Austin and we all hoped he had enjoyed his 'night of love'.

David and I were walking back to 'Oving' one afternoon when we saw a Mk 2 Beau doing some unusual flying, diving and then pulling up repeatedly. The Mk 2 was a variant with 'Merlin' engines as used in the Spitfire and was being tested at Ford by the highly experienced pilots of Fighter Interception Unit to compare its performance against our Hercules-engined Mk 1s. From our elevated viewpoint we could see what he was doing as clearly as if we were seated in the dress circle of a theatre. His port wheel was down but not his starboard wheel and he was trying to 'throw' it out by using the 'G' forces as he pulled out of a dive – a ploy we used regularly ourselves. He then dived again, but to our horror went straight into the ground and a great cloud of smoke and flame shot into the sky. Recounting this in the Flight that night Dot said 'The Merlin engine cuts out at the bottom of a dive unlike our radial engines. We had the same trouble with Spits until they fitted them with petrol injection like the Me 109s.' Poor old Donald Lake (for it was he) only left 219 in November and he must have forgotten he was not still here flying radial-engined Beaus!'

We had some well connected people on the Flight including Max Aitkin, the son of the Minister for Aircraft Production, who according to the scuttlebutt, which for once was believable, did not get the oldest Beau when he arrived, as 'Daddy' sent him a brand new one. Perhaps because of him we had a visit from Lord Halifax, newly returned from his post as Ambassador to the United States, and the whole squadron was paraded for his inspection. He was shown all round a Beau by Wing Comander Pike, who was surrounded by top RAF 'Brass', and it was explained to him that we were not permitted to fly over hostile territory, fearing that the secrets of our equipment might fall into enemy hands. After all this his parting shot was to enquire, 'How many bombs do you carry?' Perhaps he thought we were going to bomb the intruders instead of shooting them down. We were not impressed and if his brief in the US had been to talk them into entering the war on our side, we understood why they were still neutral.

Shortly after Wing Commander Pike was posted to No. 11 Group Head Quarters and Squadron Leader Wight-Boycott of 'A' Flight was promoted in his place. This was not a popular move as Tom was liked and respected by all for he had that elusive 'common touch', which was not Boycott's forte. Some time later the newly promoted Group Captain Pike decided to revisit his old squadron in a Lease Lend Havoc and we were out in force to watch his arrival. He wheeled it in and then appeared to be struggling to get the tail down. He floated across the airfield, ran out of runway, and gently the nose went down into the sunken road at the end. Luckily the civvy bus that used that road was not due for another hour! He had forgotten that the Havoc did not have a tail wheel, it had a tricycle undercarriage so its 'tail' wheel was under its nose. An explanation was given for this gaff but you couldn't fool us. It was nice to think that even the most experienced were not infallible.

The Fighter/Intruder Havoc had several variants, from the 'Boston' bomber version to the highly improbable 'Turbinlight', one of which we had on the station. It was basically a Havoc with its nose cut off to accommodate a damned great searchlight and a large petrol-engined generator in the bomb bay to power it. So desperate was the search to find an answer to the nightly bombing that all sorts of counter measures were tried, some so bizarre that they beggared belief. The idea was to take off with a Hurricane in formation, use radar to get behind a raider, switch on the light at close range and the Hurricane would then shoot it down. No chance! As soon as the light was switched on the Hun promptly took evasive action, or the Hurricane was too far away, or had even lost formation and just wasn't there. We were sent off one night to try dropping flares that were supposed to illuminate the invader and it was obvious to us, but not to whoever thought up this scheme, that it would also light us up as well, which was not the idea at all! The idea was to shoot them down before they even knew we were there, not have them shoot back at us. I know it sounds unsporting, but we were convinced ours was the best way. I kept putting the flares down a chute, which was supposed to ignite them as they fell out. But fortunately none worked, and we stopped when we saw that the woods around Arundel were ablaze, however we thought it best not to mention that in our de-briefing!

For some time there had been no 'trade' in our sector but every night we still took off in pairs and spent the next three hours doing practice interceptions on each other, boring, but necessary to keep our skills honed for we never knew when we might need them. Ford Aerodrome (now an open prison) was nearer the coast than Tangmere, and they would phone our ops to say that the sea fret was coming in and we would be recalled. If we didn't get home sharpish we would have to divert, usually to Middle Wallop or West Malling, the two adjacent sectors. One such night this happened to us, and although we lost no time responding the mist came in quicker than usual and we did a silly thing – we tried to dive through it whilst still out to sea thinking we could get under it. We nearly got under it when I shouted to Danny 'Pull out, pull out' for from my position I saw we were diving straight into the sea! I saw the waves just as the last wisps of mist were thinning; another 100 feet and we would have dived into them. The trouble was that Danny could not see anything because his windscreen had misted up and if my blister had done the same it would have been the end of us. It was a salutary reminder that you could never relax. It was also proof that your luck was still holding out – but for how long? No doubt those who 'bought it' had thought the same.

Every month or so Tangmere and Ford combined in a church parade on Goodwood Racecourse. We went in lorries through the woods of Goodwood Estate, where a French Canadian Army Regiment was encamped, and stood in the grandstand to listen to the Padre give his sermon. The parade was optional but the Padre was so sincere and articulate that he attracted a large following each month, looking for spiritual guidance or perhaps something to hold on to in a precarious, unpredictable world. Whatever it was he had the knack of reaching out to comfort and reassure. So different to the Padre at Yatesbury, who enthusiastically led the applause in the NAFFI on Saturday nights for a conscripted, foulmouthed, club circuit comedian, to prove how trendy he was. On the way back Danny said 'He's the man I'd like to bury me!' I was shocked to hear him say this as he had never spoken like that before, and in view of recent happenings, I wondered if he had some premonition. But he would say no more and I soon dismissed it from my mind, until much later.

'B' Flight entertained some submariners from a base on Southampton Water and showed them around our beloved Beaus, which they professed to greatly admire, but when we offered to take them up with us on a night flying test, not one accepted. A week later we made a reciprocal visit to their depot and were shown round their claustrophobic craft but when they offered to take us out on a test dive our response was exactly like theirs. Not on your Nellie! It wasn't cowardice, just every man to his own poison.

A short time later 'B' Flight received an invitation much more to our liking – to tour Henty and Constable Brewery in Chichester and afterwards take tea with some unspecified ladies' circle. We did not question if this was a 'thank you' for the enthusiastic support we had given to their products over many moons, we just accepted with alacrity. We were conducted through the brewing process by a director and finished up in the 'Test House' where he explained that a keg of each brew was kept so that it could be checked if a complaint was made by one of their pubs that a barrel was 'off'. Some of the bulkier, taller lads managed to hem our guide in at the far end of this treasure house, asking him detailed questions about fermentation and the like, which gratified his ego, thinking how interesting his tour must have been to them. Finally it dawned on him that while he was valiantly trying to answer these decoys, we at the other end, had been doing our best to assist the firm by sampling every brew in the handily placed mugs. By the time he was able to intervene we had emptied the lot! We made a garrulous exit, thanking our hosts profusely, but we suspected that 'A' Flight would be unlikely to get a similar invitation!

Fate, however, soon extracted its revenge for the Ladies' Guild we were to take tea with, turned out to be the Bishop Otter College for young ladies aspiring to become physical training teachers, and I found myself at the head of a table of twelve of these eighteen-year-old ravishing Amazons! They were all agog to hear of our exploits and I cannot describe the difficulty I had replying with one hand over my mouth trying to deflect my alcohol laden breath, which would have felled a grown man at forty paces! 'Dot' and the other senior aircrew were seated at the top table with the instructresses who, being more worldly wise than their pupils, swiftly realised our intoxication and you could see that on their table the atmosphere was, shall we say, strained. This added to our delight, knowing that we, the lesser mortals, had for once come off best. The lads voted the expedition a great success and the prominence of the telephone number of the college in the Mess and in every kiosk for miles around confirmed their assessment! We always aimed to please and as the old song says 'Love will find a way'!

I was so happy flying that I used to sing all the time and being a jazz fanatic my favourite was the '2.19 Blues', a song about the Wild West Railroad and of course it was our squadron number. 'The 2.19 took my baby awaaay,' I wailed 'the 2.17 will bring her back some Daaay', giving my soulful rendition of this long forgotten dirge! I loved Nat Gonella and his signature tune 'Georgia on my mind' and I sang all the popular ballads of the day. The big American bands had not yet made an impact on the British public as America was not in the war and we only heard them on the wireless. British artists and bands could still make the old 78 rpm vinyl records but the terrible loss of shipping inflicted by the U-boats meant that there were no US records for all imports were restricted to food and munitions. There was one American band led by 'Snake Hips' Johnson that performed at the Café de Paris in London until one night in an air raid a bomb killed him and half his band and the survivors came to Tangmere as the station band. They were a revelation, especially one of their saxophonists who was so 'hot' he had the dancers jumping – literally! They all seemed to have tall blonde wives with incredibly high heels, leopard skin coats, and toy poodles. I just could not hear that band often enough!

I was sent on a navigation course at Cranage, the only one on the squadron to be selected, and came back a fully qualified navigator! Immediately Danny and I were sent with a detachment of four aircraft, under Flt/Lt Aitkin, to Valley in Anglesey to provide night cover for Liverpool while 456 (Aussie) Squadron was forming up. The only thing I remember about Valley was that the Sergeants' Mess fronted onto a small lake from whence emanated an all pervading stench because raw sewage was discharged into it! We were glad to get back to Tangmere, where we had to have a long bath, wash our hair and change our clothes, to get rid of the smell that seemed to cling to us before we managed to regain our appetites

Whilst I was away David had been commissioned and he found new friends in the Officers' Mess. However, a new crew, Pilot Officer Peter Oakes and his navigator Sergeant Johnny Walsh arrived on 'B' Flight. Danny hit it off with Peter, I did with Johnny, and from that time on they became an integral part of our lives. Peter was slim and somewhat diffident in demeanour, with a nice little two-seater MG he called his 'Hoover' because it picked up bits of fluff! Johnny was the son of a Lancashire mother and an Irish father. He was untidy, maybe even scruffy, and like me, a bit of a rebel! All four of us soon became firm friends.

One night we were in the Crew Room with those next in line for take-off wearing their night goggles to aid their night vision when three officers came in, took over 'Dot's' office and started to interview us separately. They asked us to complete an intelligence test and after we had all finished they called me back and told me I had excelled in the test and asked if I wanted to be commissioned. 'Yes,' I said, when there was some muttering in the darkened background and I was asked to leave for a moment and I can imagine what then transpired. 'You cannot commission *him*! He has a Yorkshire accent, he's a bit bolshie and his father is a *bus driver*!' they would have said. Shock, horror, *a bus driver's son* in the Officers' Mess! Unthinkable! Intolerable!

I would have pleaded guilty to the first charge as, yes, I was a Yorkshireman and proud of it. My accent was not nearly as broad as some for Auntie May's elocution lessons had 'taken the edge' off the usual comedy caricature portrayal of a Yorkshire accent though I might have conceded that my vowels were still a bit flat. 'Bolshie' I certainly was not! Like all Yorkshiremen I spoke my mind having been brought up to 'always speak the truth and shame the Devil' but this did not always go down well in the RAF where toadying had been brought to a fine art by some creeps. What really got to me was the bus driver bit! How could they? How dare they? Mum and Dad were the salt of the earth and to me had twice or thrice times the value of those who were passing this judgement. I was also riled because I knew, without being conceited, that I was one of the best navigators on the squadron. Why else would both Tommy Pike and Wight-Boycott have selected me to stand in for their own navigators when they were on leave or otherwise engaged? In every assessment I had been given to date in the RAF I had been rated as 'above average' or 'well above average' yet they had ignored my record because I came from 'the wrong side of the track'. So I was called in again and politely told I would be informed when a vacancy occurred. But of course I never was – as a realist I never expected I would!

This class distinction was endemic in the RAF at that time. There was a tacitly accepted order in every aspect and facet of the Service and aircrew in particular were traditionally drawn from the socially privileged. The pecking order began with the aristocracy, followed by the nobility, the landed gentry, then professions like law, high finance, medicine, and the church, and then artisans who engaged in 'trade' (which in itself was almost a dirty word). At the bottom of the pile came workers, especially manual workers, who were so low they scarcely rated any consideration at all. As a rule of thumb, if you received an allowance (from Daddy), a yearly or monthly salary or stipend you were 'in' – but if you earned a weekly wage you were 'out'.

Accents were assessed similarly. At the top was 'cut glass' (which was surely inbred), followed by 'posh' (which was supposedly acquired). Dorset, Wiltshire, West Country and other rustic dialects were considered quaint. Scottish, Australian, New Zealand (but not South African or Canadian) were acceptable, but only Brummie, Scouse, Irish and Welsh came below Lancashire and Yorkshire. Based on these prejudices I was never in with a chance. I was near to the bottom of the pecking order and judged by that and not on my ability. I did not complain as I knew it would be pointless. You could not buck the 'system'. Oh yes, the old 'them' and 'us' I had hated so much from my childhood in the Depression was still thriving here and I had become its latest victim.

Johnny Walsh and I were walking back to 'Oving' one bright moonlit night, having done our stint, when we saw an aircraft flying down the road towards us, at no more than 100 feet. We knew it was a Jerry by the distinctive sound of its diesel engines. We could not dive into the hedge bottom as there was a water-filled ditch on both sides of the road, so, ridiculously, we sort of cringed as it passed over us and we recognised it as a Heinkel 111 bomber. He was so low we could clearly see a gunner with a light on in his under belly position. With a light on inside he would have been unable to see anything outside and that saved us from being machine-gunned for we were sitting ducks in the middle of the road. I realised that Luck had been with me once more.

Lord Nuffield, owner of the Austin/Morris car conglomerate, must have been told that night fighter crews flew all night, slept all day, and therefore never saw the sun. In a magnanimous gesture he sent a sun lamp to every night fighter squadron to compensate for this deprivation, including 219. We were told to report to the sick bay at 14.00 hours when the MO (Medical Officer) would administer the first dose (or whatever it was called) and we were happy to oblige, hoping a Hollywood-type suntan would make us irresistible to the opposite sex. The MO was not there when we arrived so we waited, and we waited, until at 14.40 hours some bright spark said, 'Blow him, the damned thing is here and plugged in, let's switch it on and do it ourselves'. In those days there were no sun parlours so we did what we thought was the 'done thing'. We stripped to our trousers and, well, sunned ourselves. Then the MO turned up at 14.55 hours and went berserk. 'You idiots,' he shouted, 'how long have you been like that?' 'Oh, about fifteen minutes,' we said, at which he really exploded. 'Two minutes! Two minutes! That's the maximum for the first session!' he screamed and collapsed into a chair frothing at the mouth – someone with a hip flask had to revive him. Alas he was right for as the dusk patrol tried to get out to their aircraft they promptly fell into a slit trench, blind as bats. The outcome was that, for the first time in its long history, 219 Squadron had to report to Group that it was unable to operate that night due to unforeseen circumstances and the Sick Bay ran out of cream to treat sunburn victims. Thank goodness that I was at the back and so suffered less than some. The sun lamp was never used again but I hope someone had the decency to write to Lord Nuffield explaining that it was a much appreciated gesture – but a mistaken conception.

Peter Oakes and Johnny Walsh were going through the preliminaries prior to being accepted for operational duties. Johnny had been one of the air gunners impressed on squadron to use the new AI with only local training. As he had been operational before, Johnny found this familiarisation process a bit of a doddle and he denigrated Peter's efforts until now Peter was afraid that if he did anything wrong it would provoke another outburst. Danny and I talked this problem over and decided that what we had at first thought was Peter's diffidence was actually a lack of self confidence, which Johnny's constant carping was making worse. What he needed from Johnny was encouragement not criticism and Danny asked if I would fly with Peter to try to bolster his battered ego. I readily agreed and we took off to test a Beau after it had just completed a major overhaul. We got off the ground nicely, without any of the Beau's incipient swing, but at once I noticed that we were heading down again instead of upwards, and I called to Peter to use the trim tabs on the elevators to make the aircraft rise. He replied that he was fully trimmed but the plane was going further down towards the perimeter hedge and we were too far down the runway to abort the take-off. I swung my seat round to face the tail and saw the trim tabs were right down, not up as they should have been and, knowing we were heading for disaster, I yelled to him 'the other way, the opposite way!' I was just in time and we scraped over the hedge with only feet to spare and climbed away into the sky – two very relieved, sweating airmen. It was discovered when we landed that during the overhaul some erk had connected the trim controls the wrong way round so it had not been Peter's fault at all. The way Peter had handled the crisis brought congratulations from Johnny, did wonders for Peter's confidence, and soon they were fully operational. Again my luck had held out, but it did no good to dwell on it, far better to have another pint and forget it!

It was 23 December and I was laid snuggled in my bed at 'Oving' after a heavy night out in Chi knowing I would be flying on Xmas Eve, when some wag came in and said 'Gos, the Adjutant wants you to phone him – you have been posted abroad'. Thinking the lads were pulling my leg my reply was monosyllabic and plural as I pulled the blankets further over my head. Ten minutes later someone else shook me and said, 'The Adj wants to know why you haven't phoned him. Honest, it's true, you've been posted overseas!' Still unconvinced I dragged myself downstairs and phoned the Adjutant, who was a bit short, but when I explained what had happened, he was almost apologetic. 'Terribly sorry old chap,' he said, 'Xmas and all that you know but I will try to get it put off till the festivities are over, you had better see the MO though!'

I had dressed when Johnny walked in and said 'We are posted overseas' with a massive grin on his face. 'I knew I was, but what luck you are too!' I replied and we slapped each other on the back and shook hands gleefully. We set off to walk to the Mess for dinner and on the way we passed the local pub. Well, in truth we didn't pass it, in fact we rarely did. It was a regular port of call for us, and inside were several of our lads and WAAFs of our acquaintance. With the festive season on us and to celebrate our posting, one drink led to another and we left in a blissful state of intoxication. After dinner we presented ourselves at the sick bay to see the MO for the strict medical we needed for overseas duty. If our inebriation caused any problems we had decided to blackmail him with innuendoes about the sun lamp fiasco, but to our surprise, he reeled away from us and said 'Jeez! If you can sup that much ale, you're *fit*!' He gave us a couple of jabs and that concluded our Overseas Medical. A piece of cake!

We had a riotous Xmas, serving the Airmen's Dinner and then being entertained in the Officers' Mess, before we sat down in our own Mess to eat a truly gargantuan meal. We could tell that the officers were having a particularly riotous time for every now and then the tannoy would burst forth with the news that the Station Commander's wife had presented him with a baby. From the din in the background it sounded like they were all helping him to celebrate!

All too soon Johnny and I handed in our parachutes and other kit, were given our clearance from the station and warrants to travel to No. 1 Ferry Training Unit at Honeybourne in the wilds of Worcestershire. I was sad to be leaving but once again I felt the adrenalin rush of entering into a new, unknown adventure. We were taken to Chichester station in the same Hillman truck that had first taken me to Tangmere. We humped our gear on to the platform, and finding our train wasn't due until two hours later, we decided to put our kit into the Baggage Room and have a last noggin in one of our favourite pubs. This was a mistake. The landlord was so sorry to see us go, as you would be to lose your best customers, that he pushed the boat out with free beer. Subsequent train times came and went until we were lucky to scrape onto the last one to London, where we arrived to find that the next train to our destination was the next day. There was nothing else we could do but book into the YMCA for the night. This provided us with an opportunity to explore the capital and its jazz clubs in particular. I do not remember how successful we were but my next recollection was waking up in the YMCA to find a cleaner sweeping round my bed. 'What a terrible night wasn't it?' she said, 'Was it?' I enquired, wondering if she knew more about our exploits than we did. 'Yes,' she said 'I think half London is ablaze!' 'Oh is it?' I replied, 'I never heard a thing!' When we went outside we saw what she meant. There were fires everywhere, and we had a job to get through to the station, only to be told that they were not sure if we could get through to our destination even if we changed twice on the way. Being already overdue we had to take a chance and boarded a train that wandered, apparently aimlessly, through the countryside at a snail's pace, until we eventually arrived at 16.30 hours to find our old SWO from Tangmere waiting to meet us. 'Where the blazes have you been?' he asked 'this is the second day I've waited for you!' Quick as lightning we replied 'We got caught in the London Blitz', which was nearly true.

He drove us to the camp and saw to it that we had good billets, which was extremely kind of him. He told us that we would be going to Filton, a suburb of Bristol where Beaufighters were built (there were also shadow factories building them too) to pick up a brand new aircraft and after we had done some consumption tests, we would fly it abroad. The aerodrome was comparatively new and set in beautiful agricultural country but our billets were so widely dispersed that we were issued with bicycles to get to and from them.

That night when I went to bed, I laid awake thinking over my time at Tangmere. I knew Johnny would sleep well and I envied the way he could detach himself almost as if he was an observer of the passing scene rather than being a part of it. I, on the other hand, always felt deeply involved, perhaps because I was young and impressionable. Maybe my upbringing had taught me to be so caring and concerned for others that they became part of my extended family. Whatever it was I could not sleep as I went over the past, with its highs and lows, its triumphs and tragedies, its fun and its frustrations. I went over the commissioning saga and decided that I ought to have taken into account that, as the premier fighter station, one could expect it to zealously cling to its RAF traditions. More importantly I had learned my trade and I was now the 'finished article', wise to ways that the Beau could snap at you if tried to take liberties with it, and never forgetting to expect the unexpected.

I remembered the glorious nights when the moon lit up the towering cumulus clouds, breathtakingly beautiful, fantastic, dreamlike, which had so enchanted me that I knew I had found my metier. We, the night fighters, were a breed apart, proud of our unique skills, and an exclusive fraternity! I also recalled the nights when low cloud, driving rain, and minimal visibility tested our abilities to the utmost, but that was part of the learning curve. I laughed to myself when I thought about our brewery visit, Bishop Otter College, and the submariners, and I remembered those who had 'bought it' and the times when I could so easily have done the same. I decided that Tangmere had been good for me and good to me. It had prepared me for what was to come, whatever that might be, and although I was still four months short of my twenty-first birthday I felt I was man enough to handle anything. And the prospect excited me!

CHAPTER SIXTEEN

Journey into the Unknown

Honeybourne was a lovely spot, in countryside so beautiful we began to wonder why anyone would want to go elsewhere in the whole world. It was typically England at her best, halfway between Evesham and Stratford-upon-Avon in rolling Worcestershire pastures, fruit orchards and strawberry fields. Its southern end was appropriately called Cow Honeybourne, and cows there were aplenty. But best of all the natives were friendly. Even in February it was a delight to cycle around the camp hinterland to explore this haven of peace and plenty. We did not care to think how loathe we might be have been to leave it in summer. But this was January and we knew not where we would be by then, hopefully in some exotic Eastern land, yet the portents were not good. Our SWO friend from Tangmere told us that the demand for new Beaufighters from the factories was so great that we should prepare ourselves for a considerable delay before our turn came.

Johnny and I only saw Danny and Peter, our pilots, when we were waiting around the Flight Hut in the vain hope that our turn would come sooner than expected. When we were dismissed we were at a loose end for the rest of the day and our pilots drove off in Peter's 'Hoover' and we rode off on our bikes to admire the pretty villages and the scenery, getting back in time for supper in the Sergeants' Mess.

On our way back to our billets one warm evening, hot and weary from a day's cycling, we decided to call in at the local pub for a refreshing pint before having another early night. 'Two pints please,' we said to the landlord. He replied 'No beer, but we have some cider!' We were staggered. We knew there was a war on but no beer! Things must be getting desperate! He looked at our downcast faces and taking pity on our dilemma but a trifle reluctantly, as if he really would prefer to keep it for his 'regulars', he advised 'It is a very good local cider, I can recommend it, we have sweet or rough.' Anything being better than nothing we decided on his cider. When he asked 'Sweet or rough?' we (tough little so-and-sos as we thought we were) disdainfully chorused 'Rough!' After all it was only cider – kids' stuff! I recall the amused but knowing look he gave us! Three pints later we staggered out, tried to get on our bikes, failed, then wheeled them back to our billets, and fell into our beds. In the morning I was wakened by a knock on my bunk door from one of the lads in the hut asking if I was all right and did I know it was 11.30 hours. I tried to raise my head from the pillow but couldn't so I weakly replied 'Come in'. I explained to him how I had been introduced to rough cider last night and that was how I now felt – *rough!* He laughed and said 'I'll get you some tea and a wad (bun) from the NAAFI.' He also did the same the next day until I finally got up and went to Johnny's bunk to see how he was. He was not there and when I enquired about him from the lads in his hut they burst out laughing 'Oh he is in the sick bay!' So off I went to the sick bay where he lay in a bed and a sorrier sight I have never seen! 'Bloody cider,' he moaned and I castigated him for ignoring my advice and having a pint more than me. I never mentioned the state I had been in myself thereby establishing my superior appreciation of our alcoholic capacity. The MO saw me on my way out and taking one look at me he said 'You will not be flying for a bit so I will give you a week's leave – you look as if you could do with it!' I did not go to tell Johnny but when I got back he was furious. 'I get ten days in dock and you get leave,' he said and for a week our relationship was definitely strained. The episode gave us a timely warning to beware of local booze we might happen upon abroad and some who had firsthand experience advised us to be particularly wary of Anisette-based drinks. These came in different guises in various countries but could be easily recognised as they all turned white when water was added to them and taking a drink of water up to twenty-four hours later made you intoxicated again. Wise counsel indeed and we never forgot it and Johnny in particular needed no reminding.

It was 12 February before our call came to collect our new Beaufighter and on the following day we were flown down to the Bristol works at Filton where we proudly took delivery of X7807. While the paperwork was being sorted out we had a chance to wander round their airfield to see virtually all their present production of Blenheims, including the Mk V, which I later flew as a 'Bisley' although the name was never officially adopted. There were also a number of Bombay transports and Beaufort torpedo planes from which the Beaufighter was spawned using the same rear fuselage and wings (not the Blenheim as was mistakenly believed). They had Taurus engines giving about 1,000 hp in total less than our Beaufighters, a bulky forward fuselage to house a crew of four and an 18- inch torpedo or 1,500 lbs of bombs and two gun turrets. I later flew one myself, for it was easy to change seats in the air, and with all that weight it was so slow to react to the controls that it sort of wallowed about and I felt sorry for those who had to fly it on operations. We called it 'The Flying Cow'!

Most exciting, however, were the prototypes of the future generations of our Beaufighters, later called Buckinghams, Buckmasters and Brigands, which we were kept some distance from as they were secret at that time. What was obvious was that they all had twin tails showing that the dihedral tail plane modification on the latest Beaus designed to get the straight tail out of the main plane's wash was only partially successful. Only the Brigand achieved any real success and that was in an anti-insurgent role in Malaya and Iraq but really it was the jet age that overtook them. However, at Filton that day we wondered if we would ever fly them.

Danny and I took three hours to get back to Honeybourne just twenty-five minutes away for Danny had to carry out a consumption test and I had a complicated navigation exercise to complete. The next day we flew the same exercises for over six hours before being told to land at Bobbington as our base was closed by bad weather. This came as no surprise to us as we had flown through some foul stuff on the courses we had been ordered to fly at near ground level. We had been up in the mountains of Scotland and the down draughts in the glens had created problems we had never before encountered. We were told our maximum height was to be 500 feet so that our range could be accurately calculated for our transit flight because the engines consumed differing amounts of fuel at other heights. Aircraft built by Bristol also varied from those built by Fairey or Rootes shadow factories and Bristol-built engines were so superior to shadow factory builds that they used up to 300 rpm less for the same output. This meant that on some aircraft it was not necessary to lead with one throttle to cancel out the Beau's incipient tendency to swing on take-off. All these foibles had to be fed into the maximum range equation before we departed on our journey with different calculations for every aircraft. The navigators' problems were no less complex for no radar navigation equipment was to be carried lest it fell into enemy hands and the only maps we had were basic in the extreme for security purposes. These calculations had to be checked and double checked so we carried out long flights using different engine boost and propeller settings over routes using AA-type road maps covering the length and breadth of the country. Each night when we got back, cold and stiff from our travels, we had to wait our turn to be debriefed and the day's events were discussed in detail. Johnny protested that such subterfuge was unnecessary to keep him away from cider as he was already cured.

Danny and I flew to Tangmere for a weekend to show off our brand new Beau and to say 'Cheerio' to old friends. By special invitation we did a 'weather test' for them on the Sunday and so that they could get a better view of the latest modifications to our aircraft we beat up the Control Tower in a breath-taking high-speed pass. The Beau was almost noiseless when making a ground attack and it later became known as the 'Whispering Death' for by the time the sound reached you it had already gone – very impressive. We flew back to Honeybourne on Monday after a convivial break and then on to what was to become our Forward Base from whence we should leave for an as yet unknown destination. It turned out to be a new satellite airfield to the Coastal Command Station at Portreath called Trebelzue and when we got out of the plane we were amazed to find ourselves surrounded by reporters and cameramen. We frantically racked our brains to think what we had done. Why had we suddenly become famous – or was it notorious? We learned the answer was much simpler, for after taking photos of us stood in front of our aircraft they gathered round a middle-aged Squadron

Leader who had been made Station Commander of what had previously been his own farm and ours was the first aircraft to officially land there.

We flew a few times from Trebelzue on various tests often in company with Peter and Johnny and the scenery was quite spectacular for you took off over a 200 foot cliff into the Godrevy Heritage Coastal Reserve. One day there was a slight haze and it was an eerie feeling as we hung seemingly motionless over the sea with these massive cliffs towering above us as far as the eye could see to the north whilst to the south we could just make out the lighthouse on Godrevy Head There had been little radio chat between us and when we landed we were strangely subdued. I think we were all so overwhelmed by this timeless grandeur that we realised how puny and insignificant mankind was in the presence of Eternity.

Our aircraft had developed a few niggling faults for my logbook tells me we flew it to Filton several times to get them fixed and we tested them again until we were satisfied that we had prepared ourselves against any foreseeable eventuality before we set off on our ferry flight – but of course you could never be 100 per cent certain. We now left Honeybourne for good and used our new base at Trebelzue ready to make our trip and were finally told our destination was Egypt. We were issued with our tropical kit including our pith helmets, shorts, and I got a long barrel Smith and Wesson .45 revolver, probably a WWI weapon (I wondered if some gallant officer had brandished it going over the top at the Somme) and was told it was to be worn at all times. It did not cause the same hilarity as when we got our flying kit but we had a good look at our knees to assess if we would look sexy in our shorts. I managed to wangle a flight to Finningley to see my parents and reassure them that I would take care of myself. The four days I had at home just rushed by for I had to allow time to make the long train journey back and failure to arrive on time would be a court-martial offence. I managed it with a day to spare, which was spent going over our route via Gibraltar and Malta. We were to fly well out to sea over the Bay of Biscay to avoid Ju 88s patrolling to cover U-boats returning to their French bases and as we were completely unarmed it seemed a sensible thing to do. We were then to keep outside Portuguese territorial waters, and to make our approach to Gibraltar from the west.

We were not to attempt formation flying as this just wasted fuel but to try to keep loose formation for mutual support and help us to communicate in an emergency as radio transmissions could reveal our position. So now we were ready to go whenever the weather was right and for three days we waited for the early morning call, being abstemious in the Mess, only to be roused at 06.00 hours by an orderly who informed us that the weather over the Bay was unsuitable. On the third night the weather was worse than ever so we knew we had no chance of getting away next morning and we really had a big night in the Mess making up for our abstinence and retiring at about 01.00 hours. We negotiated our way back to our billet with difficulty in pitch darkness and successfully crossed the small bridge over the stream and began climbing up the hill towards where we could see the sparks coming out of our hut's chimney when suddenly I heard Johnny cry out in pain. 'Johnny,' I shouted, 'where are you?' 'At the bottom of the air raid shelter,' he replied. 'I climbed up the side thinking it was the hill and fell down the middle. I thought it was a bit steep!' He was lucky to be unhurt for he had fallen at least eight feet At 06.00 hours you could hear the rain lashing down and the wind howling outside when the orderly shook us 'You are off,' he said. 'Don't be silly, it's the worst morning we have had,' we protested. 'Yes, but today it's clear over the Bay,' he said. So this was *it*. It was 27 February 1942 and the beginning of the adventure!

We got airborne at 08.45 hours my logbook says but it makes no comment on the weather, which was terrible with a cloud base of 250 feet, lashing rain and a strong headwind we certainly didn't want. It was going to be some job to keep together in these conditions. We set course at once and I saw Land's End pass below me as I sang 'I'll be with you in Apple Blossom Time' and I thought how incongruous that was. I might never see England again. As if to cheer me we suddenly ran out of the murk into bright sunshine and in the good visibility I was amazed to see all our Flight was in view. So we followed our westerly course for thirty minutes before turning due south for the crossing of the Bay of Biscay, which was a high risk stage due to the German activity. We kept low to the sea and a sharp look out for we were unarmed so our best defence would be to run for it but that would gobble up our fuel and we were already perilously close to the limit of our endurance.

Three hours later things seemed to be going to plan and we had almost cleared the Bay when Peter's aircraft started to emit smoke from his port engine. We pulled up alongside him and he broke radio silence to say laconically 'Oil leak' so we stayed close to him and watched as the leak obviously got worse. Danny and I discussed the situation and decided our best option was to lead him to Gibraltar by the shortest route before his engine packed up so we got in front of him and just said 'Follow'. I told Danny to turn thirty degrees to port and as we headed for Spain I hoped I would be able to get us there with the basic maps I had and the Beau's confounded 'back to front' navigating not helping. We figured that if we could get them over the coast at least they would be on dry land if they had to bale out. We were quite chuffed when we managed that and I gave Danny a new course to steer for Gibraltar.

I think I was the only full blown navigator on the Flight and I certainly earned my keep from now on for I had never been taught to navigate with only a road map and a compass as I guided us over mountains where it would have been impossible to land even a helicopter. I anxiously watched Peter's engine and was glad to see the leak looked no worse. I knew we would eventually get to flatter ground and when we did it was a revelation for there were bomb craters from the Civil War clearly visible around every cross roads where the Germans and Italians had honed the tactics they later used to such devastating effect. In some places the bombing had been so intense that the road was totally obliterated and tracks in the sand showed that traffic was now making a ring road around the centre. These reminders continued until at last the unmistakeable outline of the Rock appeared dead ahead so I changed course to make our approach from the west as we had been instructed and we made our way round its southern tip to land on the flat isthmus that joined the Rock to the mainland.

The eastern side was a truly impressive sheer rock face and we saw a Naval Swordfish nearer to the Rock but took little notice as I shepherded Peter to make his landing in front of it knowing that we would be clear of the runway before it landed. I was watching it to make sure of its position when it suddenly fell out of the sky from about 400 feet. It did not dive or crash but fell as flat as a pancake and on hitting the sea the wings sort of folded up over it. I called to Danny 'Did you see that?' but as he was looking in front preparing to land he had seen nothing, although he knew it had been there and now it was gone. I reported the incident on landing and the Controller who was unfazed said 'He must have got too close to the rock face and been caught by the turbulence. It sometimes happens.' We never heard how the crew had fared but it seemed likely to us that they survived and we imagined the difficulty they would have later trying to convince their Messmates that it wasn't a colossal lineshoot. We were then interviewed by the Intelligence Officer who gave us a roasting for violating Spanish airspace. 'It's not that I don't understand your decision,' he said, 'but it means that our Ambassador will have to entertain the Spanish Ambassador to lunch to explain and he hates the man.' We were not impressed as inspection had shown that Peter had virtually no oil left so if we had not taken our short cut he would have been forced to ditch in the Atlantic somewhere off the Portuguese coast. As it was we had been in the air 5 hours 40 minutes and at that he had only just made it Gibraltar but the others had taken just over 6 hours.

We were shown to our billets on the aerodrome in a bare Nissen hut with no door and no glass in the windows but because of its metal roof it was swelteringly hot. It did not really matter as we knew we would soon be on our way again and our priority was to see as much of Gibraltar as we could. After a scratch supper we went into the town intent on buying some keepsake to send home but we were disappointed for the 'shops', many of them like garishly lit grottos, had little to offer other than brass trinkets all stamped 'Made in Birmingham', which wasn't really redolent of this Bastion of Empire and they could have been bought more cheaply at home. We had to wait until the following day for two Coastal Beaus to arrive, which had the navigation equipment we lacked to lead us to the Middle East. Before we left we were briefed by the Intelligence Officer who took us to a window to point out a house across the water in Algeciras. 'That is the German Embassy' he said 'and when you take off tomorrow they will immediately alert the *Luftwaffe* to intercept you before you arrive in Malta.' A right Job's comforter he is we thought. He did not tell us, perhaps he did not know, for it was long after the war before it was revealed, that the hulk of a half sunken merchant ship at the quayside outside it had a trap door below the water line through which frogmen were released to attack the mass of Naval vessels in Gibraltar harbour. The regular detonation of depth charges throughout the night should surely have been a clue that they were guarding against the possibility of some such activity after being caught by the attack on the Fleet at Alexandria harbour in Egypt.

Peter's oil leak had been fixed and he was soon beside us as our armada of eight Beaus took off at 09.15 hours in our usual loose formation at 500 feet into a heat haze that eventually developed into low cloud with virtually zero visibility. We tried to keep sight of one another but it was impossible. All our pilots could do was to concentrate on flying the exact course and height whilst we navigators strained our eyes, looking in all directions, hoping to be able to give warning if a ghostly silhouette appeared in time to avoid a collision. We were in this cloud for over thirty minutes and when we came out of it one Beau was missing. We hoped he had simply strayed away from the formation but it was far more likely he had become disorientated in the cloud and being so low we reckoned that he must have flown into the sea – or perhaps he had been trying to avoid a collision. It was sad but we were lucky it was no worse for we still had seven aircraft not too widely dispersed, hastening to close up into loose formation. One thing we were grateful for was that the cloud had concealed us from hostile attack, or at least we thought so until we approached Malta and we saw it, or rather the barrage over it from a great distance. The whole island seemed to be under a heavy air attack. We could see bombs exploding, a mass of AA shells bursting and great clouds of dust and smoke blotted out the contours of the island. Our Job's comforter at Gibraltar had not exaggerated, the Jerries had laid on a welcoming party specially for us. Of this there could be no doubt for looking astern we saw a dozen Vichy French and Italian single-seater fighters trying to catch up with us probably from bases in North Africa, Sicily or on one of the Italian islands to the south. We called up Malta to tell them we were coming in and they told us to not to come any nearer until they gave us permission as they were presently in the midst of an air raid. They did not have to tell us as we were watching it and it was clear they were taking a hell of a pasting. We replied 'For God's sake be quick, we are almost out of fuel.' We had to circle round with one eye on the approaching fighters and the other on the needles of our fuel gauges, which were registering nil. Malta Control obviously appreciated our situation for they called us in whilst the raid was still raging with bombs and AA going off until we were about a mile offshore when it suddenly abated. Their timing was immaculate for the engines of two of our aircraft ran out of fuel and stopped as they rolled down the runway and the rest of us had a strong smell of petrol in the tanks. We had been in the air for 6 hours 40 minutes which was 10 minutes more than had been calculated to be our absolute maximum at Honeybourne.

The Controllers had impressed us with their efficient handling of our arrival but we did not know that they were located in a deep underground shelter, whereas the poor erks and soldiers who were now frantically trying to get our aircraft away from the runway did not enjoy such a luxury. They knew that it would not be long before the bombers returned to destroy our Flight whose arrival they had only just mistimed with their first raid and all they had were slit trenches. Malta was at that time the most bombed place in the world, even counting the London Blitz, and the harbour and aerodromes were their prime targets. Luqa was the main airfield so every day they had to endure raid after raid so no wonder the ground staff were jumpy. They had just got our aircraft to comparative safety, manhandling those without fuel, when sure enough the sirens went again. We were surprised to hear Warrant Officers shouting angrily 'Take cover, take cover, you stupid so and sos' to airmen who, we realised later, had become 'bomb happy'. The raid lasted about thirty minutes and we were relieved to find all our aircraft were intact when they departed.

We were shown to our beds in a large building just off the aerodrome and learned that all the buildings on the site had been a leper colony years ago. It mattered not to us for we were dog tired and ready for a good night's sleep, but we did not get one as three times we were awakened by the wailing sirens and we heard bombs falling nearby. We were roused at 06.00 hours and airborne at 08.15 hours having been hastily briefed on our flight to Egypt and it was clear that Malta was anxious to be rid of us as our presence was attracting the German bombers like bees to a honey pot.

This was by far the shortest leg of our journey so we decided to use a closer formation as our fuel situation was not likely to be a critical factor in reaching our destination – No. 108 Maintenance Depot at Fiume. There we would hand over X7807 and then proceed to a Holding Unit pending posting to a squadron hopefully with Peter and Johnny for we now had a sort of vested interest in them apart from our friendship. We pottered along nicely keeping a not too tight formation for about four hours when we noticed our fuel was disappearing at an alarming rate. We wondered if we had encountered a head wind until it dawned upon us that flying in formation was the cause so we stopped juggling our throttles and went back to the settings recommended at Honeybourne. We were little more than halfway to our destination and the problem was of our own making but that did not make it any the less worrying. We turned to the south and were glad when we sighted the North African coast, which we followed until we saw a Landing Ground. It was just in time for we had been in the air six hours and on landing we found it was LG 104 (El Daba).

The occupants of this barren strip were delighted to see us as they had been bombed the previous night and were gratified that we had been sent to protect them so promptly. We were sorry to disabuse them of such wishful thinking but they still treated us like royalty as they had never seen a Beau before. They climbed all over our aircraft and wanted to know when they might expect them as replacements for their Blenheims. They found us beds in their tents and gave us a night to remember in their Sergeants' Mess marquee. We could not get away in the morning until 12.30 hours and then only on condition we gave them a chance to photograph our Beaus as we left. It would have been churlish to refuse and we really did our best for them. Our departing beat up blew down their marquee but they could not have cared less for they waved, danced with delight and by hand signals made it clear they wanted us to make another pass. How could we refuse such a grand set of lads!

The flight to Fiume took us 1 hour 30 minutes so you can see our profligacy had put us in real jeopardy and the regime of seemingly pointless tasks we had performed at Honeybourne we now realised had been vital and raised the staff there high in our esteem. Fiume was vast and from the air it seemed that the Middle East could not possibly be short of aircraft but a closer inspection revealed that the aircraft park was half full of obsolete types, including prehistoric Virginias, Vincents, biplane fighters, and clapped out Marylands. But not a single Beau. While Danny and Peter handed over our contribution to this menagerie of ancient relics Johnny and I were put into a truck and taken to Almaza transit camp, which was just outside Cairo, and the next time we met was on the train to our new squadron. On the way we caught our first glimpse of the mystic East – and it was far from enchanting. True, we did see camels but they were spitting, shaggy, recalcitrant beasts being beaten into line by drivers dressed in rags and not a bit like the ones I had seen in the movies. The transit camp was a let down too. It was a large lump of desert wired off with rows of tents with a marquee for the Sergeants' Mess with others for administration use. We had only been there ten minutes when we dived for cover as a flight of Me 109s swept low over the camp and were shamefaced when it was explained that they were Egyptian Air Force planes, supplied by Germany as a diplomatic ploy hoping to break British domination in the area, taking off from their nearby base at Heliopolis.

We were allotted one of the tents that were dug into the ground with a fly sheet over them to keep off the sun and the first morning as I was shaking the sand from my boots a large spider scuttled out of them, which I hoped was not a scorpion. Scorpion or not I was already disenchanted with the Middle East and if I had seen a snake I would probably have tried to swim back to Blighty. Every morning there was a crowd of tattered locals sat on the ground outside the main gates waiting for the Sudanese Guard Commander to select fifty or so of them to be allowed into the camp to clean the sand up and they fought for the privilege. You had to be careful not to leave anything of value in your tent or that would be the last you saw of it. Yet you had to be sorry for these poor hapless souls whose living was derived from selling the empty cans, bottles, paper and even orange peel they collected but if out of charity you tipped one your tent was immediately surrounded by twenty more with outstretched arms baying for 'Baksheesh'. We learned that they had a sort of sub-culture with a currency based on one hundreth of a piastre, which was worth about two and a half old pence, and the dejected look on the faces of those who had been turned away really upset me. They reminded me of the ragged wretches in a Dickens novel.

Johnny and I took the tram into Cairo daily and watched the laundry men on the pavements take a swig of water from a mug and then blow it over the washing before ironing. The marvel was that they did a really good job if you could forget how they had done it. Their barbers were the best, giving you a lovely shave followed by hot towels and then they put some gunge on your face that was so astringent you looked as if you were puckered up to kiss someone. It would not have been the women who dressed so that you could only see their eyes leaving you to imagine what they looked like and judging from those we did see they were all raddled old hags – which left only the spitting camels. I met a few of my old school friends in the *patisserie* of Groppes Hotel whose wonderful cream cakes had earned them a worldwide reputation. These were the lads who had joined the Queen's Own Yorkshire Dragoons before the war to ride horses and were now on leave from Palestine where they had a peacekeeping role with no involvement in the war. Mounted on Bren Gun Carriers, with never a horse in sight, they were thoroughly p—d off and sought to drown their sorrows in copious amounts of booze before returning to their boring duties.

We were warned to be careful where we ate or drank as four soldiers had died of an obscure fever and the military were trying to discover where they had been on their last night out in Cairo. They narrowed it down to a bar whose owner had placed his dead brother's body on a block of ice and after his burial had chopped up the ice to put in drinks he served to his customers. I had been brought up to be thrifty but this had proved to be a deadly virtue.

In our quest for Egyptian culture we decided we simply must see a belly dancer so we asked around and were directed to a club where this ancient ritual was the nightly floor show. By the décor that greeted us on entering we knew that it was going to be expensive but we wanted to see these fabled erotic dancers regardless of the cost. We did not enquire the price of the proffered Greek 'escort' as such a beauty was plainly way beyond our means, and then the dancer came on. She had a group of 'followers' who greeted her with thunderous applause but we nearly fell off our seats laughing. She certainly could shimmy and shake but she had so much to shake she looked like a quivering blancmange teetering on the edge of a table. She wouldn't have lasted two minutes in a Sheffield working men's club at Sunday lunchtime and she did not last so much longer here for she soon ran out of puff and beat a gasping retreat to loud cries of approbation from her fans. We left at once as we could not afford to stay for the next show but the £2.10 shillings for our one (and only) round of drinks gave us a 'belly' laugh for a week.

We took a photo of King Farouk's yacht on the Nile where the stench from the river was so appalling that we hurried away but the truth was we had tired of Cairo, which had failed to live up to our expectations, and we were impatient for our next posting. After a week we were told that we were going to 89 Squadron at Abu Sueir down by the Bitter Lakes close to the Suez Canal. It was commanded by Wing Commander George Stainforth, a former member of the team that won the Schnieder Trophy Cup outright for Great Britain and we were delighted that Peter and Johnny were going too. We were given tickets for the train and set off next morning on the worst train journey of our lives. The ancient engine wheezed its way out of Cairo at 20 mph and then settled into a bone shaking 15 mph, stopping frequently and inexplicably, seemingly indifferent to any timetable if there ever was one. When we went up to the engine driver to enquire what the hold ups were for he said military trains had priority and he had to allow them to pass. The hard wooden lathe seats cut into our backsides and although there was no glass in the windows it was unbearably hot. We had nothing to drink but did not dare buy the suspect water offered for sale by the gangs of urchins who gathered at every stop. We could not interest ourselves in the passing vistas for there was nothing to see but sand, and sleeping was out of the question for we would have sworn the train had square wheels.

After six hours of this torture we arrived at Abu Sueir Station – only it wasn't a proper station, just some sidings obviously to handle supplies for the camp. There were no buildings or platforms, just some hardcore between the rails where we sat for another hour before a lorry arrived. There was the usual gang of urchins who squatted on their haunches and giggled, probably at our discomfort. On reaching the camp we were met by the CO who told us what he really wanted was aircraft. What he did not need was more 'sprog' (novice) crews as he already had far too many. This infuriated us, and being already in a black mood, we let into him without any thought of the possible consequences. We told him we were experienced crews who had almost completed a tour of duty at Tangmere and that we deeply resented his remarks. Our outburst clearly embarrassed him and though he did not apologise he was most conciliatory as he explained that we would have few opportunities to fly at Abu Sueir. He said he hardly dare let his preponderance of sprog crews fly lest they broke an irreplaceable aircraft, and the frequent sandstorms so affected serviceability that even more competent crews had to take turns to fly. It was obvious that this distinguished aviator was under great stress but we were gutted that the 'great adventure' and all our dreams seemed to be heading to a premature ignominious end. We had come a hell of a long way to finish up in a job with no prospects. We could not know that the man who dealt the cards was laughing demonically as he shuffled and prepared to deal a new hand – from the bottom of the pack.

We awoke the following morning to find ourselves in a blinding sandstorm, which reduced visibility to ten yards and stung our faces as we leaned into a gale force wind on our way to the Mess tent for breakfast. The Egyptian waiters had flies crawling round their eyes and mouths that they made no effort to swat away. There were darker patches on their already dusky skins, which we were assured by the scuttlebutt brigade was due to a hereditary sexual disease. We spent the morning in the Mess endlessly going over our prospects, hoping to come up with a feasible solution, but it seemed we were doomed to be here for the foreseeable future – doing nothing. At dinner time we trooped into the dining tent where the fly-ridden waiters dished up a plate of suspicious-looking stew meat with *pink* potatoes. We looked at them in disbelief until someone explained they had been soaked in Condis Fluid to make them safe to eat. That was enough – we left them uneaten. My spirits sank to an even lower ebb when we looked at the Duty Board on our way out to find I was to be Duty Sergeant tomorrow.

The sandstorm was still raging with unabated fury when I reported to the Guard Room at 08.00 hours where I was given a neatly folded RAF ensign and the SWO told me to march the Corporal and eight men waiting outside to the gate to 'raise the flag'. The Corporal and I managed to attach the flag to the lanyard and I stood rigidly to attention saluting as he solemnly raised it to top of its pole. I marched the party back to the Guard Room, dismissed them, and went inside to enquire if it was just the usual that was required of me. They looked at me in surprise and said do it as you normally would. So at dinner time I went to the airmen's dining marquee and asked if there were any complaints but they were so busy scoffing down a disgusting-looking hash they scarcely bothered to reply. I had no further duties until dusk when I took the flag party to 'lower the flag'. I stood saluting as the Corporal took the flag down but when he brought it to me to fold up the fun really started. I could hardly manage to keep hold of it never mind fold it and even when the Corporal came to my assistance we were both defeated by the wind. Darkness was closing in fast so I gave up the unequal struggle – I rolled the damned thing up, put it under my arm, and marched the party back to the Guard Room. The SWO looked at me aghast as I offered him the rolled up flag, speechless at the insult to this time honoured, almost sacred tradition. Before he recovered I said 'Well go outside and see if you can do any better.' I walked out to find the Corporal and airmen had hung about to watch 'His Fearsomeness' tear strips off of me and were tickled pink that I had been a match for him. It was the nearest thing to entertainment they had for ages.

Next day dawned and, glory be, there was a blazing sun and airmen shovelling away sand threatening to cover tents, marquees, and even the aircraft. But we were not interested for scuttlebutt had it that a detachment of four aircraft was needed for Malta and we did not even wait for confirmation, we just rushed headlong to the Adjutant's office determined to be the first to apply. Danny, Peter and I pestered the Adjutant to let us see the CO and when we got into his office we saluted smartly and said 'Sir, we request to be posted to Malta.' Johnny was not able to join us as he had been scheduled to navigate a Flight Lieutenant at 10.30 hours on some local flying. Johnny said they started to take off and immediately swung violently off the runway as the Beau was notoriously prone to do if you did not lead with one throttle. 'Oh sorry old chap let's try again, eh what.' They taxied back, started another run and the same thing happened. 'Dash it old boy,' his pilot said, 'don't seem to have got the hang of the thing, better luck next time eh.' He finally made it, albeit at some twenty degrees to the runway, and what he said we shall never know for Johnny had absconded while he was going through his third cockpit check. Johnny recounted his dereliction of duty, told us the pilot had refused point blank to see the funny side of the thing and was insisting that he should be court-martialled. He had expected us to be rolling in laughter or at least sympathetic. Instead we glared at him and told him he had likely just cost us the chance of a lifetime, a posting to Malta. We reminded him of all the fruitless nights of patrolling we had spent at Tangmere and now with the prospect of unlimited 'trade', the dream of every night fighter, almost within our grasp, his indiscretion had scuppered our golden opportunity. Like us he was gutted but we were being too hard on him for no one knew who the lucky quartet would be – it was just that we had set our hearts on this plum posting. Convinced that we had 'blown it' we had a right booze up that night in the Mess to drown our sorrows. When we went for breakfast we looked at the notice board and there was the list of the fortunate few. It read:

89 Squadron crews posted to 1435 Flight Detachment Malta
Flight Lt Hayton and PO Josling
PO Daniel and Sgt Gosling
PO Oakes and Sgt Walsh
Sgt Miller and Sgt Tearle

Johnny and I stood in front of it transfixed, it could not be possible. We read and re-read it and then I rushed to the phone to ring Danny at the Officers' Mess not just to tell him but to find out if the same list was there too. Thank goodness it was and we spent ten minutes on the phone telling each other what an opportunity this was before I went back to Johnny to confirm our luck. He was sat eating his breakfast as if this was nothing to get excited about, and though it meant he had escaped a court-martial to boot, he took it all in his stride. With me it was different, I could not conceal my excitement, and it showed. Goodbye to Abu Sueir and its sandstorms. Goodbye to stinking Cairo. Goodbye to the Mystic East. No matter that we were on our way to the most bombed place on earth, this was the adventure we had craved.

Of course the crews who had lost out were openly hostile as you would expect, especially the sprog crews, who had been clicking their heels for weeks hoping that they would get a chance to prove themselves. Now we had leapt over them after being only six days on the squadron, like ships passing in the night, and it was hard to blame them. More experienced crews wondered what was wrong with them. The answer lay with Wing Commander Stainforth and we could see the logic of his decision. He had bravely resisted the opportunity to offload some of his sprog crews. He knew they would simply have been out of their depth in Malta, and he had retained a nucleus of experienced crews to build his squadron round, if he ever got sufficient aircraft. He had chosen the crews that, at least on paper, had sufficient experience to cope with conditions in Malta but were an unknown quantity to him. We felt for the man as he was losing four aircraft he sorely needed to fulfil his obligation to provide night cover from the big Naval base at Alexandria in the north to the vital port of Tewfic (Port Said) in the south where the harbour teemed with merchant ships bringing in vital supplies and troops for North Africa. After what must have been deep thought he had discharged his responsibilities cleverly and efficiently and we were genuinely sorry when he was killed in a flying accident later in the year.

At 09.00 hours on 6 March we set off for Edku (Alexandria) on the first leg of our journey to pick up two Coastal Beau escorts for we still had no navigational capabilities and no rearward-firing gun. The Coastal Beaus had one token .303 rear-firing machine-gun, which would not have frightened off even the most timid attacker for it was the same as the Fairey Battle had in 1940. We had our full armament of six .303 machine-guns and four 20 mm cannon so it was reckoned we had all round protection. The flaw in this supposition was that the Coastal Beaus would be at the front of our formation not at the back to protect our rear. At 14.30 hours we were led to LG 10 (Sollum) ready for the last leg to Malta in the morning for without consumption tests we had to make sure that our fully laden aircraft had sufficient fuel for the flight. The airstrip at Sollum was certainly not long, neither was it particularly short, so you can imagine our surprise when the first Coastal Beau made a decent landing and then ran and ran until it went into a deep wadi at the end. We followed in and no one had the slightest problem with landing. By the time we taxied in the crew rolled up in a truck and grinning broadly they declared 'No Malta for us' and strolled off to the Mess. It was the most barefaced, brazen act of cowardice I have ever seen.

The five of us remaining set off from Sollum at 07.45 hours next morning and had a trouble free journey of 4.30 hours to Malta where we landed not at Luqa but Takali, a 'grass' airstrip without any night flying facilities. We waved goodbye to our escort wondering if he would report his despicable mate on his return. We decided probably not for it would be hard to prove his act was wilful and intentional but we were sure he would never rely on him in a tight situation in future.

We were taking in our surroundings, impressed by the ancient battlements of the medieval capital of Mdina towering over us and were looking round our dispersal when the sirens sounded and we watched from a slit trench as a raid developed over Valletta. We were not too close to the bombing but on such a small island you saw, heard, and felt the blast of the bombs wherever they fell. The main thing was that we had arrived and were itching to do our best for this gallant island and its people – their fortitude deserved all the assistance anyone could give them.

CHAPTER SEVENTEEN

Malta, George Cross Island – March 1942

As soon as we emerged from the slit trench we were hurried aboard an ancient bus with its top cut off above the waistline to take us to our billets. It wheezed its way up the hill towards the battlements we had seen from the airfield, through a village that the driver told us was called Rabat, then over a deep moat, and through a splendid archway a bit like Marble Arch, into the walled medieval capital of Mdina, sometimes referred to by its ancient name of Citta Vecchia. Turning right it stopped outside the Port De Vue hotel, now requisitioned as the Officers' Mess, built into the walls of this former fortress, and unloaded the officers. It continued into the main square opposite a beautiful church and drew up outside our billets, which were in the Casa Testaferrata, the home of Baron Testaferrata, a scion of the Maltese aristocracy. We went a short way down a passage at the side, through a small door in the wall and then up some stairs to a large room full of beds, one of which was to be Johnny's, and a smaller room at its furthest end where I was shown my bed. This was unheard of luxury and as we started to unpack our gear several chaps came in to greet us. They were day fighter pilots who were delighted to find we were night fighters flying the first Beaus to come to the island with radar, or AI as it was still called. They wanted to know all about our aircraft, which had acquired an enviable reputation in the Service for its speed and firepower and they crawled all over our planes at the dispersal. Clearly they expected we were going to perform to their high standards and I hoped we would not disappoint them. They told us that the rush to get us off the aerodrome was due to heavy raids being expected as that morning fifteen Spitfires flown from the aircraft carrier HMS *Eagle* had landed there. They had proved that it was possible to operate Spits from an aircraft carrier and plans were rushed ahead that resulted in the 'Seafire' naval fighter, with an arrester hook to enable them to replace the Fulmars, which were no match for land-based opposition. We were delighted when we were told that Group Captain Woodall had arrived to become the island's Fighter Controller. 'Woody' as he was affectionately known to all, had been our Station Commander at Tangmere and was acknowledged to be the best in his trade, always getting his fighters 'up sun', which was a vital advantage in the ensuing dogfights. He was eminently 'the man for the job'.

When we wanted our supper we were taken down the stairs, across the passage, through a door in the wall opposite and upstairs into the Sergeants' Mess facing that lovely church, but the fare was frugal and our new friends told us that Malta was starving. I had a quick drink afterwards and then made my way to bed and I was so tired that I was asleep in no time. I must have slept for almost an hour when the sirens went but no one seemed to bother so I lay awake turning over the events of the past few days in my mind – the seeming hopelessness of our position at Abu Sueir had been replaced by the euphoria of our Malta posting but was it going to prove a mixed blessing? Was the man who dealt the cards playing games with us?

I considered our little band – our Flight Commander Flt/ Lt Hayton, who came from 89 Squadron, was a pipe-smoking New Zealander and seemed like a nice chap, if somewhat taciturn for a Kiwi. His navigator, P/O Josling, was an even greater enigma for I knew nothing about him. 'Dusty' Miller had been in 'Oving Manor' at Tangmere at the same time as me, but he was on the other ('A') Flight so I had never seen much of him and only recalled his nickname, 'the Welsh Womaniser', due to his prowess in ensnaring the opposite sex. He was dark, handsome, enthusiastic and I was glad that he was with us. His navigator's name, Sgt Tearle, did not ring a bell with me and I wondered if they were a new pairing. That left Peter and Johnny and of course I had no doubts about them. So that was us – the eight little Night Fighter Boys of Malta Night Fighter Unit No. 1435, and I fell asleep again wondering what the future would hold for us. Three times that night the sirens went and when I got up in the morning I was still tired, but I soon found out that every night was the same so I learned to sleep through these interruptions like the 'old hands'. With practice you could 'tune out' the sirens and only waken if bombs fell nearby, which was quite often, and even then they brought only curses or grunts from the stressed-out sleepers.

I went for my breakfast and was dismayed to find it was the same stuff I had been given for my supper. I say 'stuff' for there is no other way I can describe the, well, stuff! It was an American concoction in a tin about the size of a small tin of salmon, which rejoiced in the name of Machonachies (I do not remember how it was spelt, in fact I would prefer to forget it altogether). It came in four varieties, No. 1 ('THE ORIGINAL' as the label proudly trumpeted), was a sort of Irish stew, No. 2 added peas, No. 3 had carrots, while No. 4 with haricot beans was particularly horrible. If we got potatoes with it we deemed it a special treat and shortly after our arrival we were rationed to half a tin of this 'stuff' per meal making a maximum of one and a half tins per man per day. This was part of a new belt-tightening regime shared by the already half-starved civilian population. After a while we were so hungry we would eat anything we could lay our hands on and regularly paid two shillings and sixpence for egg and chips in Valletta though the scuttlebutt brigade swore that they were not always hens' eggs. Eating in establishments that paid little heed to even basic hygiene was a sure way of contracting dysentery. It was rife in the Middle East where there was a military hospital outside Cairo with massive wards full of victims, many of whom succumbed to this debilitating disease.

When we were being bussed to the aerodrome we were warned that since the Spits had arrived, Takali had become the prime target for Ju 88 bombers and strafing from low-flying Me 109 fighters. When we got to our dispersal, which was a one-room hut, we set about making it fit for our requirements. Johnny and I were told by Flt/Lt Hayton to put up a Serviceability Board and we were struggling to get a nail into the breeze block when the sirens went. We heard the coastal batteries open up, then the Ack-Ack guns, but when we heard the aerodrome defence 20 and 40 mm guns start firing I thought it was time we should see what was happening outside. I tugged at the door but our hammer was wedged under it so Johnny pushed me aside. 'Don't panic, take your time,' he said, as he calmly bent down, freed the hammer and opened the door. I heard him shout 'Run' and I looked up to see bombs half way down from a Ju 88 right above us. We dived into a slit trench on top of some of our ground crew as the bombs straddled our narrow pit and we were showered with stones and sand. Johnny had been winded crashing onto a tin-helmeted head as he dived into the trench and the man he fell on cursed him roundly. When we saw our dispersal hut had taken a direct hit, the unflappable Johnny said 'Well, that's saved us a job' and we burst out laughing. We did not know then that it would have been no more than a useless ornament anyway for we were rarely to have more than one aircraft serviceable for ops each night, and sometimes we had no aircraft at all. We packed up work and retired to our Mess for dinner and as we talked over our narrow escape we tucked into the predictable dose of Macs No. 4, which somehow seemed more palatable, and we agreed that we were jolly lucky to be alive.

We had decided to operate the two-shift system used on night fighter squadrons with Danny and Peter taking one shift and Hayton and 'Dusty' the other but that too went out of the window in the light of subsequent events. Takali had no night flying facilities so every night we were obliged to make a dash to Luqa to operate. This was only a short hop but it was fraught with danger as we could get caught taking off or landing in the half light when we were most vulnerable. It was also the favourite time for Me 109 fighter bombers making their final sweeps of the day across the island. On the night of 8 March 'Dusty' and his oppo drew 1435's first blood when they claimed one Ju 88 destroyed and one He 111 damaged (which they might have destroyed had their guns not jammed). At dusk on the 9th Danny and I flew from Takali to Luqa taking two of our ground crew in the aircraft with us. There had been a trawl of maintenance personnel on the island before half a dozen men had been found who had worked on Beaus previously so we took them in case our aircraft needed servicing at Luqa. We did not call for the landing lights to be lit until we were on the final approach and they were extinguished as soon as we were rolling down the runway. Even in that short time you could get shot down before you landed by a bomber who also had seen the lights and was waiting for the opportunity to make an easy 'kill'. If the bomber was too late to get you in the air it usually dropped a stick of bombs on the runway, hopefully behind you. To be on the safe side when we landed we made a dash for 'G' shelter and ran down several flights of steps to the Operations Centre deep underground. I think bombs blew me down those steps as often as I walked down them.

We had been in our sweaty underground crew room a couple of hours sitting out another raid when the Bomb Disposal Officer, Flt/ Lt Fisk, popped his head in and said 'The moon is quite bright so we had better clear the debris from around the runway.' so we followed him 'up top' and with others that he had rounded up we formed a line across the runway and twenty yards or so at each side of it, throwing off pieces of shrapnel and spent AA shell caps that might puncture aircraft tyres on landing causing a crash. I was on the extreme left of the line and I drew Fisk's attention to a bomb the size of a beer barrel. He came over and said 'Oh that one is OK, I took the fuse out of it this afternoon,' gave it a peremptory kick, and walked away. We had gone twenty-five yards further when there was a terrific bang and we threw ourselves to the ground. When we got up we saw this 'defused' bomb had exploded showering us with stones and rubble. Fisk stuttered 'Must have had two fuses – it's one of their tricks,' and walked nonchalantly on. Flt/Lt Fisk was a former WWI observer who reckoned the safest place to be in a bombing raid was the middle of the target area, which he told us he had attempted to bomb many times but, try as he may, he had never managed to hit! After our recent experience we were not inclined to trust his judgement and we wondered if he got his stutter trying to prove his theory.

We went back to 'G' shelter and as we arrived someone came running to tell us our aircraft had been damaged by a delayed action bomb. It had been there as we walked the runway but in the moonlight it had not been spotted. Even if it had been seen nothing could have been done except to cordon off the area to safeguard lives for it might have exploded without warning at any time. It was a blow to Danny and me as we had hoped to emulate the success of 'Dusty' the previous evening and a blow for 1435 Flight to lose an aircraft only two days after our arrival. We were especially upset because X7642 was the Beau we had flown to Malta but fortunately daylight revealed the only damage was due to splinters from an anti-personnel bomb and in a couple of days these were patched up. With our hearts in our mouths we then ran the gauntlet in broad daylight to get it back to Takali so that it would be available for ops that evening. We flew it three times afterwards and apart from the draught through some unpatched holes it was fine. On the 11th we were scrambled, but when we called GCI (Ground Control of Interception) they said they had troubles and eventually declared themselves unserviceable, so we 'freelanced' for a while until our intercom packed up. Without my 'commentary' Danny was 'blind' so we had to land, frustrated once more. The next night Hayton and Josling claimed a Ju 88 damaged, but when we flew again on Friday the 13th GCI could not find us a target – an unlucky Friday for us! Two days later X7642 took a near hit from a bomb in another raid on our dispersal and was burnt out. With the Takali fire engine having long ago been bombed itself there was no chance of saving it. On that same Friday our last remaining petrol bowser suffered the same fate, after which our aircraft had to be fuelled from five-gallon cans, through chamois leather, to get rid of water and other impurities. These cans were flimsy things made of tin, which leaked profusely and compared badly with the robustness of the excellent German 'Jerry cans'. To fill a Beau right up took eight hours but we did not put in more than we might expect to use that night because petrol was scarce and if, for any reason, we lost an aircraft we did not want to lose a full load of petrol as well.

At night when we were in the air we were controlled by one of the new mobile GCI stations, which were still in the development stage at that time, so they were very temperamental and naturally suffered from teething problems. The operators took time to get accustomed to using and servicing the equipment, which was housed in a caravan. By day they had to be prepared to pack up and move quickly to another location if their aerial arrays were spotted by the Germans who would realise we had AI on the island and swiftly call in the *Stukas* to give their site an almighty pasting. The Controllers relied on their information for they were able to report the strength of the build up over the Germans' Sicilian bases. Armed with this knowledge the Controller could judge how many fighters would be needed to deal with the threat and when to scramble them – not too early but still in time to get them into the best position to meet it. The incoming raids were increasing in size and hordes of 100 hostile aircraft at a time became commonplace and now three or four times a day. Their bases were only sixty miles away and photo-reconnaissance, probably done by the legendary Adrian Warburton, showed that new formations were arriving daily. The GCI was as essential and effective as it was in the Battle of Britain, but the tactical advantage it gave could not outweigh the massive disparity in numbers.

Between these major attacks there were always solitary raiders about for it was part of the enemy strategy to ensure we were not given time to prepare for the next onslaught. The result was that after the first siren went there could be no 'All Clear' sounded until every raider had left. A new policy of blowing a whistle when hostiles were virtually overhead was brought in so that essential work was not interrupted. Consequently it was sometimes twenty-four hours before the sirens wailed to tell us we could finally relax and assess the damage that had been done.

On the 17th, despite Takali being under bomb attack all day, Danny and I managed to sneak over to Luqa and were airborne for two hours but GCI were unable to provide us with any targets. One of their problems was that the Night Controllers were largely novices, one of whom had even turned us to port instead of starboard during an interception and another potential 'kill' escaped. Clearly he did not have a naval background!

On the 18th Takali had so many bomb craters that it had to be declared unusable whilst in a raid on the 19th we had one Beau destroyed and another damaged, leaving us only one serviceable. If we had complained to Field Marshal Kesselring, assembling his armada at Catania, I am sure his gleeful reply would have been (translated from his native tongue) 'You ain't seen nothing yet!'

Peter, Johnny, Danny and I went down to the airfield at about 18.00 hours on the 20th giving us time to examine the strip and see if the craters had been sufficiently filled for us to operate our one remaining Beau. We were discussing our prospects with one of our ground crew when the sirens went and almost at once Takali came under attack. The crewman we were talking to started to run shouting 'This way' and, as they spent all day on the airfield and obviously knew the best boltholes, we sprinted after him. He ran to the remains of the old underground hospital, now abandoned as it had been almost demolished in a previous bombing. We cowered between two thick brick pillars holding up a concrete beam in what had been the operating theatre as this seemed to be the strongest part. There was so little room that Johnny had to sit on Peter's knee and I on Danny's, whilst the crewman squatted on the floor between us. What followed was ninety minutes of sheer hell. The noise of the bombs dropping all round us was deafening, making the earth shake, showering us with plaster from the roof, as one wave of bombers after another dropped their deadly cargoes in what seemed to be an endless procession. The bombs fell continuously and from the noise we could tell how close they were to our refuge. Suddenly there was an ear-splitting explosion and blast from a bomb almost on our shelter sent large rocks hurtling into the one and only entrance. We should have died but the pillars deflected the blast wave round us or we would have been found, with no signs of injury other than a trickle of blood from the ears and nose telling of collapsed lungs, like so many we were to see. We sat for a long time before we were sure the raid was at last over, still half expecting another wave of bombers might yet appear, and we started to clear the blocked entrance. Some of the rocks were far too heavy for us to move, but by clawing lumps of earth and rolling away smaller rocks we managed to make enough room for us to wriggle our way out. We emerged, dazed and shaken, into the darkness outside. There was no one about and we wandered, disorientated and lost until we heard someone shouting. It was 'Dusty' Miller who had come to see what had happened to us and were we pleased to see him – you bet we were. We made our way up the hill, said a backslapping goodnight to our crewman who was billeted in Rabat, and arms around each other's shoulders we staggered like drunks into Mdina and fell into oblivion on our beds. In the morning, when we went for our breakfast, Johnny said 'Well, at least we proved old Fisky was right' and 'Dusty' and I gave him a playful pummelling.

We listened amused as scuttlebutt was having a field day with their lurid accounts not knowing we had been in the thick of it. The truth needed no embroidering for Intelligence gave a grim enough account. More than 140 aircraft had been involved, more than half of them Ju 88 bombers, who had dropped over 100 tons of bombs on the aerodrome. For the first time they had used rocket bombs to try to pierce the caves where our stores were kept and we wondered if they had suspected our underground chamber too and used one on us – the one that so nearly killed us. No one had been allowed to go down to Takali until daybreak as unexploded bombs, delayed action bombs, and bomb craters made it too dangerous in the dark, which was why we were alone when we were staggering about. How we managed to avoid those hazards I shall never know but it made us even more grateful to 'Dusty' who had talked his way through the road blocks and selflessly put his life at risk to see if his friends were alive or to fetch help if it was needed – but that was typical 'Dusty'! We were told we had survived the biggest raid on Takali to date, but this dubious distinction lasted only hours for at 09.00 hours the onslaught began again.

We rushed to the battlements, with our steel helmets on as out in the open there would be red hot shrapnel and AA fuse caps coming down, but we would have a grandstand view of all the action on the plain below. We were joined by dozens of helmetless Maltese men and women, young and old, who regularly gathered there to watch the bombs raining on Takali and the aerial battles being fought over the island. When an aircraft came plummeting down trailing smoke and flame they would pray that it wasn't one of ours, fingering their beads and crossing themselves. In the melees above it was difficult to distinguish friend from foe but when they did they cheered our outnumbered Spits and Hurricanes. If they saw a parachute floating down they always cried 'Inglis, Inglis, Hurray' and we hoped they were right. Only today there were no intricate contrail patterns from the battle being waged high in the sky for none of our aircraft appeared, leaving the Huns to bomb without hindrance. The raid lasted almost two hours and nearly 200 tons of bombs were dropped, which broke our unwanted record of being in the biggest raid on Takali yet. We got back to the Mess to hear that nine Spitfires would be arriving soon and we reasoned the fighters had been held in reserve to cover their landing. Reinforcements were badly needed for the fifteen Spits who came to the island on the same day as us, just a fortnight ago, were reduced to just two. The newcomers touched down in the middle of another heavy raid on Takali in which a bomb fell in Mdina outside the Officers' Mess, the Port De Vue.

When Johnny and I heard this we rushed to see if our pilots were safe but there was so much mayhem going on we could not get near the place. We stopped an officer hurrying by to ask about them and to our relief he said he had seen them and they were all right. The Mess had windows built into the battlements and through them everyone inside would have been watching the onslaught, as we had done, when the front of the hotel had been blown in. Scuttlebutt said that the first rescuers found three bodies seated on a sofa with their heads blown off by the blast wave and other stories they told were too gruesome for me to recount. It was later confirmed that seven officers had been killed by what was possibly a stray bomb intended for Rabat just outside the gate into Mdina. Why Rabat had been targeted was a mystery, perhaps they thought the people there worked on the aerodrome. Several civilians were killed and the village suffered heavy bomb damage. It had not been by accident but part of a deliberate tactic as Mosta had also been attacked, and the loss of life there had been even greater. Mosta was a village just outside the perimeter of the aerodrome, which boasted a church with the world's third largest unsupported dome. During raids the locals used it as a refuge rather than going into an air raid shelter. They figured that it would never be bombed in case we retaliated by bombing St Marks in Rome, which had the largest dome. It was a sensible assumption but the villagers were not spared for bombs were dropped on the entrance and exit of an air raid shelter nearby, collapsing the lungs of those inside – the fate we might well have suffered on Takali. Amazingly a large mansion, built by an eccentric nobleman with the stables on the roof well inside the aerodrome perimeter track escaped intact. Naturally we called it 'The Mad House' and although hundreds of bombs fell around it we finally had to blow it up ourselves as blast had rendered it unsafe. At last light we went onto the battlements to look at the state of our aerodrome; every yard was pockmarked so that it resembled a moonscape from a second rate sci-fi film. We saw there were hordes of airmen, troops and civilians scurrying about like ants filling in the craters and they were obviously going to work all night to get Takali operational again. It had been a terrible, disastrous, tragic day for the island, and for Takali, Rabat and Mosta in particular.

That night we went to bed, stunned by the day's events, apprehensive of what the morrow might have in store for this island and its gallant people but determined we would fight to the end – whatever or whenever that might be. One thing the Germans would not have expected was that their efforts would stiffen our resolve and strengthen our bond with the admirable Maltese people. Daily we shared their perils, for bombs do not discriminate nor the insidious effects of gnawing, debilitating hunger. They treated us like the knights who had defended their island against would-be invaders in the long distant past and our admiration for them was unbounded. Our tribulations had made us blood brothers. We no longer thought of Malta as *their* island – we now we felt it was *our* island too. We genuinely loved these indomitable people and the way they bravely bore the Nazi attacks reminded us of the way our own kin had reacted to the London Blitz. The comparison was a legitimate one for Malta was roughly the size of Greater London, yet it had been even more regularly and more heavily bombed without the massive fighter defence London had to defend it and now they were facing starvation. The Maltese had a tradition of serving in the Royal Navy, which for years had a large base in Valletta, and sometimes their loyalty to the Crown seemed greater than our own. Even though it was no longer tenable as a naval base the island was a vital staging post to the Middle East and beyond via the Suez canal. It was also a base for planes and submarines attacking the supply lines from Italy to Rommel and his Africa Korps. For all these reasons it was known as the unsinkable aircraft carrier and as long as it held out it stood in the way of Hitler's and Mussolini's plans to conquer the Mediterranean and make our convoys use the much longer route around South Africa to supply our troops in Egypt, Burma and the Far East. Although it wasn't their war really they were certainly paying a desperate price – 'God bless 'em!' we said and we meant it.

I have to admit that describing the days up to the end of the month has proved difficult for me even though I can still recall them vividly and indeed they will for ever be in my mind. My problem has been to get them in proper chronologically order, a problem compounded by some news being two or three days old before we learned of it, especially if it came from the other side of the island. Rumours were rife, scuttlebutt abounded, and bad news was kept secret so the enemy could not profit from it. One rumour was that another convoy was on its way and this was given credence when overnight the air attack switched to the Grand Harbour and the two naval aircraft bases of Hal Far and Kalafrana – or was it because they thought they had bombed Takali out of existence? Whatever the reason it gave us some respite as did a change in the weather with torrential rain and a cloud base of 1,000 feet. This latter was a mixed blessing for bombers could easily nip back into it giving them immunity from fighter attack. Not that we had a credible fighter force for often after a long day battling against overwhelming odds only five were left. This sometimes rose to as many as twelve or so by the morning as mechanics toiled overnight trying to find and fit what they needed from the dwindling stock of spare parts scavenged from totally wrecked aircraft.

Our aerodrome was still unusable so time hung heavily on our hands and as we wandered aimlessly around we came across more signs of the damage the raids had caused. Great piles of masonry from bombed buildings blocked the streets of Rabat and round the Port de Vue hotel in Mdina. Less apparent, but of greater consequence, were the shattered pipes, which had cut off our water supply, and for the same reason the sewage system had broken down too. The power station had been put out of action so we now had no electricity. Previously we had electricity for an hour each day around teatime so that we could listen to the BBC World Service. The Maltese made this concession so that the population was kept up to date with trustworthy news of the progress of the war. We had received no mail from home since we arrived and we suspected that our families did not even know where we were, which probably saved them much heartache. As soon as the broadcast ended we would tune in to the Italian 'Lord Haw Haw' to hear his biased account of the day's events. He vaunted the feats of the glorious, gallant, Italian army in North Africa boasting how many British prisoners they had taken in the desert that day and he always finished with 'This does not include 250,000 prisoners on the island of Maaltaa!' Of course it was transparently propaganda and we rolled with laughter – he 'made our day'! The Italians were a Gallic nation, at their best when things were going well, strutting about in natty uniforms and plumed hats but when the tide turned against them they needed stiffening. In WWI the British came to their aid to stem the Austrian advance and now they relied heavily on the Germans – but they were good at making ice cream!

In the pouring rain we gathered at our observation point on the battlements to watch as the Germans pounded the Grand Harbour at Valletta, Luqa Airfield, and other places on the horizon too far away to identify but we had a fair idea of who was 'getting it'. The AA gunners were putting up a dense barrage and kept on firing even as they were being dive-bombed by Ju 87 *Stukas* – very wise really for short of going down the nearest deep hole, their own gunfire was the best defence they had. We could see the flashes and then great spouts of earth erupt as the sticks of bombs rained down, sometimes from a single aircraft, sometimes from a whole squadron at once. This was usually from those gallant Italians, flying at high level where the air was filled with so much AA they sometimes dropped their bombs in the sea and hastened home. The Germans dropped an assortment of bombs including rocket bombs, delayed action bombs, and whole bomb loads chained together, which caused such a mighty explosion it made the earth tremble and was really spectacular to see. After a raid the whole island went dark as a pall of dust and smoke almost blotted out the sun punctuated by delayed action bombs exploding, which scarcely cleared before the next raid began. Even at mealtimes we felt loath to leave our vantage point overlooking Takali as if our presence would encourage those below who were still striving to get it operational again, forgetting that we had no fighters to make use of it when they eventually succeeded.

Our topless bus had been another casualty and on the 23rd our Flight was issued with pedal cycles. Danny and I were as delighted as kids who had just got the Fairy Cycle they had wanted for Xmas and like those children we wanted to try them out at once. We decided to have a ride to Luqa to see how the repairs to our damaged Beaus were progressing. We asked Peter and Johnny to come with us but Johnny did not share our enthusiasm, particularly the prospect of cycling in the rain, and Peter had a cold so we went alone. We were surprised how far it turned out to be but we were enjoying this unexpected exercise and the rain kept us pleasantly cool. The Luqa people told us that the bombing had wrecked their workshops so our aircraft had been moved to Hal Far where there were still facilities. This was unexpected news but we were not to be deterred for having come this far we figured we might as well go the whole way. The ground crews at Luqa told us the quickest way to get to Hal Far was to go down the Safi strip and though we had heard of the strip's fearsome reputation we took their advice. Our route took us down a narrow track, a favourite playground of marauding Me 109s, flanked on both sides by dozens of burnt out, crashed, horribly mangled, barely recognisable remains of Marylands, Blenheims, Wellingtons, Hurricanes, Swordfish, Gladiators and every type you could think of piled two or three deep. We had an eerie, spooky feeling for though there was not a soul in sight we felt someone was near us and we had an urge to get away as quickly as possible. Instead, for the next half mile, we were so fascinated we cycled slowly as if hypnotised by this amazing sight. We wondered how many men had died in these wrecks and how they had met their fate. Did their dreams of glory end in a blazing inferno as they plunged to earth or was it in some other catastrophic way, best not to speculate upon, that their young lives were taken? It was said that at the end more had died with an oath on their lips than a prayer but I hoped not in their cases. The chills were still running down our spines when we were brought rapidly back to reality by the air raid sirens sounding so, keeping a sharp eye open in case we got caught in the open by enemy fighters, we peddled like fury to get the hell out of this vale of tears. Unsurprisingly we had seen no Spits among the wrecks for they had been strategically sited on our airfields as decoys in the hope that they would trick the Germans into believing they were really serviceable aircraft.

We had just got clear of the strip when hostile aircraft appeared overhead apparently heading for Hal Far so we dismounted and took cover in a roadside ditch as bombs began to fall on our destination. It was a full-scale raid of forty or so Ju 88s and maybe twenty *Stuka*s and we watched as they gave the place a thirty-minute pasting. Then, suddenly, they were gone and the 'All Clear' sounded so we got on our bikes and rode until we came to a Guard House on the perimeter. The guards waved us through the gate and we cycled along a rough road looking for a vantage point from which we could see the hangars. When we did a shocking scene of devastation lay before our eyes. The hangars had been completely demolished and their massive concrete roof beams had crashed down on the aircraft within twisting and crushing them into unrecognisable shapes. We sat there for quite a while trying to identify what type some were which had been blown through the shattered hangar doors and thought they might be Fulmars or Hurricanes but Beaus they certainly were not! Danny and I looked at each other in dismay and agreed that with such destruction there was no chance of anything being salvaged let alone repaired. We were about to get on our bikes to go home when a soldier rushed up to us shouting 'Where do you think you are going?' We pointed to the track we had come down and he shook his head. 'Sorry sir,' he said, 'that road is closed, there's a delayed action bomb on it. When we protested that we had only just come that way he went pale. He said 'Jeez! You must have cycled right over the b—y thing. I will tell you how to get out now.' We followed his directions, which thankfully did not take us anywhere near the Safi strip, and got back to Mdina in the dark. I said 'Goodnight' to Danny and went straight to the Mess hoping I was still in time for supper, which I knew would be Machonachies, but even that would be welcome, and a drink after to relax me. The Mess was awash with rumours and scuttlebutt and it was difficult to sort out the wheat from the chaff. One thing was indisputable, the relentless pounding of the last few days had virtually neutralised Malta so I gave up trying to sort it all out and retired to my bed.

I was dead tired but sleep would not come for my mind was in a turmoil going over and over my strange experience in the Safi strip. I knew there would be no rest for me until I unravelled its meaning. I pondered for ages before I came to a conclusion that, though it may seem preposterous to you, I believe is the true explanation. From the beginning I had felt no fear for I instinctively knew that the 'presence' was not malevolent but perhaps a little irritated at being disturbed. After a very short while 'it' had realised that this was not some moron come to take a morbid look but someone who empathised deeply with these fallen comrades in arms. Thereafter 'it' seemed to be saying 'There is nothing you can do for us, our race is run, leave us to our eternal rest but remember us.' Was it fantasy? Maybe. Psychic nonsense? Perhaps, but I truly believe it was the spirits of the departed who spoke to me that day. You can take your pick, I only know that I felt a tremendous contentment as if 'it' was glad that 'it' could leave me having finally been able to make me understand, and I fell into a deep sleep.

The 24th dawned and the weather improved slightly as the cloud base lifted a little but the conditions favoured the attackers still more with their overwhelming superiority in numbers against our pitifully few fighters gallant though they were. We went to our 'grandstand' on the battlements and watched raid after raid on Valletta, Hal Far, and Luqa so it was safe to assume that Grand Harbour and the remains of the convoy straggling in were the target. We saw a few inconclusive

My 'brother' Peter and self.

My Mum and Dad.

A group photo at
Yatesbury – Bert Izzard
standing extreme right,
and Archer 2nd from
left standing. Self far
left front row.

My first flying kit at
Yatesbury Signals
School.

Aged 19 – a newly
promoted Sgt
WOP/AG.

Waiting for the train at Abu Sweir station. R to L: Flt Lt Hayton (Flight Commander), Peter, Johnny Walsh and myself seated.

A Beaufighter at Luqa in 1942, although not a night fighter variant. (Bill Lazelle)

Newly arrived Beaufighters at Luqu in 1943. (Bill Lazelle)

Wrecked Beaufighter at Luqa in 1942. Spares were salvaged from written-off aircraft. (Bill Lazelle)

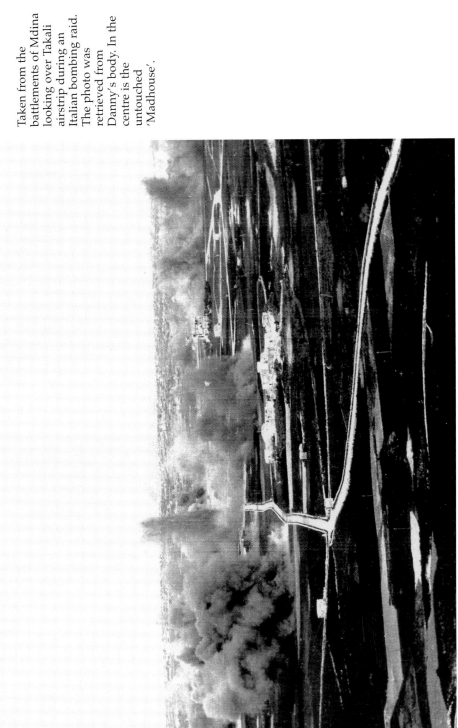

Taken from the battlements of Mdina looking over Takali airstrip during an Italian bombing raid. The photo was retrieved from Danny's body. In the centre is the untouched 'Madhouse'.

A burnt-out Hurricane – the result of a German attack. (Bill Lazelle)

Flares and tracer over Luqa during a night raid. (Bill Lazelle)

An anti-aircraft night barrage over the Grand Harbour.

MALTA

Time carried forward :— 204·33 | 86·45

Date	Hour	Aircraft Type and No.	Pilot	Duty	Remarks (including results of bombing, gunnery, exercises, etc.)	Flying Times Day	Night
APR 6	19·00	Beau Fighter X7752	P/o Daniel	Patrol	AI u/s		1·15
APR 6	12·00	Beau Fighter X7752	P/o Daniel	X Raids	R/T u/s		1·30
APR 10	07·15	Beau Fighter X7752	P/o Daniel	Luqa To Takali		0·15	
APR 10	19·50	Beau Fighter X7762	P/o Daniel	X Raids	AI u/s		0·45
APR 10	23·00	Beau Fighter X7750	P/o Daniel	X Raids	1 Ju 88 Damaged		2·30
APR 13	09·15	Beau Fighter X7750	P/o Daniel	Daylight Scramble X Raids	Returned R/T u/s 1 BR 20 Destroyed 卐		2·00
APR 14	06·15	Beau Fighter X7752	P/o Daniel	Luqa To Takali		0·20	
APR 14	20·00	Beau Fighter X7750	P/o Daniel	X Raid	Contact & Visual — Then AI u/s		2·15
APR 17	18·50	Beau Fighter X7750	P/o Daniel	Patrol	AI u/s — back hatch open		0·30
APR 17	20·00	Beaufighter X7750	P/o Daniel	Patrol	AI u/s — broke tail wheel landing		0·45

No flying till April 25th

Total Time ... 205·10 | 97·15

The author's logbook, 16 May to 21 May 1942.

MALTA

Time carried forward :— 206:40 | 100:10

Date	Hour	Aircraft Type and No.	Pilot	Duty	Remarks (including results of bombing, gunnery, exercises, etc.)	Day	Night
MAY 16	23:00	BEAU FIGHTER 7744	P/O DANIEL LAC ROSSITER	AIR TEST	AI OK		0.15
MAY 17th	02.45	BEAU FIGHTER 7744	P/O DANIEL	X RAIDS	THREE BR 20's DESTROYED 〄〄 〄〄 〄〄 (flamers)		2.15
MAY 17th	05.15	BEAU FIGHTER 7744	P/O DANIEL	LUQA - TAKALI		0.20	
MAY 19th	20.30	BEAU FIGHTER 7744	P/O DANIEL	TAKALI TO LUQA	A/c u/s - Wheels would not lock down!		0.35
MAY 20th	02.45	BEAU FIGHTER 7744	P/O DANIEL	SCRAMBLE	R/T u/s		0.13
MAY 20th	03.20	BEAU FIGHTER 7744	P/O DANIEL	X RAID	1 CANT 1007 DESTROYED 〄〄 (flamer)		0.40
MAY 20th	06.15	BEAU FIGHTER 7744.	P/O DANIEL	LUQA TO TAKALI		0.20	
MAY 20th	14.30	BEAU FIGHTER 7750	P/O DANIEL DFC MAJOR HARRISON	TAKALI TO LUQA CANNON TEST.	3 CANNONS OK. (STOPPAGE.	0.20	
MAY 20th	22.00	BEAU FIGHTER 7750	P/O DANIEL DFC MAJOR HARRISON	PATROL			2.00
MAY 21st	0030	BEAU FIGHTER 7750	P/O DANIEL DFC	PATROL AND ATTEMPTED LOCATION OF LOST WELLINGTON	UNSUCCESSFUL		2.00

TOTAL TIME ... 207.40 | 109.10

MALTA

Time carried forward :— 207.10 | 108.10

Date	Hour	Aircraft Type and No.	Pilot	Duty	Remarks (including results of bombing, gunnery, exercises, etc.)	Day	Night
May 23rd	08.30	Beau Fighter 7750	P/o Daniel DFC	NFT	109's around!	0.05	
May 23rd	21.00	Beau Fighter 7750	P/o Daniel DFC	Scramble	Back Hatch Opened		0.20
May 23rd	23.00	Beau Fighter 7750	P/o Daniel DFC	Patrol	No Trade		3.25
May 26th	19.30	Beau Fighter 7744	P/o Daniel DFC	Air Test and Cannon Test.	O.K.	0.23	
May 26th	20.30	Beau Fighter 7744	P/o Daniel DFC	Scramble	Lost Port Airscrew and Reduction Gear — Twice Ordered to "Bale Out" — Good Landing		0.40
May 27th	00.30	Beau Fighter 7224	P/o Daniel DFC	Search for "E" Boats.	Unsuccessful		2.00
May 27th	05.30	Beau Fighter 7224	P/o Daniel DFC	Takali from Luqa		0.20	
May 31st	19.20	Beau Fighter 7224	P/o Daniel DFC	Takali to Luqa.	Cannons OK	0.23	
					Total Flying For May	20.15	3.15
					Total Day	17.00	
					Total Night		3.15
					Total Day and Night to Date	323.00	

OC
Beaufighter Flight

Total Time ..... 208.25 | 114.35

MALTA

Time carried forward :— 208·25 | 114·35

Date	Hour	Aircraft Type and No.	Pilot	Duty	Remarks (including results of bombing, gunnery, exercises, etc.)	Flying Times	
						Day	Night
JUNE 1ST	00·20	BEAU FIGHTER 7224	P/O DANIEL DFC	X RAID	AI U/S		0·40
JUNE 1ST	01·30	BEAU FIGHTER 7224	P/O DANIEL DFC	AIR TEST	AI OK		0·20
JUNE 1ST	02·40	BEAU FIGHTER 7224	P/O DANIEL DFC	X RAID	VISUAL ON JU 87 IAS 90MPH! UNABLE TO GET A 'SQUIRT' IN. MUCH RETURN FIRE INEFFECTIVE BECAUSE WE STALLED.		1·10
JUNE 1ST	05·30	BEAU FIGHTER 7224	P/O DANIEL DFC	LUQA TO TAKALI		0·20	
JUNE 1ST	17·30	BEAU FIGHTER 7224	P/O DANIEL DFC	TAKALI TO LUQA		0·20	
JUNE 1ST	20·15	BEAU FIGHTER 7224	P/O DANIEL DFC	DAYLIGHT SCRAMBLE AND X RAIDS	1 JU 88 DAMAGED		2·20
JUNE 2ND	00·10	BEAU FIGHTER 7224	P/O DANIEL DFC	PATROL			0·40
JUNE 2ND	02·15	BEAU FIGHTER 7224	P/O DANIEL DFC	X RAID	AI U/S		0·50
JUNE 2ND	06·30	BEAU FIGHTER 7224	P/O DANIEL DFC	LUQA TO TAKALI		0·40	
JUNE 3RD	10·50	BEAU FIGHTER 7144	P/O DANIEL DFC	TAKALI TO LUQA - AIR TEST	OK	0·30	

TOTAL TIME ... 210·15 | 120·35

The author's logbook, 1 June to 3 June 1942.

The author's logbook, 14 July to 25 July 1944.

COLERNE

Time carried forward :— 683·30 | 253·55

Date	Hour	Aircraft Type and No.	Pilot	Duty	Remarks (including results of bombing, gunnery, exercises, etc.)	Flying Times Day	Night
14th July	15·40	Mosquito XIII C-MM517	F/O Truscott	N.F.T.		0·30	
14th July	19·15	Mosquito XIII W-HK527	F/Lt Hayhurst	N.F.T.		0·20	
14th July	22·20	Mosquito XIII W-HK527	F/Lt Hayhurst	Fighter Pool 2	No Trade		3·05
17th July	15·15	Mosquito XIII W-HK527	F/Lt Hayhurst	N.F.T.		0·20	
17th July	22·15	Mosquito XIII W-HK527	F/Lt Hayhurst	Fighter Pool 2	1 Ju 88 Destroyed 15m S. Carteret. In Flames. ⵜ		3·00
21st July	17·25	Mosquito XIII W-HK527	F/Lt Hayhurst	N.F.T.		0·40	
21st July	03·35	Mosquito XIII W-HK527	F/Lt Hayhurst	Fighter Pool 1			2·25
22nd July	15·30	Mosquito XIII W-HK527	F/Lt Hayhurst	N.F.T.		0·30	
22nd July	22·10	Mosquito XIII W-HK527	F/Lt Hayhurst	Fighter Pool 2	D/F on AI jamming		3·20
25th July	14·40	Mosquito XIII W-HK527	F/Lt Hayhurst	To Zeals		0·15	

Total Time :— 686·05 | 265·45

The author's logbook, 20 February to 24 February 1945.

Time carried forward:— | 728.50 | 318.05

LILLE – VENDEVILLE   B51

Date	Hour	Aircraft Type and No.	Pilot	Duty	Remarks (including results of bombing, gunnery, exercises, etc.)	Day	Night
20th FEB	12·50	OXFORD N3299	F/LT WELFORD F/SGT MASSEY F/LT TROMAN	NAV	NORTHOLT TO B51	1·10	
22nd FEB	14·00	OXFORD X724	CAPT KRISTIANSEN P/O BAIRD F/LT MASSEY	PASSENGER	ENGINE TROUBLE – LANDED MERVILLE CONTINUED TO DEFFORD VIA NORTHOLT	2·45	
24th FEB	15·00	OXFORD X7241	CAPT KRISTIANSEN P/O BRAD F/O MacDONALD W/O HUGHES XXV DFC F/LT DIXON DFC	PASSENGER	TO BASE VIA DEFFORD	2·00	

TOTAL FLYING FOR FEB.
DAY 8·30 HOURS
NIGHT 5·40 HOURS
TOTAL FLYING TO DATE
DAY 734·45 HOURS
NIGHT 318·05 HOURS

SENIOR NAV/RAD.

"B" FLIGHT 604 SQN

O.C. 604 SQUADRON

LILLE – VENDEVILLE B51

Has completed a very satisfactory tour.
Well above the average.

Total Time ... | 734·45 | 318·05

The author, aged 24.

Medals, citation for the DFC and a model of a night-fighter Mosquito.

Irene, Dennis's beloved late wife.

Dennis in retirement at his home near Doncaster.

dogfights in the distance but the AA put up a tremendous barrage, which was now our only real defence. How many ships had got through we did not know but their safe arrival was vital for the AA were obviously using up our precious remaining ammunition at an unsustainable rate, and we were so desperately short of food we could think of little else. At the end of the day we went to the Mess for our meagre fare, tired and despondent, and when the scuttlebutters claimed only two ships had made it vicious fights broke out at such blatant defeatism. I went to bed depressed wondering what the man with the cards had in store for us next.

The 25th brought the same weather but better news from the ants at Takali who had performed a minor miracle for with no machines to assist them they had toiled day and night to make the airfield usable again – by hand! Those airmen, soldiers and civilians deserved a medal for their efforts and when we called on them later on they responded magnificently, especially as they too were starving. Danny and I went to the airfield to see for ourselves if the take-off strip was usable and on the way down we could scarcely believe our eyes. From a distance it looked horrendous with not a blade of grass in sight, just sandy holes strung together. When we got closer we saw that there was a somewhat more level run where the old strip had been and when we walked the full length of it we decided we might just manage to get airborne from it. It would be a gamble but worth a try and if it could be done there was no one was more capable than Danny, so we decided that we would operate that night. However, we did so in an aircraft whose number does not appear in my logbook before or after that one night and I can only guess why. It had been made clear to us that the prime reason for sending us to Malta was to protect the aircraft landing on the island every night on their way to the Middle East thus keeping the vital transit route open. Due to the bombing there were times when we had no serviceable aircraft to fulfil our commitment, which was considered so important that we were given permission to commandeer Beaus in transit. We then put the crew on one of the Wellington bombers, which passed through every night operating a sort of 'Postman Pat' service. This may have been how we acquired the aircraft we flew to Luqa that night and it seems likely it too was later destroyed in a raid. Our efforts were in vain as we flew for three hours without making a single contact and when we twice flew to Luqa later that month our one Beau was kept grounded as the island was considered too dangerous for transit aircraft to use.

The weather had improved on the 26th for the cloud base had lifted but the wind was still strong and blustery. The raids began at breakfast time and we could hear the bombs and continuous AA fire, which told us that Valletta, shipping unloading in the Grand Harbour, its docks and ships trying to hide in the many creeks, were being targeted again. The two ships from the convoy that had got through were attacked and sunk at their moorings, luckily in shallow water. The number of pilots in the Mess told us there were no aircraft for them to fly, like the problem at Abu Sueir only ten times worse. Of course there were rumours aplenty but now things were happening so fast all over the island that almost anything was believable. We were saddened by the news that the gallant HMS *Breconshire*, hero of so many nocturnal supply runs, had been sunk. HMS *Penelope*, who had shared the same dangers bringing in desperately needed supplies, and was affectionately known as 'The Pepper Pot' from the bomb splinter gashes she had suffered, was grievously wounded and in dry dock.

There was also a persistent rumour that two submarines had been sunk at their moorings, and the whole flotilla was withdrawing from its base on Manoel Island. At first I discounted this as I knew the submarines usually submerged during the day to escape the bombing and leaving altogether would remove a major threat to the Axis lines of communication. On the other hand I knew that minefields sown indiscriminately by the Italians had made a dangerous task even more perilous. They had been using 'U' class boats, which were small and considered the most suitable for use in the crystal clear waters of the Med but they could still be seen from an aircraft even when laid on the bottom in certain conditions. Their job was hazardous yet courageously they had created havoc with the supply lines to Rommel's famed Africa Corps. Their presence had forced the Italians to tie up fleets of escort vessels, and resort to using convoys to protect their merchant ships. If they left the Med the Suez Canal would be denied to us making even greater demands on our U-boat-ravaged shipping who would have to take the much longer route around South Africa to supply Egypt, India, and the Far East.

A new rumour was now being bandied about and over the weeks ahead it became ever more persistent – the likelihood of an invasion. In its present parlous state we knew Malta would be a pushover and with the fall of Crete to German paratroops in our minds we were aware that they were well versed in the art of airborne assault. There would never be a better time to rid themselves of this unsinkable aircraft carrier whose indomitable fighting spirit had been a thorn in their side for so long. Isolated by more than a thousand miles in both directions we could expect no succour from the east or the west and if Malta fell they would have complete domination of the Mediterranean. True the island would put up a fight but invasion was the obvious solution and it was hard to believe that the Germans would spurn such a golden opportunity. It would also raise Mussolini's waning popularity among the Italian people who instead of his promise to build an Italian Empire around his '*Mare Nostrum*' had delivered them only a succession of humiliating defeats.

The weather was still poor on the 27th so it seemed that it might be worse in Sicily for there was little activity from the Germans but ten Hurricanes managed to get through to us from North Africa. They were badly needed for pilots were having to take their turn to fly what few fighters we had left as the attrition rate had been so high both in the air and on the ground. It was a welcome respite but could the Hun simply be reorganising before renewing his attacks with even greater ferocity – who could tell? The scuttlebutters had their own theories.

On the 28th there were no attacks at all and although the weather was really bad even I had to admit it was puzzling but on the 29th the heavy raids on Luqa were resumed probably prompted by the arrival of seven Spits from the aircraft carrier HMS *Eagle*. One thing you could rely upon was that the Germans would always respond to the arrival of Spitfires.

On the 30th the weather was absolutely foul and scuttlebutt had it that many transit aircraft had failed to arrive from Gibraltar and others which did arrive had been seen to crash trying to land at Luqa and some crews had been killed.

The 31st saw a return to normality for despite low cloud damaging raids were made throughout the day on Luqa, Hal Far and the Dock area where even underwater attempts were being made to salvage everything possible from the two sunken ships and HMS *Breconshire*. So desperate were our needs that the unloading did not stop despite being targeted by large numbers of Ju 87 *Stuka* dive-bombers. With the new arrivals we were able to put up more fighters but the low cloud made it easy for the bombers to escape and claims for 'kills' were hard to confirm. That night the Mess was buzzing with scuttlebutt, which they assured us came directly from the Intelligence Section. Through wireless intercepts they had found out that Kurt Student who had been in command of the invasion of Crete had arrived in Sicily with orders from Hitler that Malta was to be invaded in April. For once it was so feasible that we had no reason to doubt its veracity but Student could not invade on his own and there were no signs of the necessary forces gathering as yet. However, to maintain the element of surprise until the last minute it was always possible that the assembly was taking place elsewhere ready to be moved to Sicily, their obvious jumping off point. It was not a happy prospect but sufficient to the day is the evil thereof so we consoled ourselves by dismissing it all as just scuttlebutt – we hoped!

So ended March and I reflected on the twenty-four days since I arrived in Malta and what a desperate twenty-four days they had been. I had hoped it was going to be a great adventure but I had never dreamt it would be anything like the nightmare it had turned out to be. In the month of March Malta had received twice the tonnage of bombs that London had in a whole *year* I had been told and I believed them. I had certainly earned my 'Hard Lying Allowance'. On the 7th I had high expectations as we brought in our four aircraft but they had all been destroyed by the bombing. The unit had been incredibly lucky that we had all escaped unscathed but I had spent as much time in a slit trench as I had in the air. Despite all the tribulations I decided that I much preferred to be here rather than in fly-infested, filthy Egypt where I was constantly pestered by beggars, shoe blacks and pimps trying to sell their 'very young, very clean sisters'. In complete contrast I had found the Maltese to be hardworking, keeping themselves and their homes spotless despite having no sewage or running water and I admired the way they contended daily with the all pervading dust from the shattered buildings around them. It reminded me how my folks had donkey stoned the front doorstep every day lest the neighbours outshone them. The Maltese had convinced me that they were proud of their island's long, varied history and were almost fanatically loyal to Britain. I had already become friendly with some of them and had been welcomed into their houses. Often they had shared their last crust, which really embarrassed me for I had no way of repaying them – not even a tin of Machonachies! Human nature being what it is I suppose they must have had their share of bad eggs but I had never encountered one, maybe the war brought out the best in them. Our relationship was one of mutual respect and I felt so comfortable with them it was like being at home and certainly they treated us better than the Welsh had in Pwllheli.

With all the bombing it would have been foolhardy to travel to Valletta but I had taken to cycling out and then walking around the villages where the architecture reflected the distinctive features of the many civilisations who had occupied the island in the long distant past. It was obvious that the Maltese were staunchly Catholic for the churches were always the predominant feature, being large, impressive and beautiful both inside and out. They were made of the local sandstone and like the great domed church in Mosta many were raised on a plinth of five or more steps and some had massive Grecian-type pillars as a façade. Inside they exuded religious opulence with fantastic frescos, ornate ceilings, altars adorned with gold crosses and vessels worth a fortune and the all pervading scent of incense had left me breathless. The overall effect had been so stunning that even as an Anglican I had been so overwhelmed by the splendour that I had an urge to cry out loud 'Glory be to God'. Sadly I had found evidence of the bombing everywhere and there were blockages in many places where the lovely buildings had collapsed into the street and my hatred of the Germans grew as I surveyed the wanton damage they had done. They were too obsessed with spreading death and destruction in their quest for domination to think of the hundreds of years it had taken for those towns and villages to develop into the unique and picturesque places they now were. I remembered seeing plate glass shards embedded like daggers into the soft honey-coloured stone by bomb blast and I thought it was somehow symbolic of their barbarity. I was concerned for their fate should the Germans ever overcome the island who I felt they would be hell bent on retribution for their stubborn resistance.

I was convinced that the possibility of an invasion was uppermost in all the defenders' minds but the thought of being starved into submission was what they hated most yet it was becoming more likely with every passing day. I was worried because I could see no hope of any relief effort being attempted let alone succeeding. I had to accept that the Med was effectively closed and mounting another Malta convoy was beyond the Allies' capability. I thought of the thousands of Maltese, young, old, and even children who had been killed in the pitiless bombing and the privations they had endured during three years of stubborn defiance. I thought of the courageous defence, on the ground, in the air, on and under the sea against overwhelming odds and my heart bled for them all. The old adage 'that it is always darkest before the dawn' came to my mind as I looked forward to April but I feared that there might be a long wait before the sunrise and time was not on our side. How cruel, how unjust it would be if all their sacrifice was to be in vain – and I cursed the man who dealt the cards.

CHAPTER EIGHTEEN

Recognition Too Late? – Malta, April 1942

Seamlessly March slid into April but no one thought of April Fool's Day leg pulls; we were too concerned about our apparently hopeless plight. We awoke to the sounds of the inevitable morning attack on the harbour by Ju 88s, Ju 87s, and their clouds of escorting fighters. We had only a handful of Spits and Hurricanes, so outnumbered that they really should not have been scrambled at all but had they been left on the ground they would have been destroyed by marauding Me 109s. After the catastrophic fate of the last convoy we could not foresee any chance of the Admiralty risking their precious carriers and capital ships again. In fact it was difficult to imagine how any means could be found to strengthen the garrison, in particular the air defences, let alone relieve the island's food situation. This was becoming so desperate that any attempt would have to be made soon or starvation might bring about an inglorious end to the island's otherwise indomitable defence of this bastion isolated by 1,000 miles in every direction by hostile territory.

And it was not just the people who were hungry, the AA guns were also hungry. They had put up an intense barrage to salvage something from the few remnants of the last convoy who had managed to get to Malta. Despite their efforts the two or three survivors had been sunk at their moorings and though the dockers and salvage squads hastily put together by the Army had worked night and day, in and under the water, only a fraction of their total loads had been saved. So much had depended on those supplies for they were Malta's vital lifeline and their loss might well prove to be a mortal blow. The AA crews had stuck to their guns even under constant attack by bombers, dive-bombers, and strafing fighters but they had been unable to protect the harbour against such a violent and sustained onslaught. The shipping losses in the harbour were grievous and the surrounding creeks were littered with the wrecks of submarines, warships and merchant vessels. One vessel was valiantly fighting for her life. Even though she was in dry dock HMS *Penelope*'s guns still blasted out defiance shooting down attackers and miraculously escaping near misses. Riddled with shrapnel, dear old 'Pepper Pot' fought on – an inspiration to us all.

The AA guns' stock of ammunition was so depleted that their crews were now not allowed to fire at bombers after they had dropped their bombs and were only permitted to fire at fighters if they were clearly attacking a target, like an airfield. What fighters we had, some days up to ten and some days none at all, were kept to disrupt the major raids but they were too few to repel them. Consequently the *Luftwaffe* roamed the island almost at will and seemingly short of military targets they strafed and bombed small villages, donkey carts, cyclists, walkers, bathers, buses – indeed anything that took their perverted fancy. It was very hard to take such blatant, wanton, sadistic destruction with no means of retaliating and we prayed for our day to come. I was standing on the roof of the Casa Testaferrata one evening at dusk enjoying the cool night air when a Me 109 flew by at rooftop height and I could have sworn he gave me the two fingers of derision. Too late I drew my trusty Smith & Wesson revolver and blazed away at his fast disappearing silhouette in the fading light. A more futile gesture I cannot imagine (David had a much better chance against Goliath), however it made me feel a little less frustrated – but not a lot!

Nearly every day followed the same pattern and even the scuttlebutters were silenced for the news was always worse than anything their fertile minds could invent. Happily there were days when our spirits got a badly needed boost but as yet we did not know this was to be 1435 Flight's day. We made our way down to Takali about 18.00 hours to prepare for operations that night. It was Peter and Johnny's turn to fly our one remaining Beau and Danny and I went to Luqa by road with the ground crew. When we arrived we found that they had run the gauntlet from Takali without incident and were waiting for us down 'G' (Operations) shelter. Just before last light 'Fisky' the Bomb Disposal Officer and erstwhile WWI observer called for us to do our runway sweeping duties. After his previous gaffe with his supposedly 'safe' bomb we had got used to doing this necessary chore and had become quite blasé as there had been no further incidents. Twenty minutes later we were back in 'G' shelter awaiting 'the call', which came about 22.00 hours when considerable activity was reported by GCI and Peter and Johnny, already kitted up, rushed to their aircraft to our shouts of 'Good luck'.

We had a link with ops that allowed us to hear what was happening and shortly we heard Peter call 'Tally ho', engage an Italian aircraft, and whoop with joy as he claimed its destruction. We were delighted for them and some minutes later they were vectored onto another but they lost it in the haze that sometimes covered the island but not before they had seen strikes on its fuselage. Great going so far; one had been destroyed and one damaged, and there was still more trade about. A short while later they engaged another target and then Peter called saying his port engine had been set ablaze by return fire from its tail gunner. This was bad news but the Beau could fly well on one engine and we had practised single-engined flying regularly so we were worried but not unduly alarmed. The combats had been at 16,000 feet and Peter had lost around 10,000 feet when he cried out that his starboard engine had stopped too. Now we were alarmed for it meant landing in the dark without engine power, which he had certainly never done before. It was imperative that he had plenty of height on his final approach and so the angle of glide indicator would be useless to him – he had to be much higher than that. We knew Peter was a good pilot but was this asking too much of him especially as the Beau had all the gliding properties of a household brick!

When he called to say he was on his final approach we rushed onto the airfield and got as near to the runway as we dare to see if we could help rescue them if fire broke out. All the runway lights were on and then the aircraft was suddenly sliding down the tarmac on its belly in a shower of sparks and then the lights went out for they would undoubtedly attract some intruder. I raced towards the wreck shouting 'Peter! Johnny! Over here! Over here!' and then Johnny appeared beside me. 'How did you get out of that so quickly?' I asked and he replied 'I was out before it stopped sliding and so was Peter!' We had no time to say any more before the expected bomber came roaring towards the stricken plane dropping bombs on the runway as Johnny and I rushed for shelter. The only cover we could find was under the wing of a Hurricane and when I said 'Some use this is – two thicknesses of canvas and a bit of wood between us and a b—y great bomb' we burst out with nervous laughter.

On the way back to 'G' shelter Johnny gave me a lurid account of their escapade and although Danny and I were now the only one of 1435 Flight's crews not to have scored so far, we were envious but not a jot jealous. We heaped congratulations on them and praised the wonderful airmanship Peter had shown in pulling off an incredible landing against enormous odds – it was nearly a miracle. They could have baled out but Johnny had shown his confidence by staying with Peter, the pilot he had so many doubts about at Tangmere until the night Peter and I had our narrow escape with the trim tabs. I was pleased that I had a hand in keeping them together and I was proud of their success. Half an hour later one of the ground crew came down 'G' shelter and dejectedly reported that our one and only aircraft was a total write-off but we were only concerned that Peter and Johnny were safe. We went back in the morning to Takali in the truck tired yet happy as sandboys.

Johnny and I talked over the previous night's encounters. In fact he was on such a 'high' he could talk of little else, and we agreed that the Germans seemed to be concentrating their efforts on daytime bombing and leaving the night raiding increasingly to the Italians. We wondered if the pressure of flying three or four sorties a day was taking its toll at last and they were suffering from combat fatigue, which would not be surprising. Perhaps they were saying to the Italians 'We have softened them up now it's time you pulled your weight' or was it 'You take over at night while we prepare for the invasion' for they were receiving fresh reinforcements daily. Whatever the cause it was clear that there was something in the wind – but what?

The following day there were the usual raids on the harbour and the airfields including one on Takali, which destroyed a Beau we had hoped to get repaired to enable us to resume our night operations. It looked as if Danny and I would never get a chance to get our first 'kill' – why did they have to hit our precious Beau instead of the 'Mad House', which still enjoyed a charmed life? The next day was a comparatively quiet day but still a happy day for HMS *Penelope* had managed to sail away and we wished her luck and God speed to calmer waters. Yet somehow her going left us feeling even more alone as if we had lost a friend, which indeed we had. Things were relatively quiet the following day too but on 6 April Danny and I got airborne and my logbook shows it was in an aircraft with a serial number new to the Flight so I can only assume it was another transit aircraft we had commandeered. It didn't bring us any better luck for the first flight we made in it the radar packed up and having got that fixed we took off on our patrol only for the radio to fail. We stooged around for over an hour hoping to come across a hostile by chance or maybe caught in a searchlight but we did not and so we landed thoroughly brassed off and convinced we were jinxed. I could imagine the man who dealt the cards was watching our frustration and laughing his head off as he said 'Thought you were going to be a hero, eh? Well no chance!'

The heavy raids were incessant and we were so used to them that we came to accept them as part of our daily lives. The raids on 9 April were the same as we had become accustomed to every day but today differed in one respect – the Germans had dropped bombs on Mosta Cathedral. Mosta was so close to our airfield perimeter they might have been intended for Takali as we had a Beau damaged in the raid or it could have been another act of intimidation. It had exploded the myth that the church would never be bombed for fear of a reprisal raid on St Mark's in Rome and they were reminding us that we now had no means of carrying out such a threat. Although few of us were Catholics we felt deeply for the Maltese people who revered the beautiful edifice as part of their heritage and we were outraged on their behalf. What did not explode, however, were the bombs, including one that went through the dome, ricocheted around and came to rest near the high altar. It was rolled out of the church, bounced down the five steps of the plinth and with the others that also failed to explode, was carted away into the marshes. The scuttlebutters insisted that dear old 'Fisky' the Bomb Disposal Officer from Luqa had been the one who had driven them away, allegedly on a donkey cart, but it seemed unlikely as Luqa was miles away and he had more than his hands full there. The bomb that went through the Dome was discovered years later, the explosive was steamed out, and it was returned to the church as a souvenir – doubtless with a slot cut in it for donations. Of the 300 or more people taking refuge there not one was injured – a vindication of their faith.

On 10 April we were lucky that Luqa had recovered sufficiently from a 90+ raid for us to fly there in the new aircraft and once more on the air test the radar went on the blink. We landed and the mechanic tinkered with it for ages, finally declaring it serviceable but it was too late for us to test it again. With no other aircraft available we had no option but to accept his assurance of its serviceability and anyway we were desperate to get into the air. At 23.00 hours we were scrambled to intercept an incoming 'X' raid and as we raced to the plane we were determined that this was going to be our day at long last. Under GCI control we were vectored to 13,000 feet some twenty miles north of the island and five minutes later I got my first contact on the intruder. It was coming towards us, which made it the trickiest interception of all to execute as you could easily lose it in the ground returns (we called it 'clutter') as we turned. I was sweating trying to keep it on my radar screen but I managed to get behind it. I immediately realised it was going very fast so I told Danny to go flat out to close the range as quickly as possible and we steadily narrowed the gap until we got a visual on it. The onus was then on us to make a positive identification for being classed as an 'X' raid meant GCI had not ruled out the possibility it might be a transit aircraft desperately looking for Malta to land on. This happened often for navigating 1,000 miles over the sea in the dark from Gibraltar without any landmarks called for great skill and not a little luck. There was no way of checking for crosswinds and even a one degree compass error could put them twenty or thirty miles off their course. If they failed to locate the island they ran out of fuel and with the nearest friendly landfall 1,000 miles further on they would inevitably have to ditch in the sea. To make it worse the island was often covered with a sort of haze somewhat like a sea fret, sometimes low to the ground and at others up to 15,000 feet. It was like that now as we sat behind our target for what seemed to me to be ages before Danny satisfied himself that it was a Ju 88, which I confirmed, and we closed for the kill. Danny gave it a ten-second burst with our four 20 mm cannon and six .303 machine-guns from about 250 yards when the Jerry did an unexpected thing. Obviously the pilot was no novice for he extended his dive brakes and went straight down like a *Stuka* dive bomber. Had we tried to follow we would have overshot and finished up in front of it, which was a dangerous place for a night fighter to be. We tried to get another contact on it without any success and then the radio packed up just as it had four days ago. We had to return to base but at last we had broken our 'duck' for we had seen many strikes on it and we claimed it as a 'damaged'.

After a day of massive raids 'Dusty' Miller and Sgt Tearle got another destroyed on 11 April and again it was an Italian Breda, confirming that night operations were becoming their responsibility.

The 12th was a really happy day for I shook hands with Air Marshal Tedder – with nothing on but my shirt! He was on his way to the Middle East and had asked to meet the island's night fighters when he was down 'G' shelter ready to board his plane. I had just flown and was trying to get to sleep on the floor of our hot and stuffy crew room far underground so I had stripped to my shirt when the door opened, the light came on, and there stood Tedder. He shook hands with each of us as he moved round and asked us questions about our experiences on Malta. When he came to me I was embarrassed, holding down my shirt with my left hand whilst shaking hands with my right and I was glad we only had a pre-flight red light bulb in our room – it matched the colour of my face. (Of course you know of my dislike of underpants but please keep it our little secret.) Tedder was a great bloke and he richly deserved the honour of becoming Eisenhower's deputy for the invasion of France.

I was born on 13 May and I had always regarded thirteen as my lucky number and so it proved to be for Danny and me. There was little hostile activity during the day and we had no trouble getting to Luqa. We did our usual sweep of the runway, and had barely got back to 'G' shelter when we were scrambled at 19.15 hours in daylight. The GCI took us under control as soon as we got airborne and vectored (directed) us towards the north of the island at 14,000 feet where they told us to orbit (circle). Ten minutes later they said 'We have trade for you.' We were given a new course to the west, and almost at once I got a 'blip' on my screen. I told Danny to increase speed for it was now quite dark and I was anxious to get a visual before the light finally went. It took us maybe five minutes before we saw it and a minute or so to identify it as a Breda 20 bomber and we decided it was now dark enough to attack. It was flying a straight and level course, taking no evasive action, obviously unaware of our presence. Great sheets of flame from our guns engulfed our wings as Danny gave it a long burst from about 200 yards but it continued flying straight and level so we gave it another long burst and watched in amazement as it still flew steadily on. Puzzled, we cautiously moved nearer in below and to its port side to get a closer look. What we saw left us in a state of utter disbelief for although the blinds were down all round we could see bright lights were on inside the cabin as if the crew were having a party. We speculated that all the crew were dead and the aircraft was flying itself on autopilot for it never deviated from its course. We were discussing what else we could do to finish off this ghost ship when it started to lose height and we followed it down for some time as if in formation we were so close. We were almost in sight of Sicily before we saw a dull red glow start in its port engine, which soon became a fierce fire and it dived steeply towards the sea. We followed it down to 1,000 feet on our altimeter until we dared go no lower for the haze had cut the visibility and pulling up sharply we began our triumphant way home. Just as we knew the German pilot we had encountered before was a seasoned campaigner this Italian was clearly a complete novice or a fool. Surely the pilot must have known that with lights on inside he could not see anything outside and having the blinds down as well meant that no one was keeping a lookout for which we could think of no credible explanation. No matter, it looked as if at last our luck was changing and we were delighted. Just two hours after take-off we landed back at Luqa to receive the congratulations of Peter, Johnny and the ground crew and at last we felt we were full blown members of 1435 Flight. A couple of days later the euphoria wore off and I began to torture myself with thoughts of the anguish of the five Italian mothers who had lost their beloved sons. I was glad that Mum had no idea I was in Malta for with the news being widespread I knew she would have been frantic with worry. I guess I was just homesick!

The next night Danny and I were scrambled on an 'X' raid and over an hour later we were vectored into a position where I was able to get a contact. The adrenalin began to flow as we closed the range sufficiently to get the visual we needed to identify the aircraft before we could attack when the radar packed up and in the mist Danny lost it. We were devastated at getting so near to perhaps another kill only to be thwarted at the last minute by these recurring faults on X7750. Was the aircraft jinxed or was it us? It made no difference, the opportunity had gone. It was probably a hostile for the time gap suggested that GCI had first picked it up near to Sicily and plotted its approach towards the island, but they had to rely on us to ensure it wasn't a lost transit aircraft.

The 15th brought tremendous news for the island, its inhabitants, and its garrison when His Majesty the King awarded it the George Cross. The Governor, General Dobbie, read the citation:

> To honour her brave people I award the George Cross to the Island Fortress of Malta to bear witness to a heroism and devotion that will long be famous in history.

The whole island was ecstatic for such an award had never before, and has never since, been made to a community and it could not be more richly deserved, but I hoped the gracious gesture had not come too late. Hunger was gnawing at everyone's guts as the rations had been reduced again and the fear of invasion was ever present. For a while our spirits were lifted but when we faced reality we could see that nothing had changed. I doubt there was a man, woman, or child on the whole island who would not have exchanged the honour for a good old English breakfast, and we salivated at the very thought of traditional Sunday dinners. It was not that we were ungrateful – we were just terribly, desperately, ravenously hungry. For the next three days all bombing ceased and as if to mark his approval of the award the Lord gave us a respite by sending such absolutely foul weather it even grounded the birds. It was nice to feel He was on our side – we needed all the help we could get!

On 17 April Danny and I tried twice to get on patrol in X7750 but twice the radar refused to function and on landing after yet another test flight the tail wheel broke. We now had no aircraft available until the 25th when we were scrambled to deal with a bandit (hostile) only for it to drop its bombs into the sea and scurry home. This was a not unusual Italian ploy but for us it proved beyond doubt that the damned aircraft definitely had a jinx on it.

We were not alone in our enforced idleness, the fighter boys had no planes to fly either because of the massive odds they faced in aerial combat or the incessant bombing and strafing of the airfields, which had daily reduced their numbers. All the Spits from the aircraft carriers and the sundry small packets of Hurricanes that had dribbled in from North Africa, probably over a hundred in all, had been destroyed. The situation was more than desperate – it was absolutely dire and there was nothing we could do about it. The island now relied on the stringently rationed AA guns for its defence aided by an issue of rifles to the Army in the vain hope that someone might get lucky. We were in this parlous state until the end of April.

About this time a certain Squadron Leader Westmacott got himself and Pilot Officer 'Timber' Woods, who I knew well as he had been billeted in our room before his commission came through, attached to 1435 Flight. This was not too difficult as some squadrons had been disbanded when all their aircraft had been destroyed and their crews absorbed into other squadrons. They were both Hurricane pilots but after flying across to Luqa one night with Danny and me Westmacott prevailed upon Danny to let him go solo. To our astonishment with no proper tuition he took off, flew round for a while, and then landed perfectly thereby earning our great respect for the Beau was notoriously tricky to fly. Our situation was so serious

Westmacott decided that he and 'Timber' would attempt to disrupt the enemy on the night of the 26th by intruding on Sicilian airfields in their one remaining Hurricane. Westmacott went first and on his return the aircraft was refuelled and rearmed and 'Timber' took his place. It was a gallant but tragic attempt to take an offensive initiative for 'Timber' was shot down by AA and killed.

There were several other NCO pilots in our billets, many of whom made a name for themselves in Malta. I particularly remember the tall dark Australian Sgt Virgil Paul Brennan and the small puckish New Zealander Sgt Ray Hesselyn. They had arrived on the island the same day as us from a carrier and the appearance of the Spits had triggered the subsequent German Blitz. They were both fighter pilots but Hesselyn specialised in shooting down Me 109s fighters whilst Brennan concentrated on destroying Ju 88 bombers. They were great pals with a robust, irreverent sense of humour typical of their Commonwealth origins and listening to their verbal exchanges had us all in fits of laughter. Hesselyn would taunt Brennan 'Why go for the bombers when they have rear gunners who try to shoot you down. The fighters cannot do that. Want to be a dead hero?' It usually ended with Brennan chasing him round the bed spaces but he rarely caught him. In 1943 they had a book ghost written about their escapades called *Spitfires over Malta* a copy of which I still treasure. After the war Hesselyn became a 'high up' in the RNZAF with a DFM and Bar. Brennan was awarded a DFC and a DFM but was killed in a flying accident before the war ended. That's how the cookie crumbled for them and for many others.

I had somehow acquired a fan club of seven or eight children who tagged on behind me like the entourage of boys from twelve to eighteen years of age who followed behind the priest riding in his sunshade covered Karozzin (horse drawn trap). The eldest of my 'gang' of boys and girls was a sixteen-year-old lad called John Gatt with whom I used to play tennis on a court in the moat of Mdina. We were so debilitated by lack of food that we only ever managed one set before we became exhausted. There was also a quiet young girl of eight or so who I noticed was treated by the rest with great deference and years later I discovered that she was a niece of Baron Testaferrata with whom we were billeted. It transpired that she possessed a title in her own right and had to be addressed as 'The Noble Mavina' for that was her name. Having no aircraft to fly I took them on long walks in the countryside and occasionally they stopped to rest by sitting down in the long grass at the roadside – but not me for it caused a great rustling and dozens of lizards shot out. They were perplexed by my reactions but anything snakelike sent a shiver down my spine. On other days we went to the battlements to watch the bombing where I donned my tin hat against the AA shrapnel and fuse caps that rained down with their distinctive whizzing sound. They scorned wearing tin hats, which they regarded as a sign of cowardice despite my warnings, and laughingly brought fuse caps to me that were still so hot they juggled them from hand to hand to avoid getting burnt. I guess they must have been disappointed that their hero was such a cissy but they still waited outside my billets for me every day and I was really pleased to see them for they were lovely kids and great to be with. They gave me religious icons and made 'Good Luck' dollies out of wool and showed me the entrances to several ancient underground tunnels that honeycombed Mdina. Those that had not been converted into air raid shelters were now securely locked to protect their decorations from vandalism and they were of great historic importance. It was said that some of them stretched for miles to link other communities and their origins were lost in the mists of time.

Johnny and I had made short visits to Valletta before but we now had ample time to really explore the beautiful city at our leisure. We entered over a deep moat through the Porta Reale, a triumphal arch like the entrance to Mdina but much bigger and more impressive, and into the maze of narrow cobbled streets. The architecture showed the influence of former occupiers of the island since Roman times when Saint Paul had been wrecked here and converted the people to Christianity. It had suffered under the yoke of the Arabs, the Phoenicians, and the Carthaginians before fighting off the Moors in an epic siege. In the Crusades it was again besieged as it was contested by the Turks and the knights of St John who eventually were victorious and the Pope bestowed on them the title of 'The Knights of Malta'. The knights founded Valletta and built a massive fortress dominating the harbour entrance and the entrance to the many creeks leading off it, which were ideal anchorages for trading ships from all over the Med. The Barracca as it was called proved invincible against every would-be invader until the French under Napoleon seized it from the knights whereupon the Maltese appealed to England for aid to ejected his forces. This was the beginning of a close link with Britain, which in WWI served the Navy well as a base from which to control the Med. We visited our Headquarters, which were deep underground in the Barracca and were impressed by how the massive ramparts of the ancient fortifications had been adapted to make it virtually bomb proof.

Just inside the city gate was the Opera House, which had obviously been beautiful but its frontage had been wrecked by a bomb and the huge stones from the massive pillars of its Gothic façade lay in a heap in the road. It was the same everywhere; we could not walk fifty yards down a street without climbing over the rubble of bombed buildings and sometimes there was so much debris we had to turn back. There were a lot of shops open with their shattered windows boarded up and their pitiful stock of bomb-damaged furniture displayed on the pavement. The only other thing they had to sell was the lovely hand-made lace for which Malta was famous but most of it looked as if it had been rescued from the ruins of some poor unfortunate's home and bartered, probably for food. Yet every bar that had not been destroyed and others with quite severe bomb damage was open and offered a bewildering variety of shorts and liqueurs, a lot of them with names we had never heard of before. Remembering the warnings we had been given by 'old timers' at home Johnny and I refused the exotic booze and settled for a couple of beers. We ventured inside two or three of these candlelit dens on Strada Stretta (Straight Street) or the Gut as it was called by the troops and were appalled to find them thronged with sailors who had been on sunken ships in the convoys and were marooned here as they did not have the priority to get themselves flown out. Not that I think many of them had any longing to end their present existence for they knew escape would mean they would again have to face the dangers of another convoy and aerial and submarine attack. They had gone 'native' and become a scabrous lot and there were knife and broken glass fights every night. Some of them had set themselves up as pimps for the numerous usual prostitutes who abound in every port whilst others had become aggressively homosexual. It was all very seedy and unpleasant and spoilt our appreciation of this ancient city, which even in the throes of its present torment we found fascinating.

There was little fraternisation between the Forces and the Maltese girls for if they arranged a 'date' it always included a chaperone like their mother, elder sister, or an aged aunt. It was also difficult to get romantic on an empty stomach and passion was quite out of the question. Nevertheless Johnny had managed to form an association with a girl who ran a flower shop and seemed rather smitten with her as he went into Valletta nightly returning in the morning looking shattered but lauding his paramour's sexual prowess. Johnny was interrogated at length by the lads in our billet and I added my earnest entreaties but he steadfastly refused to reveal the secret of overcoming the chaperone barrier.

The powers that be had noted our inactivity and pronounced a new venture – we were to censor the Navy's letters and the Navy would censor ours, which really was a joke for no one had received any mail from home since we arrived and we very much doubted that any of our mail had ever left the island. In fact we had long ago given up writing knowing the letters were going nowhere. Nevertheless sacks of Navy mail duly arrived and to maintain confidentiality were taken to our dispersal as the most secure location away from prying eyes. Johnny and I were on the same shift and armed with a pair of scissors apiece we set about our unexpected task. We were overseen by a Navy officer who told us there was to be no talking between us but he could not stop our stifled titters, which developed into gusts of laughter at times. Even now I cannot disclose any of the contents but I can testify to those sailors' imagination and ingenuity for they had no ships (as we had no aircraft) yet tales of their daring deeds abounded. Johnny told me of one man who enclosed a (sealed) letter to his paramour in the letter to his wife. Of course he had to open both of them and what naughty Johnny did then left me creased in paroxysms of laughter. We wielded our scissors assiduously and often there was more on the floor than what we struggled to get back into the envelopes, – they had more holes than Maltese lace. One thing emerged – many folks haven't a clue about security for some men had even said exactly where they were and wrote freely of our losses and hunger.

Halfway through one of our sessions Johnny looked out of the hole where the window used to be and shouted 'Come and look at this!' I rushed and saw a sight that made me ashamed to be in the RAF. A dog had been shot through its hind quarters so it could only sit, snarl, snap and yelp at a Military Policeman firing a revolver at it. He dared not get close enough to kill it and had to reload before he managed to finish it off. Long before that I had drawn my sidearm and was blazing away at the man but he was too far away for me to have a hope of hitting him. I was shouting every foul oath in my extensive vocabulary, cursing, ranting and raving in my fury. I wasn't furious – I was incandescent with rage. Johnny had been trying to stop me and the officer sat open mouthed in amazement. 'Christ,' said Johnny, 'you've done it now – you'll get court-martialled for this.' I did not care, I ran outside, mounted my bike and raced up the hill to our Mess where I grabbed the telephone and rang the Adjutant. 'This is Sgt Gosling of 1435 Flight, I want to speak to the Station Commander,' I said. He replied 'I'm afraid he is not in at the moment, can I help you?' So I told him the whole story leaving nothing out including firing at the MP. 'Well the Station Commander ordered the shoot because rampaging dogs on the airfield are a danger to aircraft.' I almost exploded 'My aircraft weighs 10 tons – we would not feel a bump even if we ran over one. These poor mutts have been bombed out of their homes, are starving, and half deranged with fright and how does he expect to kill running dogs with pistol fire? It's shameful and the kind of thing we expect from the enemy not a supposedly humane society. If you must shoot them at least use the proper weapons and if I see anyone using a sidearm again you can tell the Station Commander I shall certainly use mine and I'll make b—y sure I'm close enough to hit whoever it is this time.' I turned around to face Johnny who had tried but failed to keep up with me on his bike. 'Now you are really in it,' he said. 'Come on, let's have a drink.' For weeks I waited anxiously for my arrest but it never came and I never saw anyone trying to shoot dogs again. As for the Station Commander after the war he probably rose to the top amongst the other nutters on the Health and Safety Executive.

April came to an end with no signs of any let up in the bombing or any hope that May might be better. There had been highs that had temporarily heartened us but in the end crushing lows had brought us to the brink of disaster. Yet the will to fight was as strong as ever. Even the scuttlebutters became belligerent as they changed their tune from pedalling gloom and doom to outrageous reasons for optimism. Once more I was amazed by their inventiveness in finding hope when sober assessment was depressing in the extreme. The chance that Malta was going to be invaded was greater than ever and Danny, Peter, Johnny and I devised scuttlebuttish schemes to escape with our aircraft if it happened. Yet invasion was not foremost in our minds – but hunger definitely was. Never in our wildest dreams did we ever expect that we would long for a tin of Machonachies yet now they had disappeared from the menu we craved for them. They had been replaced by miniscule portions of things so horrible it was best not to ask what they were but the cooks said they were good and we were famished. The people were eating anything including grass and I suppose there was a thriving black market, which we never seemed to be able to get into it but we tried – believe me we tried hard. With 850 raids Takali had been the most bombed airfield in April, only the harbour and docks had more. Yes, April had been hell and I hoped the man who dealt the cards would realise that this was beyond a joke – but he clearly had a perverted sense of humour!

CHAPTER NINETEEN

The Darkness Before the Storm? – Malta, May 1942

May started with some good news for Johnny and I for we were informed that we had been Flight Sergeants since 1 March but the news had only just filtered through and that night we repaired to the small bar we frequented in Rabat to celebrate. It was owned by a pleasant young Maltese man who stayed open as long as our finances lasted and that night it was very late indeed. There we had met a jolly crowd of habitués who were genuinely pleased and honoured that we had sought their company. Better still we were given the back pay due to us, which we shared with them, and they went out of their way to make us feel at home. This was not surprising as everyone on the island was always gracious and kindly to members of the garrison, particularly the aircrews who they had seen battling against almost impossible odds. They hated the Germans for their brutal and sadistic attacks on civilian targets but they saved their most violent invective for the Italians who they positively detested. They blamed Mussolini for seizing the opportunity to further his plans to control the Med and build himself an Empire by joining the Axis and declaring war. He had bombed them continually from the very first day of hostilities long before the Germans arrived. After we left the island we heard that 'our' bar had been bombed one night after all its patrons had left and my host had been dug out of the rubble alive and well.

Sadly there was no happy beginning for the island as the old saw that spawned so many ditties about 'The Merry, Merry Month of May' certainly did not apply to Malta in 1942. In 1435 Flight we had less than most to be merry about for on the very first day we lost X7752, which was bombed on the airfield at Luqa leaving us without a Beau once more. However, the raids were generally light and we were encouraged that there were noticeably fewer German and more Italian aircraft involved. Not that it made much difference for our fighters were still hopelessly outnumbered. Also on the down side there were intelligence reports that three Sicilian airfields had built what looked suspiciously like parking areas for gliders, which had been used to spearhead German airborne assaults in the past. It came as no surprise as it was in line with our expectations – the Germans were going to invade us.

I always spoke of 'us' for we were all in it together as the civilians were not only the unfortunate victims of the kind of collateral damage which is almost inevitable in bombing campaigns, but were deliberately targeted as often as the military. Proof of this was that the village squares where the Maltese had for centuries been wont to promenade at dusk in the cool of the evening were attracting marauding Me 109 fighters like bees to a honey pot bombing and strafing at will. Killing men and women, the young, the old and children indiscriminately who were just enjoying their only remaining pleasure, socialising innocently with their families and friends made me hate the Germans even more. If they thought these callous attacks would break the will of the Maltese people they were hopelessly mistaken. I believe that they were the cause of a subtle change in everyone's attitude – as if to say 'Don't think you can break us by such atrocities you B—ds we can take that, and more!' A new spirit became the order of the day. After all you cannot be permanently miserable and although the old defiance was still evident no one now thought of what the morrow might bring. It wasn't foolish bravado, it was far too calculated and carefully considered for that as if we all thought 'sufficient to the day is the evil thereof'. Let's get on with it and let the Germans do their worst. It made a wonderful difference to our morale but unfortunately it did nothing to fill our bellies.

Over the next two or three days the raids were comparatively light and our fighter force recovered somewhat, but still nowhere near enough to gain parity with the enemy or prevent the sinking of the Gozo ferry. Strangely, there was a frantic rush at Takali to erect blast pens for fighters we did not possess with gangs of soldiers filling used petrol cans (at last a use had been found for them) and sandbags to make three-sided enclosures about ten feet high. Close by them slit trenches were being dug and buttressed with more sandbags – all very commendable but seemingly pointless.

There are no entries in my logbook until 7 May and we must have commandeered not one but two more transit aircraft for I flew in X7744 and X8224, which were both new numbers to the Flight. Another problem now arose – our 20 mm ammunition had to be tested for the fighter boys had reported that it was jamming in the breech blocks of their cannon at crucial moments in aerial combat. It had taken a while to tie these stoppages down to the ammunition rather than the guns themselves so we now had to undertake a series of test firings to determine if all the ammo was faulty or just some of it as we could ill afford to waste any. They were only short flights to test the ammo and in both aircraft we had three stoppages in our four cannon so obviously the newcomers were not yet operational. The results confirmed our worst fears – it was all faulty and we had to scrap thousands of rounds of 20 mm ammo, which was already in short supply not only for aircraft but AA guns as well. It really was a cruel, cruel blow.

The day was, however, memorable for the arrival of Field Marshal Lord Gort VC to replace General Dobbie, the island's Governor, a move that was greeted with mixed feelings. Dobbie had endeared himself to us all by his constant involvement and commitment but his efforts were said to have literally worn him out and now he was weak and exhausted. We wished him a speedy return to full health, at the same time wondering if the gallant Gort would somehow find a way to feed us but we doubted his VC would be of any great help.

Funnily on the same day an insignificant event turned out to have a far longer lasting effect on my life than the change of Governor. I had been voted by the Sergeants' Mess Committee to be the unpaid distributor of the weekly cigarette ration, which in the past had led to fisticuffs. Probably figuring that no one would hit so small a man they had appointed me. The majority of the ration was Egyptian-made Player's but there were also a few packets of Capstan Full Strength and as the ration was only twenty cigarettes per man per week there was fierce competition for the stronger brand. So I devised a rota system, which was closely scrutinised to ensure that I was not being bribed or 'got at' in some devious way. This was my first distribution day in the job and I had a gathering round me to see if the 'Gosling Charter' worked to their satisfaction. You may think this was petty but to them it mattered greatly and when at the end they could see that all I had left was a 2 oz tin of 'Punchbowl' pipe tobacco they were satisfied. None of them was a pipe smoker and I did not smoke at all but when they pressed me to take the tin myself I was touched by their gesture. True it cost them nothing but it showed they were convinced of my impartiality. Being a canny Yorkshireman who had been instilled from birth to 'Waste not, want not' I hied myself into Valletta and bought a pipe. After lace making the island was famous for the quality of its briar pipes and to my delight I found smoking took the edge off my hunger. To this day my pipe is my greatest solace.

On 8 May we tried twice to coax the radio in X7744 to work so that we could patrol in it that night but it defied all the ground crew's endeavours and cursings and we began to wonder if it was 'jinxed' like the late unlamented X7750. But we soon had something to distract us – something so momentous we could scarcely believe it!

The American aircraft carrier *Wasp* and the British carrier HMS *Eagle* had made another sortie into the Med to launch sixty-two Spitfires to our beleaguered island. Now we understood what the new aircraft pens and the slit trenches were all about for it had been planned that the newly arrived aircraft would be back in the air in less than fifteen minutes. This time they were not going to be caught on the ground and destroyed piecemeal by the Huns as they had been before, unprepared and easy meat for the strafing Me 109s. This time a new strategy had been devised aimed at getting the new arrivals back in the air in less than fifteen minutes. The organisation had been meticulous and secret rehearsals had been held for the airmen and soldiers involved so that every man knew his part including the stand-by pilots. Each pen had been equipped with all that would be needed on their arrival to get them turned round quickly. Some ground crews were so slick they had them refuelled, rearmed, taken over by a Malta battle hardened pilot and back in the air in seven minutes and 'Woody' in ops had them in the best position waiting to meet the inevitable response.

I had been tipped off by the fighter boys that something big was afoot and my 'gang' and I were on the battlements nearly all day not wanting to miss anything for there was plenty to see and it was glorious to behold. We cheered as the Me 109s came quickly on the scene expecting to find the newcomers stranded in their pens only to be pounced upon by the already airborne Spits. It must have given them a tremendous shock for they were harried into a hasty retreat, scattering in confusion, shorn of the arrogance they had displayed when they could roam over the island with impunity, and they fled for their lives. They were back in numbers time and again throughout the day and it was so gripping to watch the dogfights all over the sky that we could not tear ourselves away until dusk fell. At the end of this epic day we had lost some seasoned pilots but we still had nearly sixty Spits left, which was a vast improvement on previous deliveries, and the Spits would be needed for we knew the fight was far from over. After the war we learned that Churchill had lauded our gallant defence with his customary eloquence and being acutely aware of the strategic value of the island had appealed to Roosevelt for help, which had been freely given. Of course we did not know all this at the time but we did know we were so very, very grateful, delighted and ecstatic. What a day it had been!

In the Mess that night there was quite a party with the fighter boys waving their arms about to illustrate how they got on to the tail of a Me 109 or a Ju 88, their faces flushed with excitement at the memory of it all. I imagined how the adrenalin must have coursed through their veins in the maelstrom of the battle raging in the sky, their necks straining to see if anything had got behind them whilst they were concentrating on bouncing an enemy in front. It was probable that they were most vulnerable then for many times they had to break off a chase as tracer came whipping past them from Me 109s trying to catch them unawares and sadly they sometimes realised their danger too late. There was no time to be afraid, they were too busy wheeling, diving and making turns, which put immense 'G' forces on them crushing their heads into their chests or even making them 'black out'. I listened to them enthralled as they recounted their experiences with glee and noted the detached way they told of seeing someone, possibly a mate, 'buying it' (being shot down). It wasn't that they were callous – it was the old self-preservation game I had seen before for there were no 'shrinks' to molly coddle us through our stress in those days. The official attitude was that we were men and as such we were expected to be able to cope – their idea of therapy was to stick you in another aircraft and send you off again before you had time to reflect on how close you had been to disaster and thus restore your confidence. Unsurprisingly it usually worked but often for the wrong reasons as uppermost in your mind was the knowledge that if you did crack up you would be classified LMF (Lack of Moral Fibre). This meant that you would be permanently reduced to the lowest rank in the RAF and spend the rest of your war peeling potatoes at the back of the Airmen's Mess. Most men realised they really had no choice at all for they knew they could not live through the ignominy and disgrace of being branded a coward. It was a brutal and unjust way to treat men, many of whom had previously distinguished themselves in combat and only needed rest and refreshment to restore their confidence.

The next day, the 10th, the gang and I were out early to watch the aerial dance of death but at times I had to repair to the toilet in the Mess for I had got the 'runs' and a severe tummy ache. I blamed it on eating a fruit introduced to me by my 'gang', which was about the size of a plum. They called it a 'Naspli' (which I doubt was its proper name). It tasted a bit like an apricot and I was so hungry I guessed I had overindulged for it was food and that was what we craved. I was speedily back at the battlements for a new dimension had been added to the spectacle – the appearance of Italian fighters, in daylight! The action was as fierce as yesterday's but it seemed from our excellent viewing position that the Spits were gaining the upper hand for the intruders' formations were being broken up by the Spits and were unable to make many coordinated attacks on our airfields. Those that did get through were pounced upon by more of our fighters, which made their incursions hasty, random 'tip and run' affairs that lessened their effectiveness. In the Mess that night the fighter boys were boisterous and happy discussing the appearance of the Italians, hoping it was a sign that the Germans, if not a spent force, were at least in need of assistance. The wags said that if the Huns were reduced to relying on Italian assistance they must be pretty desperate. Still feeling queasy I retired to bed whilst the party was in full swing, but not before a victorious Brennan and Hesselyn had recounted their latest 'kills'. Hesselyn was also furious because he was robbed of another 'kill' when his cannon jammed – apparently due to duff ammo again.

On the 11th I awoke to find my symptoms were more severe and I spent much time with three or four others sat on the winding stone stairs leading to the one and only toilet situated at the very top of a turret of the Casa Testaferrata. Clutching our aching bellies and cheap books with the softest pages we could find (toilet paper had disappeared long ago) we begged whoever was inside to come out and give someone else a chance but our pleas fell on deaf ears. I took to my bed and lay dozing until the afternoon when the boys in my 'gang' turned up with a large jug of freshly made lemonade. The girls had been told by their mothers that it would be improper for them to enter a male dormitory so they were waiting outside. The boys assured me that lemonade was an infallible cure for 'Malta Dog' as dysentery was called on the island – in Egypt it was known as 'Gypo Gut'. Up to then I had steadfastly insisted it was only a stomach upset but now I felt terrible and I had to face the truth. I had definitely been bitten by the dreaded 'Dog' and I cursed my luck getting it just two days before my twenty-first birthday. I lay abed the whole day almost comatose and Johnny sat by my bed selflessly forgoing the lure of the erotic 'Lady of Valletta' so I knew I really was ill. He had told Danny of my plight and I was surprised he did not bother to visit me. As darkness fell returning fighter boys came to my bedside to enquire how I felt and to report the day's events. They said it had been a quiet day and it looked like the storm had blown itself out but I wondered if in reality it was the lull before the storm.

The following morning I felt a good deal better and got up early to go to Luqa with Danny to collect X7744, which had been up to its old tricks and had been left there for repair. When it was finally serviceable we flew it to Takali ready for the night's operations. After what was jokingly described as dinner Danny, Peter, Johnny and I made our way to Takali and Danny and I shuttled it back to Luqa. We did the obligatory sweep of the runway and returned to 'G' Shelter when the strain of my long day began to tell on me. I had been up since 07.00 hours and on the go ever since so I was feeling distinctly groggy and when the lads told me to 'get my head down for a while' I did so gladly. The next thing I remember was Danny and Johnny shaking me to tell me they had shot down a Ju 88. They said they had failed to waken me when a scramble call came through and in the rush to get airborne Danny had taken Johnny in my place. They had been vectored on to a Ju 88 and in quick time had shot it down in flames. Still half asleep I did not know what to say so I congratulated them and from then on I flew with a bucket in the back of my Beau – I was not going to be robbed of a kill again. I never had to use it thank goodness but I wished I had thought of it sooner for missing a 'kill' was devastating. I pitied the poor Spit pilots who had been bitten by the 'Dog' like me for there was no room in their cockpits for a bucket – they must have been in agony! I went to see the Medical Officer and came away with a large bottle of chalk and quinine, which was the standard treatment for the 'Dog' and in any case he had nothing else to offer as our medical supplies were almost exhausted.

Then came the great day – my twenty-first birthday! It was much the same as any other day in Malta – hot and sunny but with not much activity save a few *Stuka* attacks on the airfields and harbour, which we were so accustomed to we took as par for the course. I decide to luxuriate with a long lie in bed as a present to myself for my birthday – probably the only present I would get. I lay in bed thinking what it would have been like at home. Mum would have wakened me with a kiss and pressed a large card into my hand, saying 'Happy birthday, come on I've got you a lovely breakfast' and the postman would arrive with more cards from friends and relatives. I wondered what present she would have for me; it would be something expensive I had always wanted regardless of the cost. Nothing was too good for 'Our Dennis'! I knew how much she would have been looking forward to this day and I was nearly reduced to tears when I thought how distraught she would be, not knowing where I was or even if I was still alive. I drifted into a troubled sleep until I was awakened by Johnny about 16.00 hours and after a shave we embarked on the biggest binge of our young lives, most of which I do not remember. I did, however, recall meeting a woman in one of the back alleys and trying to tell her how much I admired the Maltese people, but unlike most locals she spoke little English and she did not understand. Thinking she was being importuned by a drunken airman she let out a shrill cry and ran towards her house and I ran after her trying to explain myself. Her husband came out brandishing a large knife and chased me followed by Johnny who eventually caught up with him and as the man spoke good English he was able to explain the situation. The outcome was that we all finished up drinking together at a table in our favourite watering hole laughing at the episode and profusely apologising to each other for the confusion. It was a complete contrast to what it would have been like at home where at the evening party Dad would have proposed a toast to the 'Birthday Boy', now officially a man.

Then there would be much merriment and cries of 'Speech, speech' until I made a reply thanking the party of forty or so friends and family for their presents, cards and good wishes followed by a buffet meal and the inevitable singsong. Instead I had shared my big night with two strangers I had met in ludicrous circumstances and now I had wakened with a king-sized headache and a mouth like the bottom of a baby's pram. Hey ho, it would all have to wait until I got home though I had no idea when that would be.

On the 14th things were so quiet that instead of our usual low-level scurry to Luqa Danny and I took the opportunity to have a good look at Mdina in the brilliant moonlight. I had been enchanted by the moon shining on towering cumulus cloud over England but the moonlight here was so much brighter it was almost dazzling. Mdina lay below us like a picture in a book of fairy tales and I could scarcely believe it was real. We had no electricity and the blackout was total except that here and there were a few faint lights like the candles on a Xmas tree. The massive ramparts, the domes and minarets of the many churches, the winding alleys and the streets with buildings of so many cultures were all made of the local honey-coloured sandstone. In this light the stone appeared almost ghostly white making the ancient walled city look like it was frozen in a time warp. It was easy to imagine I was in some bygone age for it could have been mistaken for the mystic East or something out of the Arabian Nights and the flickering lights could have been from Bedouin tents in the desert. I half expected a turbaned snake charmer on a Persian carpet to float by playing his pipe as his snake swayed in its wicker basket. We seemed to be suspended motionless in the air gazing in wonderment at this scene that had not changed in centuries and I had a strange feeling that I was a voyeur from another age or even another planet looking at something solemn and secret not intended for prying eyes. Our most imposing cathedrals in all their splendour had never filled me with so much awe and reverence, made me feel so humble, or realise how insignificant we mortals were. I thought of all those who had passed this way in wars long past and those who had never left, staying here for ever in graveyards. Suddenly I felt as if 'they' had realised my empathy with them and had forsaken the sanctity of their eternal rest to once more gaze with me at the glories of the city they, too in their time, had loved so well. Many times they had fought epic battles against overwhelming odds to protect this island and their faith from the assaults of infidel hordes and now they were forgotten – but not by me. It put the tribulations of my contemporaries and I into perspective – our devotion and sacrifice were as nothing in the greater scheme of things. Like ships that pass in the night we would be forgotten just like them. Despite all the vicissitudes of our present situation I felt privileged to be actually living in the heart of this beautiful, ancient, magical city. I knew that in all the world this was where I wanted to be and wherever fate might direct my steps I would never forget this breathtaking sight nor how lucky I was to be here. I was left hoping that those who came after me would see Malta by moonlight and be as uplifted by its mysticism as I had been. All the time we were circling Mdina Danny and I were so enthralled we had not exchanged a word on the intercom and I wondered if he had shared my thoughts. We landed at Luqa and had a good night's sleep for it was unlikely that a raider would venture out in such perfect visibility with the glorious moon making them easy targets.

The 15th was just another Malta day with attacks on the airfields and the harbour with the Italians being increasingly involved. They did not press home their attacks like the Germans and when they bombed it was mainly from considerable height. Their Machhi fighters were not as good as the German Me 109s and their pilots less experienced so they lost quite heavily when dogfighting with the Spits but the Huns were still present in numbers and they were another kettle of fish. The Germans were more determined and aggressive and although we respected them as formidable foes in combat we could not forgive the sadistic streak they showed when they held the ascendancy. They also had an arrogance bred of having swept away all the weaker opposition they had met up to the 'Battle of Britain' but still believed they were destined to be the master race. Meanwhile I had a personal battle to fight – trying to keep the 'Dog' at bay but it was difficult for being permanently hungry I was loath to refuse the dubious offerings put before me in the Mess.

On the 16th Danny and I took X7744 to Luqa and we made two futile test flights trying to get the radar to work until finally, fuming in our frustration, we collared the technician, took him on a test flight in our aircraft and in fifteen minutes he got it to function. It was 23.15 hours when we landed but our unusual measure was justified for at 02.45 hours on the 17th we were scrambled and this time it was not for an 'X' raid (called a 'bogey') but was already identified as a hostile (called a 'bandit'). We raced to get airborne and shortly GCI vectored us behind a target at 12,000 feet and we began a long careful approach in misty conditions to enable us to identify the type before we attacked. The intruder clearly being cautious, weaving and varying height, and I tracked it for some time before I was able to get near enough and in the right position to get a visual on it. We recognised it as an Italian Breda 20 and opened fire from about 150 yards seeing pieces fall from it before it plunged straight down into the mist and we followed at a safe distance until it hit the ground. We did not linger for during the chase I had noticed another 'blip' on my screen passing from port to starboard and I was keen to get after it so I directed Danny to turn hard to starboard and was amazed to find it was still in range.

We called GCI to report our 'kill' and told them that we were now on the tail of another 'bogey'. They were obviously surprised but confirmed that it was on their display too and they wished us 'Good hunting'. I was glad that it was well within range and did not appear to be taking evasive action so I was able to put Danny in position without too much trouble. It was about 2,000 feet lower than us and we picked up so much speed as we dived to get below it that I had to tell Danny to weave from side to side to prevent us from overshooting. It took me some time to get us into position about 150 yards behind and fifty feet below, the ideal place from which to attack, and we sat there until we were able to identify it as another Breda 20. Danny pulled up behind it, gave it a twenty-second burst and it exploded right in front of us. Danny had to break away violently to avoid flying through the debris. We called up GCI to report our success and they congratulated us and then said 'Orbit at Angels 13 (circle at 13,000 feet), we think we may have more "trade" for you.' We replied 'Wilco' (will comply) and less than twenty minutes later GCI put us behind another 'bandit'. It was going west about two miles ahead and some 1,000 feet above us but as we climbed up to engage it we entered cloud, which the pilot was obviously using to cover his approach. This posed a problem for me; I could certainly intercept it but I could not disperse the cloud. I decided I would put Danny directly beneath the cloud base some distance further away than I would normally have done so we would not be seen, hoping that at some stage it would pop out of the cloud for a 'looksee'. We would then close in quickly and make our attack or if we were lucky there might be breaks in the cloud where it would be vulnerable. It was a long, anxious chase; twice it came out but not long enough for us so we kept well back close to the cloud base. After ten minutes that seemed like an age we came to a patch where the cloud was broken and I directed Danny into a position for us to attack. He gave a long burst and then began to curse. 'Run out of ammo, saw b—dy great lumps fall off it and then the b—dy guns stopped, and I lost sight of it I am sure I got it, but it will only go down as a "probable",' he moaned. Danny was particularly quiet as he reported the outcome to the GCI Controller who put us on a course for the island and soon I picked up the radar beacon and we landed back at Luqa. In the 2 hours 15 minutes we had been airborne we had destroyed two aircraft and damaged one, which was a fair night's work. We taxied to the dispersal and climbed out to be met by Peter, Johnny, and all the ground crew shouting and slapping our backs. 'We got two but it would have been three if we had not run out of ammo,' we said and there was a deadly hush. 'No, you did get three, a lighthouse keeper has phoned ops to say he saw the one you thought you had damaged crash into the sea.' We joined the celebration, jumping up and down, whooping with joy. Three destroyed on one patrol was one for the record books, but to do it in X7744 was more like a miracle. We had been the last to start our tally in 1435 Flight but now we were top scorers with four destroyed and one damaged and I couldn't even phone to tell Mum!

In the morning Danny and I flew back to Takali and in the Mess I found the news had preceded me and I could not get my breakfast, such as it was (no night flying nosh up here), for I was surrounded by a mob of fighter pilots wanting to know all the details of our feat. I was so worn out that sleep came as soon as I 'hit the sack' but when I woke I had the same old regrets thinking of the twelve or fifteen Italian mothers, just like my own Mum, who would be mourning the loss of their sons.

We flew X7744 back to Luqa on the 19th but again it was up to its old tricks with the intercom not working and the undercarriage refusing to come down. We spent twenty-five anxious minutes trying to 'throw' the wheels out by diving steeply and pulling out sharply, the manoeuvre we had watched at Tangmere when Donald Lake got killed. As we had radial engines it was relatively safe and we had done it many times but we were lucky some enterprising Hun did not spot us. We left Takali just in time for when we got down 'G' shelter we were told that the Aircraft Dispersal area had been heavily bombed minutes after we left presumably hoping to catch us before we took off.

At 02.05 hours on the 20th we were scrambled but had to return as once again the radio went 'on the blink' – give X7744 its due it was certainly consistent! However, it was soon fixed and at 03.20 hours we were scrambled to investigate an 'X' raid and as soon as we switched to the GCI channel they were screaming for us thinking that the unidentified intruder would escape. Immediately they told us to climb to 12,000 feet at full speed and I soon got a contact high above us going towards the island. The approach from below suited us for it was what we always aimed for and we were quickly underneath what we could see was a large plane but we had to match its height to identify it properly. This must have taken us about eight minutes but once we got into position there was no difficulty in recognising it as a 'bandit' for it had three engines and as the RAF had no three-engined aircraft it could only be hostile. It was a Cant 1007, sometimes used as a floatplane, but this was the land-based version with a crew of between five and seven and was heavily armed. I brought us gently up right underneath its belly, then fell back a bit, made my final height adjustment, and closed to about 150 yards, not daring to get any closer lest we were spotted and met with a hail of return fire. At so short a range Danny could not miss when he gave it a long burst and flames streamed from our cannon and machine-guns over our wings. Then I saw it explode in a massive ball of fire and again we had to pull up violently to avoid flying right through it. We watched as its burning engines broke away and plummeted earthwards followed by pieces of blazing fuselage floating lazily down and another explosion when it hit the ground. GCI Control congratulated us, told us there was no other 'trade' about and directed us to land. From take-off we had been airborne just forty minutes when we landed and the 'lads' gathered round to hear our story. I explained how we probably managed to avoid being seen by coming up from the darker background of the earth below rather than being silhouetted against the starlit sky and drawing return fire. Now we had five 'kills' to our credit and my 'gang' hailed me as 'their' hero, which tickled me pink.

At 22.00 hours that night we took a Major Harrison on a two-hour flight to observe the AA guns and searchlights in action and thirty minutes later (00.30 hours) we took off on what was to be one of the most extraordinary flights of my life. Aircraft were still transiting through Malta nearly every night and as I have already explained many were unable to find the island at the end of their long flight from Gibraltar. Apart from the difficulty of navigating by dead reckoning 1,000 miles in the dark we suspected that the Italians were using beams to interfere with their instruments, which they were good at. Whatever the reason, aircraft were going missing regularly even though they had sometimes been seen on the plot by our radar ground station. When we got airborne we called GCI and they said they had seen a Wellington on their screens thirty miles south of the island and directed us to the place where it had disappeared from their plot. When we got to the spot they told us to put all our navigation lights on and orbit flashing the 'Letter of the

Day' on our upward and downward identification lights. The 'Letter of the Day' was changed every twenty-four hours and was used in emergencies to show we were a friendly aircraft if we were challenged. So there we were going round and round lit up like a Xmas tree making ourselves as conspicuous as possible not just to the missing bomber but to every enemy aircraft between Gibraltar and Egypt. I sat tapping out the 'Letter of the Day' on my Morse key and vainly trying to see if we were about to be attacked but of course I could see nothing beyond the loom of our lights. If we had been spotted we would have been a sitting duck and this went on for ninety sweating minutes before GCI said 'He does not seem to be responding so you may dowse (put your lights out) and return to base, thank you.' We did not have time to give them the response they so richly deserved for at once Danny had put us into a screaming vertical dive and I was busy putting out the lights. We pulled out at 6,000 feet and were still shaking when we reached 'G' shelter. We never found out who had thought up this hair-brained scheme and we could only surmise we had survived because our Xmas tree illuminations had been suspected as some sort of trap by the enemy – and probably by the missing Wellington as well. Worse still it had a cumulative effect on my 'Malta Dog' and no wonder!

On the 22nd I went with some NCO pilots to see one of the lads from our Mess who was in the Military Hospital at Imtafa and as there was no public transport we had to cycle there. The hospital stood atop the next bluff to Mdina so it did not look far away but looks were deceptive and we struggled to get there, undernourished as we were. Our mate was in a large ward with forty or more patients and although his right arm was in a sling and his head swathed in bandages we soon spotted him sat at his bedside. When we asked what had happened to him he told us that a cannon shell had hit the Perspex panel at the side of the armoured glass windscreen of his Spit. He was concussed by the blast, his right arm was nearly useless, and he realised that blood was running down his face. He could hardly see for slivers of Perspex had pierced his face and his eyes were filled with blood but somehow he had managed to land safely at Takali, though he did not know quite how. Every now and then he sort of screwed up his face and with his left hand gently teased another needle of Perspex from his eyes and put it in a bowl on his bedside table. He then took us to a nearby bed, introduced us to the occupant, explaining that he was a German who spoke little English, and told us his story. He had arrived late from home leave in Heidelberg and was told the rest of his crew were waiting for him as they were due to fly immediately so he grabbed the nearest parachute and ran to join them. Over Malta they were shot down and he had to bale out but unfortunately the chute was too big for him and when it opened the sudden jerk caused the loose-fitting straps between his legs to snap together emasculating him. Our friend told us the lad was called Otto but that everyone in the hospital called him 'TT' as his accident had castrated him as cleanly as any gelding iron, which left his name with just the two 'Ts'. He seemed to enjoy the 'joke' for when he heard his nickname he laughed loudly but we were too embarrassed to join in.

On the 23rd Danny and I were told to be careful going over to Luqa as there were Me 109s about and when we were taxiing down the strip to take off into wind the aerodrome light defence guns opened up. This could only mean one thing – 109s were about to strafe Takali any second and we leapt out of the aircraft not even waiting to stop the engines. We were right in the middle of the strip stupidly cowering under our aircraft, which was exactly the kind of target they would be looking for. We saw two 109s streaking towards us at high speed and flung ourselves to the ground anticipating they would open fire on the Beau (and us cringing under it) but they swept over at fifty feet and were gone. They were probably surprised to find an aircraft out in the open and in the dusk did not see us until the last second by which time at the speed they were travelling they were too late and we had been very, very lucky. We jumped back into our plane and made it to Luqa in just five minutes – a speed record that was never beaten to the best of my knowledge but of course no one else had the same incentive. That night we were sent off on a routine patrol instead of being 'scrambled' only when raiders were showing on the GCI screens. This meant that during the recent lull we had managed to get two serviceable aircraft on the same night for the first time in weeks. We spent over three hours patrolling but there was no 'trade' about so we were told to land.

The following two days off due to our duty rota gave me and my 'gang' a chance to stroll around Mdina in blazing sunshine with little enemy activity to bother us. They delightedly took me by the hand and showed me the secret places they had found in and around their home as all children do. Mdina was known as the 'Silent City' and as the girls skipped ahead and the boys trotted beside me they displayed an amazing knowledge of its history and traditions. They taught me so much pointing out where this or that had happened and even though they had none of the usual toys kids of their age play with they were still happy and carefree. They also introduced me to 'shoats' milk', which was from the cross between sheep and goats peculiar to the island and reputed to be free of tuberculosis. Mixed with various fruit flavours it was so delicious that I spent hours with them in a café just outside the city's gates drinking this nectar and they were the most delightful company. By this time I had been introduced to most of their parents and had met them in their temporary homes for many were here only to get away from the bombing or because their houses had actually been destroyed. Some were clearly embarrassed by their inability to offer me refreshment but all welcomed me and their sparsely furnished houses were spotless. I knew that these hospitable people were starving like the rest of us and I did my best to put them at ease. The food situation was so grim that aircraft transiting through the island each night were being loaded with non-essential personnel, including surplus pilots, to make fewer mouths to feed.

On the 26th Danny was given the immediate award of the Distinguished Flying Cross and the practice among night fighters was that the navigator was similarly honoured, usually for four 'kills'. I should therefore have been awarded the Distinguished Flying Medal as a non-commissioned rank for I had five 'kills' to my credit but I had got nothing. I was naturally upset but I was too proud to ask

Danny why I had been ignored and though I could sense he was somewhat discomforted he said nothing.

That night we took X7744 to Luqa and at 20.30 hours we were scrambled to pursue a 'bandit' and on contacting GCI we were told it was flying east of the island at 15,000 feet. We were given a course to steer and we started climbing at full speed to try to catch up with it when about ten minutes later there was a suddenly a loud explosion and the port engine burst into flames. Above the roar of the fire I shouted to Danny to push the port engine fire extinguisher button for from my position halfway down the fuselage I had a much better view of the engine than the pilot who was in front of it. There were blowtorch like flames extending back beyond where I was sitting and showers of sparks engulfed the tail plane. Danny shouted back after a short while that the fire extinguisher had failed to put the fire out so I suggested we should open our escape hatches to give us some slight chance if the whole aircraft blew up or the port wing broke off. He agreed but we were both reluctant to 'bale out' as Jerry regularly machine-gunned ditched airmen in their dinghies within sight of the island and we were sixty miles from it.

As we were discussing our options I thought I noticed that the flames were losing their intensity and I told Danny that the fire seemed to be abating so we decided to hang on a bit longer. Eventually the flames subsided and the streams of sparks petered out but now the whole aircraft was juddering violently throwing us about as it wildly climbed and dived. I asked Danny what was happening and he said the port propeller was 'windmilling' (running away) so fast it was completely off the clock (the revolution counter). This was causing the plane to rise and then drop away on one wing like a falling leaf, losing 2,000 feet each time, and he could do nothing to control it. We had already lost 10,000 feet so we would have to be ready to jump before we got too low for our chutes to open. He then said 'I am going to see if I can start the port engine', which shocked me but anything was worth a try. He was under so much pressure that he made what was nearly a fatal mistake – he left the throttles fully closed as they had been when he shut the engine down. If he had used full throttle setting there might, just might, have been a faint chance of the reduction gear adjusting to the speed of the windmilling prop but now there was an almighty bang.

I heard him shouting 'Bale out, bale out' and I was sat on the edge of the escape hatch when I was brought up short by a sharp tug, which had I jumped could have broken my neck. In my haste I had forgotten to undo my intercom plug and that probably saved my life for as I climbed back to my seat to pull it out I heard Danny shouting 'Don't go, don't go, the prop has blown off.'

I struggled back into my seat and at once I felt that the juddering had ceased and that Danny had control of the aircraft. Yet we were not out of trouble for although Danny knew how to fly on one engine it was a long way back to base and I had no radar to guide us. Danny had been so occupied dealing with our emergency that there had been no time to use our radio but now he called 'May Day, May Day' (the radio telephony SOS) and thankfully GCI responded immediately. He explained our plight and asked for a course to steer for base. We now turned our attention to other pressing problems like would the wheels come down or would we have to prepare for a belly landing but we dare not test them yet as they would cause extra drag. Danny asked me if I could see any other damage in the bright moonlight but from my position nothing was evident. Next we considered trying to close my hatch to minimise its drag but to do so we would have to reduce our speed to near the stalling point. We did not know if the stalling speed had been affected by the damage we had sustained and we might go into a spin. The Beau was always difficult to recover from a spin and with only one engine it was too big a risk to take.

We talked all these things over and decided it would be advisable to maintain our height until we reached base and then Danny could find out what was and what was not working. The outcome would determine how best to make a landing and we were lucky there were no hostiles about to complicate matters. Everything seemed to be working so we started to make our approach and, glory be, the controller switched on the Chance Light (runway floodlight) when we got down to 1,500 feet. Only three weeks ago this would have brought a full scale Blitz on the airfield from German bombers but things had changed since the Italians had taken over. We were also told not to make the normal landing circuit but to come straight in, which meant there were no transit aircraft about for they were always short of fuel and would be in more dire straits than we were.

We made a perfect landing with all the emergency services racing behind us before Danny cut the engine and a tractor pulled us into a blast pen. When we got out we were confronted by a frightening sight for not only the propeller but half the reduction gear was missing. The tremendous stress caused by the massive difference in revs when Danny tried to start the engine had been too great for the unit to bear and it had disintegrated sending the prop flying. It had spun away cutting off the radar transmitting aerial on the aircraft's nose just missing the back of the instrument panel only inches in front of Danny. With Peter, Johnny and the ground and emergency crews we stood amazed looking at the damage, realising how lucky we had been to escape. We did not know whether to curse the jinxed X7744 or thank it for getting us home safely! When we got down 'G' shelter Danny phoned to thank GCI for their help and ops for the way they handled our landing. Three hours later at 00.30 hours on the 27th we were sent off in another aircraft, ostensibly to look for E-boats trying to pierce the grand harbour defences. We did not spot any intruders but 'Dusty' Miller had better luck a couple of nights later. Far more likely it was the good old RAF therapy – don't let them brood over their miraculous escape, get them airborne as soon as possible. It certainly worked for us and at 05.00 hours we flew back to Takali for a well deserved sleep and I never even had a dream let alone a nightmare.

It was the start of our two days off but I was laid low with the 'Dog' and rarely ventured far from those stone steps to the toilet, which was now in even greater demand. The 'Dog' was claiming more victims but we counted ourselves lucky for civilians were suffering from a new virulent disease caused by drinking contaminated water from the bomb-shattered drains. Nevertheless we were so enfeebled that it was an effort to do more than lie in our stinking beds. I kept wondering why I had not received my medal and could only surmise that Danny had got an immediate award and mine was delayed by having to go through the same channels that had held up my promotion to Flight Sergeant so I might get it later. There was also a chance that Middle East Command, being new to twin-engined night fighters, did not know that the usual practice was that both aircrew were honoured.

I was also concerned that an attempt was being made to 'hijack' 1435 Flight and not for the first time. We suspected that the now departed Westmacott had a longer term ambition when he showed an interest in learning to fly a Beau. The problem was that 1435 Flight had been too successful to be commanded by a mere Flight Lieutenant for we now had the best 'kills' per aircraft on the island. To command such a unit would be a feather in anyone's cap. It was an opportunity many had eyed and now a certain Spitfire Squadron Commander called Gracie had emerged as front runner. He had an outstanding reputation as a Spit pilot and we did not doubt his ability but we were loyal to Hayton and 89 Squadron. We could not understand how a Wing Commander we had never seen should be eligible to take over when we already had our own in Egypt, the much more senior and experienced Stainforth. A squadron never has two Wing Commanders so were we no longer to be a Detachment from 89 Squadron and to be formed into a new unit? It was not as if Hayton had proved incompetent for it was under his command that we had gained our distinction. We neither liked nor disliked Gracie for we had never met him but the whole business had the stench of high level RAF politics. We did not want Gracie or anyone else but there was one secret we tried to hide in case it strengthened Gracie's cause – Hayton had joined the 'Doggie Brigade'. When our logbooks were signed at the end of the month by the elusive Gracie whom we still had not met it unsettled us and made us wonder what was in store. We had been a happy band of brothers but now we were apprehensive that we were to become pawns in a power struggle. So now I had an unsettled feeling to go with my unsettled guts.

When I did venture out I was like a man sleepwalking and I felt quite lightheaded but the weather was beautiful and I hoped a walk would do me good. Since getting the 'Dog' I had lost a lot of weight and when my 'gang' saw me they rushed to greet me but they were clearly shocked by my emaciated appearance. I walked a little way with them trying to appear as normal as I could to reassure them but after half an hour I had to beat a hasty retreat for the 'Dog's' demands had become undeniable. As I dashed away with scarcely a 'Goodbye' I hoped they did not think I no longer wanted to be with them or that I had snubbed them. Far from it for now I needed them more than ever – they had been my anchor, keeping my feet on the ground in my dangerous and unreal world. They had become my surrogate family and I desperately wanted someone I could confide in and talk to about the things I had on my mind. There was the iniquity and disappointment of not getting my award, my worries for the future of 1435 Flight and my increasing debility. Of course I knew the idea of baring my soul to them was not realistic but simply being with them was therapeutic.

Danny and I flew on the 31st to take X7224 to Luqa but due to the damage sustained by X7744 on our near fatal flight the previous night we were again reduced to only one serviceable aircraft and it was Peter and Johnny's turn to use it. There was no 'trade' about so they flew our one remaining Beau back to Takali in the morning.

That was the end of May and what a month it had been with so many distressing lows and ecstatic highs it was difficult to sum it up. The good news was that the Germans had been less evident over the island and reconnaissance showed that a large number of bombers had left their bases in Sicily. We did not then know that Hitler wanted his aircraft back to use in his spring offensive in Russia and since then the Italians had given us a welcome respite by curtailing their attacks. Italian shipping taking supplies to Rommel in North Africa had sailed unchallenged since Coastal Command had to withdraw from the island due to their losses in the bombing. Now things were quieter a few had returned but their puny efforts did not hinder the flow of thousands of tons of munitions to the 'Desert Fox'. The Spits we had so longed for were unable to draw the Italians into combat and now Malta was useful only as a staging post for transit aircraft. The scuttlebutters said the reason for the lull was that the Italians thought they only had to wait and we would be starved into surrender. They speculated that we could last no longer than mid-August and it was hard to deny that for once they might be right. Everyone was lethargic and some had chronic muscle spasms that bent them double but the worst affected were the old and the young. There was no milk on the island so mothers could not feed their babies for their shrivelled breasts did not lactate and there was no baby food to wean them on to. Stories abounded that grandmas had starved to death by forgoing their pitiful rations to nourish the emaciated toddlers in their family. Even the food kitchens (like our soup kitchens) set up by the Governor to ensure a fair distribution of what food we had were sometimes unable to offer anything at all. It had to be admitted that the situation was grim and I wondered if all the RAF planes would be recalled to Egypt before the gallant island had to surrender. Having witnessed the Huns' barbarity I feared they might exact a terrible revenge on the inhabitants I had come to love and admire. The thought of what might befall them was too awful to contemplate.

But I had not reckoned with the man who dealt the cards and his twisted sense of humour was soon to become evident.

CHAPTER TWENTY

The Long Journey Back Home

I was so ill I scarcely noticed that we had entered June. The weather continued to be hot and sunny but I was in no state to enjoy it or fully appreciate the changes taking place in our battle for survival. The Italians were more and more in evidence but there was still a significant German presence to stiffen their somewhat timid resolve. The Intelligence reports of the continuing withdrawal of the *Luftwaffe* from Sicilian bases were encouraging but baffling. Post-war historians examining Nazi records have revealed that the Germans had indeed intended to invade Malta in an attack named *Hercules* and it was Hitler's personal decision to redeploy the aircraft from Sicily to the Russian front that had, temporarily at least, delayed the assault. The records also show that after the Crete campaign he was unwilling to risk incurring the same heavy casualties sustained there by the German paratroopers and they were never again used as an aerial attack force. The Italians did not have the stomach to undertake the job alone and gambled, not unreasonably, that we were so near to starvation that all they had to do was wait for us to surrender. If we had known all this at the time it would have made no difference to our reaction for we no longer cared what the Germans or the Italians might try to do, we would go down fighting. We were more concerned that the weakening effects of the lack of food combined with the diseases related to the bomb-shattered water and sewage systems were threatening to escalate to epidemic proportions. Most vulnerable were the old and young in every strata of Maltese society including my little 'gang' who were mainly well-to-do or even of the nobility (like Mavina) and I saw little of them. The garrison was equally stricken and I was no exception for at times I lapsed into a zombie-like trance (my friends say that I still do!) but some in our Mess were exhibiting even more serious symptoms.

However, there was no time for self pity as our war had to be fought and I see from my logbook that I flew three times when the first of the month was only hours old. Twice we took off before I got the radar to work and at 02.40 hours we were scrambled to investigate an 'X' raid. We were soon under GCI control and vectored at 10,000 feet onto an intruder within the Valletta Gun Defended Zone. We called to have the anti-aircraft guns hold their fire but it seemed that our erstwhile passenger Major Harrison had failed to institute the procedure we had agreed for the number of bursts increased and some were uncomfortably close. We pressed on regardless and got a visual on a Ju 87 dive bomber, which did not go into its dive but instead pulled up and began an almost vertical climb at 90 mph, way below our stalling speed. We tried to follow but without the assistance of the flaps and slats with which it was equipped we had no chance and we quickly went into a stall, the starboard wing went down first and we went into the spin for which all Beaus were notorious. We tumbled and spun down into the barrage pursued by fire from its rear gunner for about 2,000 feet before Danny got control and high-tailed it out of the Zone but we had lost contact and the *Stuka* escaped. After we landed a contrite Controller of the Gun Zone phoned his abject apologies and invited us to visit an AA site near to us so that they could make amends and explain some of their problems.

At 20.15 hours that same day we were scrambled in the half light to join in a dogfight raging over Valletta, which was really not our forte. The idea was to catch the enemy making their way home in the coming darkness but up in the air the sun was still high above the horizon and shining brightly. Before we knew it we were in the midst of hordes of Spits, Hurricanes, Me 109s, Ju 88s, and *Stuka* dive bombers madly gyrating around us and I was acutely aware that the Beau was the only twin-engined fighter with no rear armament. Night fighters were not built for daylight pursuits and I felt so useless and vulnerable having no gun to join in the fun and was only a spectator when Danny got behind a Ju 88 and gave it a good long burst, which sent bits flying off it. I was then taken by surprise as Danny suddenly stopped firing and broke sharply away shouting 'Bl—y hell, a Spit cut in front of me' and so his chance of a daylight 'kill' had gone. We claimed 'one damaged' and landed back at Luqa 2 hours 20 minutes later having caught nothing returning to Sicily. At 00.10 hours we were scrambled to intercept an 'X' raid but we stooged around for 40 minutes before GCI finally admitted they had no 'trade' for us so I guess they had received a 'dressing down' from 'Woody' (the Controller) for putting us at risk by involving us in a daylight dogfight. We were off again at 02.45 hours on another 'X' raid but had to return as our radar was unserviceable and flew back to Takali in the early morning.

Before we could get to bed we got a call from Luqa to fetch our old unloved X7744, which was waiting for us to do an air test. We had left it at Luqa to have a new propeller and reduction gear fitted after our disastrous flight but before work started a bomb had cut the fuselage in half. Undaunted, the Luqa ground crews fetched another bomb victim's rear section weighing three tons on their 30 cwt Commer truck from Hal Far and married it up to X7744's front section. This was a fantastic effort and we were hoping that as this resurrection was only half X7744 it would only be half jinxed. We got airborne and I was appalled when we went into the first moderate turn to see ripples appear on the fuselage skin just ahead of me.

119

I told Danny that the main frames were flexing under this mild strain and that under the greater stress of a violent turn there would be a complete failure of the airframe where the joint had been made and a catastrophic break up in mid air.

Danny would have none of it. 'That aircraft is all right,' he said. 'You were not sitting where I was so you couldn't see,' I retorted. 'The skin was as wrinkled as a furrowed brow.' It was the first time Danny had ever challenged my judgement and as I mulled over our disagreement I began to realise that our relationship had been changing for some time. I still admired his superb skills as a pilot but instead of the close personal relationship we had enjoyed I rarely saw him except when we flew together. I had also noticed he had developed an aura of invincibility and although self confidence was essential in our game overconfidence would eventually lead to a costly misjudgement. It was well known that an aircraft is most vulnerable just after 'lift off' so it was usual to use full throttle in a straight, steady climb to a height that gave a chance to return if an engine was malfunctioning or cut out altogether. Yet immediately after take-off Danny would go into a steep bank and turn within the confines of the airfield. To have an engine failure, or even stutter, at this juncture would result in a sideslip into the ground which, of course, would be fatal. I don't know if he did it to impress his fellow officers watching from the windows of their Mess in Mdina or from his sheer enjoyment of flying. Naturally I gave him the benefit of the doubt but it was dangerous and irresponsible and typical of his newly acquired cavalier attitude.

He seemed to have forgotten that stealth was the key to successful night interception and that it was his navigator's ability to use the long practised wiles of his trade to make an unseen approach that gave us such a vital advantage. To put it more succinctly he had become 'gung-ho' and that was a sign of battle fatigue, which was probably why we had lost so many highly experienced pilots when the new Spits arrived – Luck was a very fickle lady! I had also been surprised that even after Johnny had phoned to tell him of my incapacity he had never come to see me nor did he enquire how I felt when we met though he knew I was flying with a bucket in the back. I have to admit I was miffed that I had not received my award and he had never offered any explanation but I was careful not to let that affect my assessment of the change in him. I was mystified as to why or when our relationship had begun to deteriorate but try as I may I could think of no good reason. I decided there was nothing I could do about it – we were oppos who had been trained to become a team and that was what we would remain for there was no divorce among night fighters.

Despite my misgivings we took off to ferry X7744 to Luqa for the night's operations with Danny still stoutly averring that 'There is nothing wrong with that aircraft' but on the flight over all the electrics packed up. On our arrival we had to scurry down 'G' shelter for a raid was developing and when we came up there was a sight that gladdened my eyes – X7744 had received a direct hit and was blazing fiercely. This surely was the end of it I thought but I felt sorry for the ground crews who had worked so hard to get us more aircraft to operate so I said nothing about its unairworthiness to upset them. Later we flew for forty minutes in another aircraft but had to return when the port engine packed up (thankfully on patrol and not on take-off at Takali).

From my logbook I see that I flew for six consecutive nights at the beginning of June, which was because Hayton and some other pilot (I think it was 'Dusty' Miller) had been laid low with the 'Dog' but for five nights there was either no 'trade' or we suffered various defects in our aircraft. The sixth night, however, made up for our previous inactivity when we were scrambled for an 'X' raid and GCI vectored us some twenty miles south of the island to chase an unidentified aircraft heading further south towards North Africa. We made contact after ten minutes or so but when we reported this we were told the weather was closing in and to make full speed back to base. Intent on getting another kill they had delayed far too long for by the time we got back the whole island was blanketed in mist.

I have mentioned before that this mist was often at different heights and this night it was right down on the ground covering Luqa completely. We were confronted with a serious problem for if we could not land we faced having to bale out over the island for we had insufficient fuel to divert elsewhere within our range and would end only end up ditching in the sea. Our options were really reduced to two – bale out or try to make a completely blind landing in the dark. We decided that Danny would attempt to land and he asked the Duty Pilot to fire Very lights, which we saw pop out and arc just above the mist and then glow through the mist as they fell to earth showing the murk was about 100 feet thick. The Duty Pilot had a most hazardous job, which was usually kept as a punishment for some small misdemeanour. He had a caravan at the end of the runway and had to fire a red warning Very cartridge if an aircraft made an approach when the runway was obstructed by an aircraft wanting to take off or by a crashed plane. Being out in the open he was a target for strafing fighters and had to race to a slit trench as bomber after bomber attacked the runway – his was not a happy lot! I directed Danny to the north and lined him up on the runway heading, or rather where the Very lights kept appearing, and Danny made a long flat approach hoping the Duty Pilot would not run out of cartridges. I was able to help by homing him on the radar beacon but could only give him approximate distances to go for the beacon was unfortunately at the other end of the runway. When Danny got to where the lights popped out of the mist he pushed the nose hard down and then hauled the stick right back into his stomach and we touched down smoothly on the runway. It was a brilliant piece of flying, which very, very few would have attempted let alone succeeded to do and confirmed what I already knew – Danny was a quite exceptional pilot.

On 7 June we got a day off so Johnny and I decided to take up the invitation from the AA officer to visit one of the gun sites near us close to the Governor's Palace. It was a lovely hot day so we enjoyed the bike ride and when we arrived we were pleasantly surprised to find the four 40 mm guns in the emplacement were manned by the Durham Light Infantry. The Warrant Officer in charge let us operate one of the guns to have a crack at an Me 109 but only till it passed us as they were under orders to save ammunition. Best of all before we left he surreptitiously slipped us a very large tin of peach slices, which he had obviously been saving for a special occasion. As soon as we were out of sight of the battery Johnny and I set about trying to open it with his penknife, which was all we had. We struggled to get into that tin for half an hour but finally we succeeded and we ravenously scoffed the contents there and then as we sat on the roadside – we were not going to share them in the Mess, we were too damned hungry.

The following morning I decided that breakfast was out of the question as my poor stomach was not accustomed to the luxury of gorging on a tin of peaches and had me on the trot all night. I had not had a wink of sleep for even a sip of water had me rushing to the toilet and when I finally arose I went for a stroll hoping the sunshine and fresh air would do me good. I had not gone far when I saw an officer with a red band around his hat and in a trance I walked straight past him. His shout of 'Sergeant' in a commanding voice awakened me from my reverie and I stopped, turned round and saw he was a Brigadier. 'Sergeant why are you not wearing a hat?' he enquired. 'And do you not salute when you see an officer?' 'Sorry sir,' I stuttered, 'I did see you but my mind was miles away and it somehow did not register.' He looked hard at me and what he saw must have appalled him – gaunt, unshaven, and unwashed I must have been a sorry sight. He asked for my name, my trade and my unit so I told him 'Flight Sergeant Gosling, Navigator, Malta Night Fighter Unit sir'. At that his voice and demeanour changed and he became almost solicitous. 'How old are you Sergeant?' he asked. When I said 'I was twenty-one on the 13th of May' he sort of 'tut-tutted' said 'All right Sergeant' and walked away with me calling 'Thank you sir' after him. It was a close encounter of the bowel-moving type and I had to rush back to the toilet 'sharp pronto'.

The following morning I got a message to report to the Medical Officer and he gave me a basic examination, which left him frowning. I told him I had visited him only once because I feared I would be grounded with the 'Dog' if I went to him again. He disappeared into his office and when he returned he told me that he had arranged transport to take me to Valletta for a Headquarters Medical Examination. I was shocked and pleaded with him but he would brook no argument. 'I do not have the equipment to give you the thorough examination you need,' he said. So I was whisked away to Valletta and they gave me a peremptory going over but by the way they looked at me I knew that their minds were already made up – I was medically unfit to be flying. They tried to soften the blow by saying I needed the rest and recuperation I could only get in Cairo and in my heart I knew they were right but I hoped I was not going to be sent to that awful Dysentery Hospital.

On the way back to Takali I was almost in tears and I swiftly came to the conclusion that I had been 'shopped' by the Brigadier – or was he the earthly incarnation of the 'the man who dealt the cards'? I went straight to bed when I got back, distressed and disconsolate, fearing I might even be classified as LMF (Lack of Moral Fibre) but mainly to wallow in self pity. It was so unfair because I had never let my condition prevent me from flying as some others in the Flight had been forced to do. The medics had made it fairly clear that there could be no rest or recuperation in Malta due to the bombing and the lack of a nourishing diet. Yet I desperately wanted to stay for my 'gang' had become my surrogate family, and I had unbounded admiration for the people's fortitude and tenacity. I felt I was deserting them in their hour of need facing invasion and starvation but the die was cast for next morning I got a phone call from Valletta warning me to hold myself ready to take care of a party of civilians on the next available transit aircraft going to Cairo. I asked the Adjutant if he had any idea when this was likely to be and who these civilians were. 'Oh' he said 'they are twenty-three wives and children of medical staff at Imtafa Hospital but when the aircraft will come depends on so many things as I am sure you will know better than me, just be ready to go when it arrives. I am arranging transport for the party and I will try to warn you in good time.'

I knew only too well the unpredictability of the transit service for I had spent hours trying to guide them to the island and I suppose we were successful nine times out of ten. When they landed at Luqa they were refuelled and despatched within the hour but often they had engine or other faults, which delayed them, and when daylight came they were targeted by the enemy bombers and destroyed. It really was a hit and miss business but with twenty-three women and children in my care I hoped we would be some of the lucky ones. I had been told by the Adjutant that they had been on the island when Mussolini had declared war and for almost three years since then they had suffered almost daily bombing. There had been ample opportunity to get them out before now and only due to the change in policy were they being evacuated, not because of the danger they were in but to make twenty-three fewer mouths to feed. They were relieved for the sake of their offspring but reluctant to leave their husbands and although this was unquestionably the right policy it was too late and I thought that it was callous for it was being done for the wrong reasons. I needed no further spur to make me determined to do my utmost to get them safely to Egypt and I also reflected on those seamen who had survived from ships sunk in the ill-fated relief convoys who had the lowest priority of all. They might not have descended to such depths of Bacchanalian excess if they had some hope of early repatriation – instead the island for which they had risked their all to succour had become their prison.

Since I had been told I was leaving I had seen no one from the Flight except Johnny and this really hurt me for I thought Danny would at least have come to commiserate with me but I did receive a letter from John Gatt congratulating me on getting another 'damaged'. It arrived too late for me to reply but I treasured it for fifty years until, well, you will read later. It was now clear that once more in my RAF career I was on my own but far from being daunted by the prospect I remembered that I had coped rather well in the past and it restored my self-confidence. On 13 June the Adjutant phoned to say an RAF van would pick me up at 20.00 hours to take me to Luqa where I would meet my charges before boarding a plane for Egypt. I was surprised I rated a high enough priority to get me such a quick flight out for commonly it took about a month.

The van arrived for me and my parachute bag, which was ample for the few bits and pieces I possessed, and I began my journey home. I was glad that it was dark going over to Luqa for in the glimmer of the van's 'blacked-out' head lights I was unable to see any of the countryside I had come love and could not bear to see again. Unlike the furtive dash I was accustomed to it seemed to take ages and I wanted time to meet the seventeen women and six children I was to chaperone. They were waiting down 'G' shelter and were naturally upset to be leaving their RAMC husbands and apprehensive about flying, which none had done before, so I tried to reassure them it was quite safe – Ho! Ho! Ops told me the plane was landing and I was introduced to the pilot, F/ Lt Goodyear, who was keen to get away as soon as possible. I ushered my party up the stairs and into the aircraft, which was a Lockheed Lodestar and had just one long seat down each side of its spacious interior. I spaced them out so that they would have room to lie down, soothed the crying kiddies, and at 23.30 hours when the engines started I discovered that there was no seat left for me. Watched in amazement by my charges I curled up on the floor using my bag for a pillow and went to sleep and unintentionally it did the trick for when I had a quick peek they had all dozed off too. Five hours and forty minutes later we landed at Heliopolis where a bus was waiting to take them to a hotel in Cairo and after I saw them settled in I bade them 'Good luck' and thought it was the last I would see of them. The bus was waiting outside for me and I thought it would take me to that grotty Almaza transit camp again but to my delight it took me to another hotel. I was given a decent room, which had a wash basin and a comfy bed with a mosquito net, and when I arose much, much later I went down to the restaurant and feasted on a proper English breakfast. To my astonishment I suffered no ill after effects so I took a tram into Cairo going to RAF Headquarters, hoping I would meet someone I knew maybe on leave from the Queen's Own Yorkshire Dragoons. I had no luck and this time I had no film-based expectations about the Mystic East either for Cairo was still the same – hot, dirty, smelly, and infested with every sort of rogue you could imagine. I spent five days wandering around aimlessly. HQ had told me to report daily and on the sixth day they issued me with a warrant to Port Tewfic for the 09.30 hours train on the morrow. Tewfic was the deepwater port for Port Said and the embarkation port for England and Burma. Surely they are not going to send me even further abroad I thought. I must be going home and a wave of mixed feelings engulfed me. I had really hoped to be sent back to Malta when I had recovered sufficiently to rejoin my old Flight but when I enquired if this was possible they replied 'Oh no, all 1435 Flight are coming back here too, we expect them next week'. I was gobsmacked. Was this to do with the attempted take over of 1435 or whatever else could have happened?

I was awake much of the night pondering this unexpected news but knowing I had to be up early I had put in an early call for 07.00 hours so that I would be in good time for my train. Once more I had to face the bone-shaking journey that had taken me to Abu Sueir and this time I was going even further to Port Tewfic so I resigned myself to facing the ordeal and tried to get comfortable. I did not succeed but my mind was in such turmoil between trying to fathom the news of 1435 Flight and what was in store for me that I seemed to get to my destination quickly. There was a surprise awaiting me for on the station platform were the Imtafa lot with an

RAF Corporal who approached me enquiring 'F/Sgt Gosling?' When I nodded my assent he said 'You are to take charge of this party Sergeant, I have transport in the station yard.' I followed him outside with the women and children trailing behind me like a modern day Pied Piper. The truck took us a short distance to a dockside and among the transport ships that filled the bay was one that was unmistakeably the *Queen Mary*, pride of the Cunard fleet and holder of the Atlantic Blue Ribbon. This was the coveted award for the fastest Atlantic crossing from Cherbourg to New York, which had been hotly contested with the French super liner *Normandie* and its famous three funnels were known to everyone in Britain. We walked down a short slipway and were helped to board a smart launch, which set off with everyone's eyes riveted on this beautiful ship wishing we were going to travel on it. There were squeals of joy when we sped past all the other sea-battered anonymous ships and it dawned on us that was precisely what we were going to do. As we approached the massive ship towered above us but the launch expertly came alongside a gangway leading to an opening in the ship's side only ten feet or so above the waterline. The women and children were helped to get aboard and I followed still grasping my parachute bag with my pitifully few belongings for I had no clothing except what I was wearing plus my pith helmet.

I was shown to my bunk and was surprised that no one else was sharing it with me until the steward explained that this was the Orderly Room and that I was now the ship's Acting Orderly Sergeant, which was a shock of such magnitude that I was left speechless. The ship slipped anchor almost immediately and I went for a walk on deck as we plunged down the Red Sea in seas that came green over the ninety-foot high bows. Fascinated, I watched shoals of flying fish leap from the back of one roller into the front of the following one as if they were enjoying putting on a show for me. We were being escorted by a warship as large as a battleship with huge gun turrets but with its truncated stern it looked unlike any capital ship I had ever seen. I asked a passing seaman what it was and he told me:

That is HMS *Rodney*, one of a class of new super battleships laid down in the twenties to be called 'dreadnoughts' epitomising the race to build ever larger warships. Before they were completed the League of Nations (forerunner of the United Nations) passed the Geneva Convention limiting the size of capital ships, which was observed by every nation, with the exception of Nazi Germany. We, foolishly, complied too and cut about a third off the stern to make them conform to the new edict giving them a distinctly odd look. Because she cannot match our speed we are having to slow down but when she leaves us in the morning we shall resume our usual cruising speed of thirty knots.

I retired to my bunk but the *Queen Mary* had no air-conditioning as it was built for the cold North Atlantic run not the sweltering Gulf so it was hot and humid. I was pouring with sweat when the Head Purser appeared and said 'Come on lad and bring a blanket.' He led me to what used to be WH Smith's shop on the promenade deck where members of the permanent staff lay asleep on mattresses on the floor under the biggest standard fan I had ever seen. I thanked him and went to sleep at once for the cool air was heavenly and I never slept in my sweatbox again.

In the morning I slung my pith helmet into the sea to express my opinion of the stinking Middle East and went to seek out the Orderly Officer. I found him prostrate in his bunk groaning in agony. 'You Air Force types are lucky not getting sea or air sick,' he moaned. I could understand why he was so affected for the *Queen Mary* was unique in having long unobstructed corridors, which extended from the bow to the stern. The watertight bulkheads retracted into the walls and when the bows rose you could see the ship rising towards you like there was a giant wave beneath the carpet. Looking green he said 'I am always like this [whereupon he frantically sought to reach his bucket before vomiting] just carry on, I am sure you will cope.' He had more faith than I had so I went to see the Head Purser who told me it was the duty of the Orderly Officer to pay any servicemen aboard and to enforce discipline but as he was ill I would have to do it until he recovered. Together with my responsibility for the ladies from Malta and their kids it looked like I was going to be kept busy. So it proved for every swaddie aboard came to me complaining that he had not been paid for between one and three months. Apart from a few RAF lads they were mostly from the Royal Artillery and it took me ages to fathom their (to me) complicated ranking system but worse still there were also a couple of hundred Poles newly repatriated from Russia and only one could speak a fractured version of English. I soon realised that they were trying to take advantage of my obvious inexperience and when I told them I needed to see every man's pay book before I could make a payment very few pressed their claims. This bugged me and I suppose I became the most unloved NCO on the ship when I decreed I would only pay them from the time they boarded the ship. Some were belligerent and others openly hostile but seeing I could not be swayed they eventually gave up and became quite friendly. One even said 'Well it was worth a try'.

Below the waterline there were 1,800 Africa Korps prisoners of war who had to be brought up to the promenade deck twice daily for exercise, which it was part of my job to supervise. They had to come up the ornate main stairway for seven or eight decks and on each level there was a captured Italian Beretta machine-gun manned by the Poles. Now these Poles hated the Germans almost as much as they hated the Russians and they delighted in letting fly a burst over the prisoners' heads if the queue got out of line. In fact I had difficulty in persuading them not to fire into the crush, which was usually caused by the pressure from the ones at the back being eager to get their full time on deck. I had to dash up and down to wherever I heard gunfire and the bullet riddled decorative murals testified that my exertions really were necessary. I was surprised when I saw the much vaunted 'supermen' of the Africa Korps for they were spotty, pallid, weedy-looking specimens, younger and no taller than me.

After the *Rodney* left us the *Queen Mary* visibly put on speed although the seas were even more mountainous but the flying fish still kept pace with us amazing me with their prodigious leaps as I leaned over the rails watching them. As the ship's

Orderly Sergeant I ate in the Sergeant at Arms' Mess, which was inside the galley and what a feast and what portions the cooks served up. The *Queen Mary* had just taken 12,000 troops to Egypt and perhaps thought they were still aboard for the six-course breakfasts they dished up were gargantuan, far more than I got for a week in Malta. There were things to eat I had never seen since the war began and some I had never seen in my life so I tried them all like a child in a sweet shop. I feared I might provoke a recurrence of the 'Dog' but mercifully I suffered no reaction but at every meal, nay every mouthful, I thought of my 'gang' and how their little faces would have lit up if I had been able to share these gastronomic delights with them.

The ship had set a course sweeping far out into the Indian Ocean to avoid surface raiders constantly zig zagging, which combined with her speed made submarine attack impossible. The vastness of the ocean was awe-inspiring as I walked around the upper deck in the evening, struggling against a wind I had to lean into, seeing its heaving, endless expanse with never a vessel in sight. How far south of the Cape we sailed I do not know but I was awakened one morning when I suddenly felt there was no vibration from the engines and I realised we had stopped. I looked out of a porthole and saw we were in a bay with some other ships and there were houses and a flat topped mountain with clouds scudding over its summit. We must have rounded the Cape during the night and now we had arrived in Simonstown on the other side of Table Mountain to Cape Town. I joined a rush of people hurrying to the upper deck, I supposed to see where we were, but when I got on deck I saw they were looking at the twin-funnelled *Queen Elizabeth*, our sister ship. She was slowly heading out to sea past us with thousands of troops lining her decks cheering and waving. We may have been fewer in numbers but we cheered until we were hoarse and in our hearts we wished them all the luck in the world for we realised they were on their way to Egypt to fight in the desert. It was a memorable moment for it was one of only a handful of times that the ships had ever been seen together.

We spent two days refuelling and victualling before we set sail and it was obvious from the position of the sun that we were not heading for England unless we were again taking a circuitous route. I had got to know the permanent staff and one of them took me onto the bridge where two seamen were steering the customary zig zag courses. The one holding the wheel was looking at a large blackboard with white lines painted on it representing the zig zag course he had to follow. The other stood beside him with a stopwatch calling out precisely when to make the change and replaced the blackboard from a stack on the floor when his mate had finished the one before him. They told me that by using this system it was impossible for a U-boat to successfully launch a torpedo at them. We sailed for five days in a featureless ocean not knowing where we were heading for but when we did arrive we were amazed for the last place in our minds was Rio de Janeiro.

We sailed imperiously past the Sugar Loaf with people hanging out of the cable car waving as it took them to the top and dropped anchor in the lovely bay. It was a spectacular sight with the bright orange roofs of haciendas surrounded by lush green foliage on little islands with dozens of tiny multicoloured seaplanes flitting around them like butterflies. On our port side were luxury hotels fronting the famous Copacabana beach and behind them the high rise buildings of the city centre. Ahead, atop a mountain was the 'Christ of the Andes', a massive statue of the Son of God with outstretched arms which was floodlit at night and when clouds passed below it looked ethereal as if floating in the sky. As in Simonstown we stayed two days so no one was allowed ashore but a German prisoner had escaped and just before we departed he was brought by a police launch and made to climb a ninety-foot rope ladder hanging over the side. Halfway up he dropped his bag into the water and turned to retrieve it but a couple of shots from the cops deterred him and he was soon hauled aboard. We made our way out of this paradise accompanied by scores of boats crammed with sightseers and into the Atlantic Ocean to continue our Cook's tour. This time we had an idea where we were going for we were heading north and that meant the east coast of America where U-boats had reaped a grim harvest when the USA declared war. We knew when we entered their territorial waters for the air filled with large flying boats and dirigible airships and we were accorded an escort of a cruiser and four destroyers. We ceased the zig zagging and steered a straight course about four miles offshore through the night and 'Glory be', the Orderly Officer surfaced. We entered the Hudson river in the early morning to anchor off Staten Island, the immigration centre, and a party of American Military Police came aboard. They formed two lines, through which the scions of Rommel's Africa Korps passed and their clothing was taken from them piece by piece, thrown over the MP's shoulder, until they emerged naked at the end. Only then, subdued and humiliated, were they allowed to try to find their own clothes out of the jumbled piles behind the MPs whilst more items were still hurtling over. The onlookers, including me, really enjoyed it and shouted for more! The contraband taken from them was piled ten feet high and included hundreds of cartons of American cigarettes they could only have got from the ship's crew. There were also dozens of bottles of wine, watches, bracelets, knives galore, and several flashy Italian pistols.

The prisoners were taken off and we raised anchor to be pushed by hordes of tugs into Pier 90 New York with the burnt out *Normandie* lying on her side in the next pier. Her demise, according to the Yanks, was caused by a cigarette so they imposed a smoking ban on us but we did not care for we were busy waving to the girls in the cars, which slowed down to rubberneck from the elevated freeway. Early that evening we booed as the RAF officers left to explore the city while we NCOs were not allowed off the ship. We made such a fuss that the Captain asked to meet a delegation to explain our grievances and I and three others were ushered in to meet the great man. He was the senior captain of the line and had entertained celebrities from all walks of life at his table. He had become such a celebrity himself that he had been knighted but a nicer, more affable man, you could not meet and after hearing us out he gave us permission to go ashore if we promised to be back by 08.00 hours. He even apologised that the Purser's Office was closed so he was unable to change our British currency for us.

All the RAF lads left the ship and in the city centre we got our currency changed at ex World Heavy Weight Champion Jack Dempsey's Bar though we could not afford to eat or drink there. He was very chatty and directed us to Maddison Square Garden where I got arrested for wearing short khaki trousers, which was against the decency laws in New York. Four of my mates came with me to the Cop Shop but after explaining my circumstances they said 'Gee, you musta got bombed bad there – we had a bomb on the West Coast last week,' I could scarcely keep a straight face but they issued me with a special permit and at midnight we were in Times Square when a US Army Air Corps Colonel recognised our uniform and insisted on treating the five of us to supper. It seemed he had been seconded to the RAF before the war and had made good friends, and held the service in high esteem. When I said I had been flying Beaus in Malta he was keen to know about the new wonder plane saying the US had nothing to match it. He wined and dined us sumptuously but we wanted to get away to explore the city without offending him. We were so used to the black out that we could scarcely recall the bright lights of our own city centres pre-war but here the street lamps, bars and diners blazed all night long. We wandered round all the places whose names we knew so well from the movies – sky scrapers, hotels, restaurants, bars, theatres, streets, avenues, parks, until we took a yellow taxi back to the ship just in time to meet our deadline but two let us down by being brought in later by two amused cops dead drunk and I had to apologise to the Captain.

For the next five days my four mates and I toured the Big Apple and the curiosity our uniform aroused was a godsend. People would ask and when they discovered we were in the British Royal Air Force they vied with each other to sponsor and entertain us for we were nearly broke as our rates of pay were pitifully low being about a quarter of equivalent US ranks. We felt terribly embarrassed that we could not reciprocate their hospitality, which was, to say the least, magnanimous. When they learned we were jazz lovers they arranged for a black friend to take us to Harlem every night as American 'whities' did not dare to set foot there after dark. We, however, were greeted cordially. 'Blacks are treated as equals in your armed services but in ours they are treated like "niggers",' they said. They explained that segregation was more rigidly enforced by the military than in the Ku Klux Klan strongholds in the Deep South. In the dimly lit clubs and bars small groups delighted us with their spontaneous renditions of soulful blues and swinging jam sessions, which contrasted with the heavily orchestrated offerings of the Big Bands to be heard in the swish venues around uptown Broadway.

On the morning of the sixth day an officer arrived to take the RAF contingent to Moncton transit camp in Canada, so I bade a fond farewell to the *Queen Mary*, which had taken me halfway round the world, and we set off to Grand Central Station. We entered what looked like a concert hall with a balcony running round it with not a sign of a railway train. When the tannoy announced '11.00 train to Boston, Gate Three' the officer said 'That's us'. We hurried down a wide stairway onto the floor of the hall to doors marked 'Gate Three', which had opened in the wall and through them we could see the train. There was no platform so steps had been placed by black porters to enable us to get into the coach where seats had been reserved for us. Inside, black attendants came round selling drinks and soon the air conditioned, double glazed train slid almost silently into the sunshine giving us a last glimpse of the city that never sleeps and we gazed out as the city gave way to green pastures and tree covered slopes. When we got to Boston we were taken to a hotel and later went out to explore the city, which looked so very Olde English that the bar of another great American heavy weight boxer, Jack Dempsey, seemed somehow incongruous. We spent the following day sightseeing until we entrained at 17.30 hours on an overnight sleeper train to Canada. The views from the windows became increasingly rugged and every bend in the track revealed a small lake set amid steep pine clad slopes sometimes with a solitary house. We watched these enchanting vistas until it fell dark and at 23.00 hours the train stopped in the middle of nowhere. We were ushered into a gigantic restaurant, which we were told could seat 2,000 people, to be served supper and we wondered where the staff came from in such an isolated place. We returned to the train to find our beds had been made up and I slept until 08.00 hours, awakening to find we were arriving at our destination.

We were bussed to the camp and after breakfast I went to the Stores, handed in my khaki tropical uniform and was kitted out with regular RAF blues. I sewed on my chevrons and made my way into the town, which had a distinctly Gallic feel. I went straight to the post office from which I had been told messages could be sent home. You had to pick numbers from a card – No. 1 was 'I am well', No. 2 'I am not well' etc, etc until you used up your quota of numbers but you could not say where you were or when you would be coming home. Mum and Dad must have been frantic for they had heard nothing from me for months but now they at least would know I was alive. I asked a local where there was a pub and he told me that the town was 'dry' but it was easy to pour a gin into a bottle of 'Seven Up' under the table in the local café cum coffee shop. Having become a regular (with my under-the-table bottle of gin) I got to know Janine Legère the daughter of the owners of the coffee shop well. One day she and her brother drove me miles into the wilds to a tumbledown French Canadian shack to sample home-brewed hooch. On a table there was an ancient wind-up gramophone with a large horn endlessly playing a fiddler's reel, which seemed to be the only record they had. The drink was expensive and the whiskey was a real witch's brew but I did not say so for it was kind of my hosts to have brought me knowing their church-going parents would not approve. In any case the villainous-looking bunch of locals, dressed like pirates, were people I definitely would not want to offend.

I began to make friends among the pilots and navigators in the camp, most of whom had completed their basic training in Canada and the US and were now going home to convert mostly to operational bomber aircraft. Amongst them was a pilot who had been at grammar school with me and tentatively we arranged to team up for my third tour if he could get posted to night fighters. The embryonic pilots were keen to hear the experiences of the very few in the camp who had flown operationally and I told them of my unrewarded 'kills'. My story sounded so improbable that I believe some one high up did a check lest I was 'telling the tale' for kudos or free beer. It was then I first heard that in Danny's report on our 'kills' he had never mentioned me and it had been assumed he was flying solo. The news shattered me and initially I passed it off as scuttlebutt but on reflection I had to admit it could explain his attitude. He might have been too embarrassed or ashamed to tell me of his gaff and figured the only way out for him was to get rid of me by reporting I was too ill to fly. I was, and still am, reluctant to believe Danny would do that to me and I have never had any confirmation but for some time after I was embittered. Unexpectedly I was suddenly treated with great respect from everyone in the camp who now realised how shabbily I had been treated. The odious 'Mongolface' (the beast of Yatesbury) constantly sought my company so that he could bask in the reflected glory of having had a hand in my training. I was senior to him in rank and I used the strongest Flight Sergeant vernacular I could muster to rid myself of him but to no effect for he was so dim he simply could not be insulted.

For days I languished in this far away place and then one morning the tannoy announced that everyone was confined to camp until further notice. I knew this was a security measure to prevent the news of a convoy forming from leaking out and later that day I was told I was to set sail from Halifax, Nova Scotia, to dear old England the next day. I was beside myself with joy and I rushed to the shop on the camp to fill two kitbags with food unseen at home since the war started. In my bunk that night I was too excited to sleep and I began to wonder just what the man who dealt the cards had in store for me this time. I was soon to find out!

CHAPTER TWENTY-ONE

The Longest Mile

As I boarded the train in Moncton my heart was singing the old song 'The longest mile is the last mile home when you've been away' knowing that I was about to embark for dear old England. I did not sing it out loud for great pains had been taken to keep our departure secret; telephone communication with the outside world had been cut and we had been confined to camp. The implications were obvious, U-boats were active on the Atlantic route we were about to travel, which was not good news. I imagined the welcome I would get from Mum and Dad and from my family and friends when I appeared on our doorstep unexpectedly. For months they had not known where I was or what I had been doing, and did not even know if I was alive until the telegram I had sent from Canada arrived. No prodigal son would ever receive a more joyous homecoming and boy oh boy would I be pleased to see them! Looking out of the train window I saw another chapter of my life close as the town slipped away and I looked back over the time I had spent here. I had found it hard to realise there was no rationing but I quickly adapted to the abundance of American-style gizmos like juke boxes and electrical gadgets in the predominantly wooden buildings. Because of the fire risk there was no smoking in the cinemas and other public places and as there were no pubs the liquor store did a roaring trade. What surprised me was that what appeared to be a pair of wooden semi-detached houses were occupied by four families – two upstairs and two on the ground floor – when there was obviously no shortage of building land. Indeed, what had impressed me most was how far away the town was from what we would call civilisation and the way this was reflected in the attitude of the population. The people were nice enough but having been born and brought up in this isolated place they were content to live out their lives quietly in this small town with no desire or aspiration to widen their horizons. In those days every town back home was as insular for holiday air travel abroad was yet to come and direct Atlantic crossings had only been undertaken by pioneers like Lindberg – the difference was that in Britain there were other communities relatively close at hand. No, this part of Canada was not for me and I was leaving with few regrets but many pleasant memories of the friends I had made.

By now the train had moved out into the surrounding countryside, which was flat and featureless with none of the charming lakes and pine forests we had seen on our way to Moncton. It travelled through miles and miles of barren windswept sand hills so monotonous it lulled me to sleep and when I awoke I saw there were big ships sailing among them. I realised they were passing along the St Lawrence seaway, which is the shipping artery to the busy ports on the Great Lakes and the maritime gateway into the heart of Canada. Darkness fell and we waited for some time in open countryside outside Halifax before the train slowly moved on eventually stopping under bright lights on a dockside close to where a large ship was waiting. We were hustled aboard and at once tugs moved the ship out into the night and we saw another ship was already being pushed into our place at the dock. All this was cleverly planned to thwart prying eyes and had become a well practised routine. We were taken below into a large space filled with row upon row of Mess tables, which had hammocks hanging above them. We stowed our kit bags under the tables and tried to get into our hammocks. Laugh? We were in stitches as man after man entered one side only to fall out of the other on to the tables below. Several (including me) decided it was easier to sleep on the tables and competition for spaces was fierce. At first light I went on deck and saw we were in a wide bay with dozens of other ships all weighing their anchors to take their appointed place to form a convoy. It was all done so slickly that we had scarcely cleared the bay before they were in three lines astern heading for some warships on the horizon.

I enquired what ship we were on and was told it was a P & O boat called the *Strathmore* with a Lascar crew and British officers. It was part of a twelve-knot convoy, which was the cruising speed of the slowest vessel, so none of them were laggards. Further ahead I could see several warships, which I presumed were to be our escorts, but I was told breakfast was being served so I went below. 'Served' turned out to be more of a lie than a euphemism for on each bare wooden table there was a basket of bread pieces, a large metal jug of sludgy porridge and a pot of jam. Memories of the *Queen Mary* came flooding back and I was happy to join the general outcry against this gastronomic offence to the palate – but worse was to come for it was reported the 'heads' (toilets) were overflowing. It seemed that in the absence of toilet paper the troops had been using newspaper whereas the seasoned travellers like me used books with nice soft pages. These news sheets gummed up the main drain so that the toilets and urinals were inches deep in – well I'll leave it to your imagination. I had to laugh remembering how reluctant occupants were to vacate the 'throne' in Malta; now they were trying to get in and out without having to inhale. The washing facilities were not much better for there were no mirrors and trying to shave from memory in cold water was an art I had yet to acquire. By the time I got back on deck a US battleship was heading the convoy whilst a battle cruiser brought up the rear and both flanks were guarded by destroyers but I could not count how many there were for they were dashing about whooping with their sirens – I guessed a dozen or so.

My two mates and I found a place on deck out of the chilly wind and watched them as they fussed around like headless chickens until it was time for dinner. We went below to find there were the same bread chunks and the same metal jug but this time it was filled with stew but I cannot remember what there was for 'afters' – I had lost interest. Supper was forgettable too but we decided that we would be better on deck in our windbreak for the night so we put on all the warm clothing we could muster and took our hammocks on deck. We were NCOs but we were sharing our accommodation with the 'other ranks' in the noisy, smelly Mess Deck, which we had christened 'The Ghetto'. Our bolt hole was infinitely better even though it was cold and draughty but at least it was quiet and we slept undisturbed. When a Lascar crewman tried to move us on during the night we didn't half pull rank on him and we were never challenged again during the whole trip.

The following day we spent on deck marvelling at the tremendous bulk and massive guns of the battleship leading the centre column that we were in but we were still perplexed by the antics of the destroyers. The convoy too was fascinating for it must have covered miles of ocean with all types of ships and we particularly noted a beautiful petrol tanker five or six vessels to port and astern. The food did not improve but the 'heads' were made almost bearable by being cleared with a pressure hose every hour. So came the evening and as being in the fresh breeze all day had made us really tired we settled down to a good night's sleep. Next day followed the same pattern but at dusk just as we were laying out our hammocks there was a loud bang and we saw flames shooting up from the tanker we had admired. We were watching the inferno grow when there was a tremendous explosion on the starboard side so we rushed across to see what was happening but apart from a thin cloud of smoke astern of the troop transport level with us in the outer column there was nothing to be seen. Clearly it had not been another torpedo strike for the line was keeping station unlike the tanker, which was dropping astern with the flames getting higher and lighting up the whole convoy. We watched until the tanker was out of sight before we settled down for the night praying for its crew and mystified by the cause of other massive explosion. There was little to distinguish the succeeding days until in mid-Atlantic our armada of American escorts withdrew, handing over their duties to four puny British minesweepers. As they struggled to keep pace with us in the heavy Atlantic swell it showed the massive potential of the Americans compared with the British who had spent so much of their strength fighting single handed for the survival of freedom in the world. It struck me that Britain relied on this lifeline to bring in the essential food, munitions and reinforcements needed for survival but if this was all we could scrape together to guard a large convoy such as ours then we might well face starvation like Malta.

Despite feeling naked with only our Mickey Mouse escort we suffered no further alarms and about 16.00 hours on the first day of September we entered the Firth of Clyde, docking at Greenock just after 17.00 hours. What today is a three-hour flight to Malta had taken me eighty days but I dare not think how much my world sightseeing cruise would cost nowadays! Everyone aboard was buzzing with excitement at the news that a special train was to take us to the reception centre at 23.00 hours – even then it could not be soon enough for some who had been overseas for three years. Imagine our dismay when heartless dockers began walking out as they said they could not unload the ship before their shift ended at 17.30 hours and we would have to wait their return in the morning. The dock workers' union was so strong that on many occasions they held the country to ransom and off they went making rude gestures in reply to our boos and curses. There was mayhem on the ship and sympathetic Customs Officers went to the yard's management and got permission for us to use the runabout trucks with their trailers ourselves. To the many tank drivers aboard this was a piece of cake and with the help of the customs men who showed their disgust by waiving their checks we caught our train making a riotous exit on time. It was not long before the dockers got their desserts for airlines replaced the great ocean liners and they were no longer indispensable, instead they were made redundant in their thousands. I hope they sacked the lot at Greenock! We travelled all night to a camp near Derby and when it came to my turn to be 'processed' I told them I had lost all my kit in Malta. They looked at me sympathetically and said 'Go to the Adjutant and get a travel warrant to Doncaster.' I had to wait a couple of hours to catch the last train at about 20.00 hours, which I hoped would get me home in time for supper but when I got in the train as I had been excitedly on the go for forty-eight hours I promptly fell asleep. I awoke with a start and when a fellow traveller told me we had past Donny and were nearly in Retford I gathered my kit to alight there. I stood forlornly on the platform thinking there would be no train back until morning when I was befriended by some train drivers. Hearing of my plight they invited me to join them in the guards' van of a goods train, which came in an hour to take them back to their base in Donny when they had finished their shift. Outside the station I paid for a taxi to take them to their homes after it left me at my doorstep and they waved out of the window shouting 'All the best' as I dragged my kitbags to the porch. It was 01.30 hours and the house was in darkness. Fearful of waking the neighbours I tossed pebbles at the upstairs bay windows until a light came on. Mum looked out and I heard her shout to Dad 'It's our Dennis, it's our Dennis' followed by much scuffling before the front door opened and she flung her arms around me. I was dragged inside and excitedly asked did I want a cup of tea, did I want any supper. I was asked all sorts of inane questions until, calmer at last, they wanted to hear my whole story. I tried to give them a short version but they interrupted me many times wanting to know when, where, how and why that I might as well have gone into all the details from the start.

Mum made us a cup of tea and then she brought me up to date on the happenings at home, her main concern being the food rationing. Uncle Charles had been made Traffic Superintendent on the buses, Mum was worried about the stress Dad was under having to drive in the blackout even in the dense fog and Cousin Peter was abroad as an armourer in the RAF. My pal, Dennis Potter from six houses down the road was reported 'missing, presumed lost' in his submarine operating out of Malta. His mother was devastated as he was her only child and since the telegram came she had become a recluse, ageing almost beyond recognition. I think he was in the *Ursula* but I did not tell them that I knew about the 'U' Class boats and the heavy losses they had suffered from unmarked minefields or how visible they were from the air in the clear shallow waters. It was plain that they had already gone through hell fearing they too would get a dreaded telegram that would shatter their lives for ever. When I eventually managed to unpack the food they had not seen since the war started and I got to the Number Seven gift boxes I had bought for Mum and Auntie Elsie she burst into tears. 'It's all lovely' she said 'but the best present is you.' It must have been dawn before they let me get into my gloriously comfortable bed so I slept like a log till late in the afternoon and that night we just talked and talked. I was *home* and it was every bit as wonderful as I had imagined, maybe even better for in my pocket I had a chit giving me three weeks' accumulated leave.

Next morning I did the rounds of relatives on my bike to give each of them an account of my adventures, which was time consuming but they wanted to know all about Malta for the siege was headline news in Britain. They lapped up every word and I guessed they would proudly tell their friends how 'Our Dennis' had been there and in the thick of it. It was still daylight when I got home and for the first time I saw that Mum and Dad had changed the house name from 'Glen Avon' to 'Glen Dennis' – I was so embarrassed I swear I blushed! I visited my old workplace but apart from the old timers there were only young women whom I did not know. The town centre was unchanged but whereas before the war we were all on nodding acquaintance now there was no one I knew. When I went to my old church, which had been wonderfully supportive with parcels of woollies and hard to come by razor blades, it was the same story. I went to the movies and the roller skating rink but it wasn't much fun being on my own so I stayed home and played my jazz records but I wondered if Donny would ever be the same again. Mum and Dad positively cosseted me and it was great being with them but the days had begun to drag and daily I became more impatient for news of my next posting. I felt I was being selfish and ungrateful but the truth was I was bored – I had got the old wanderlust and I wanted to get back to the war and new challenges.

When the news of my posting came I tried to assure them that I was only going Cranfield in Bedfordshire for my long overdue rest as an instructor in No. 51 Operational Training Unit – a piece of cake really, no need to worry. The letter enclosed my travel warrant with details of the trains I should catch but someone had got things wrong for I found myself on a deserted Bedford station at 04.30 hours. The waiting room was locked so I waited two hours on the platform before a postman arrived to meet the early morning mail train and I managed to cadge a lift in his van. He meandered through umpteen villages making his deliveries sometimes at remote farms in the pretty rural countryside and it was 10.30 hours before we arrived at the camp. I reported to the Adjutant who seemed genuinely pleased to see me 'Oh you are the one just back from Malta,' he said. 'Welcome, we are short of instructors with operational experience.' He got a clerk to show me my billet though he scarcely needed to for Cranfield was a typical Expansion Scheme aerodrome and they all had basically similar layouts. Apparently I was to share a room with another Sergeant who was out on duty so I stowed my kit and went to the Stores to draw my flying gear. I returned to lay it on my bed before going to the Mess in time for dinner. It was a pleasure to get a decent RAF meal after what had been 'served' on the *Strathmore* and as I tucked into my bangers and mash with a cup of scalding tea I had strange feeling that this simple meal was somehow special – as if it marked the end of my odyssey. Yes, my world tour was indeed finally over! Now I began to wonder what the man who dealt the cards had in store for me. I no longer thought of him as malevolent but more like a guardian angel protecting me. This was a feeling that grew stronger as the fates of my comrades unfolded – fates I could so easily have shared.

CHAPTER TWENTY-TWO

A Rest and Tragic News from the Past

I reported to No. 3 Squadron and was cordially welcomed by the CO who immediately put my mind at rest regarding my demotion (as I saw it) to flying Blenheims again. 'You must be wondering why you are back to the old kites,' he said. 'Well our job is to make you into an instructor and for that we first have to assess your competence in the air before we teach you how to lecture pupils. With your record I am sure you will find the first part easy and I see no reason why the second part should be any obstacle.'

Thus reassured I entered into the training with gusto and after three days the CO called me into his office and said 'No need to have you flight tested any more, you will now commence teaching pupils in the air whilst learning lecturing.' So I started flying in the morning and became a pupil myself in the afternoons learning lecture room techniques. This I did for three weeks before the CO called me in again. 'You have done very well, which has saved us two weeks' training time, and so that you can start at the same time as the next intake of instructors I am giving you a fortnight of the accumulated leave you are entitled to. When you come back you will go straight to No. 4 Squadron. Well done, and I hope you will enjoy your leave.' When staffing levels permitted aircrew leave was normally one week at the end of every six weeks on operations and since departing England I had been unable to take any leave at all so there were now forty-eight days due to me. When I was on leave from my squadron friends would greet me on the street with 'You home again? When do you go back?' This was very irritating as you could not explain to everyone that the system had been adopted because it was found that efficiency declined sharply after six weeks of ops due to stress. I collected a travel warrant from the Adjutant's office and was on the train to Donny early the following day. The several changes the journey involved made it long and tiresome and though all the name boards had been taken down at stations I could not mistake dear old Donny and did not oversleep like last time. I had heard my old mate Jack Dye was now a Flight Lieutenant in charge of navigator instructors flying Ansons at Usworth, which was where my old *alma mater* had been transferred when Church Fenton became a front line night fighter base. After passing out their pupils came to us at Cranfield to polish their newly acquired skills and to be 'crewed up' with a pilot before going to a squadron. I phoned him and had a long natter catching up on the gossip from Tangmere and he wanted to hear the full details of my exploits in Malta. He was incensed that I had not been decorated and when I told him of my recent train journey saying I wished I had been posted to him as I could get a direct mainline train from there to Doncaster he said 'Leave it with me.' Like me Jack was a Yorkshireman (from Sheffield) but I thought no more about it – perhaps I should have remembered that a Yorkshireman's word is his bond.

I was delighted to find that my old mate Fred Hardy was home on leave too and we arranged to meet in a pub in Donny that night. The place was full of aircrew from Finningley and among them were several lads from the transit camp in Canada. They had been aboard the transport level with me on the starboard side and explained the colossal bang that had mystified us. Apparently when the tanker on the port side was torpedoed a US destroyer had tried to cut through the convoy and their ship had sliced it in half. It had bounced along the side of their ship until when it was just astern its depth charges went off blowing it to smithereens, hence the smoke we had seen. I doubt if anyone survived from the destroyer but had the explosion happened alongside their ship it could have caused a major catastrophe for it was jammed full of troops and, of course, we could not stop to pick up survivors. All their kitbags were quickly tossed into the forward compartment to stem the water gushing into the gaping hole in the bows before the bulkhead was closed behind them sealing the forward compartment off. They had lost all their kit and worst still all the goodies they had intended for their families but to the great credit of their crew they had never lost speed or station, which would have thrown the whole convoy into utter confusion in darkness. One option would have been to stop the whole convoy but 20,000 tons of ship take some stopping and lit up by the burning tanker they would have been sitting ducks for the attacking U-boat pack but had they not kept going in a convoy three miles long God alone knows how many would have collided causing more mayhem. The proverbial bull in the china shop would have been nothing by comparison! They told me that they had heard the stricken tanker had managed to quell the inferno and make its way back to Halifax on its own. They also had heard that I had not got my award because Danny had never mentioned me in his post combat report. Now they had been posted to Finningley or Lindholme on Bomber Command, which was suffering increasing losses at that time, and I wondered how long their luck would hold out. The odds were against them for the German AA and night fighters began to take such a fearful toll that 60,000 aircrew had been lost by Bomber Command by the end of the war, sometimes over 500 in a single night.

I returned to No. 4 Squadron at Cranfield and it was obvious that questions had been asked in high places as to why I was the only undecorated navigator with more than four 'kills' in the UK. I was often asked to fly with the CO or his deputy and when we entertained distinguished visitors I was detailed to demonstrate our equipment on the static trainer in one of the hangars. The Simulator Instructor tried every wile he could think of to make me lose contact but he only succeeded in making me hoarse shouting my instructions to thwart him. Two or three times a week we (or should I say I?) entertained politicians, diplomats, embassy officials and high-ranking military officers and once I was offered a five shilling tip for my performance. I was certainly being given star billing – 'Come see the great Gosling, three performances a week, try to escape him if you can' – and I have to admit I lapped it all up! I had one other asset that made me indispensable – I was the only instructor in 51 OTU who was able to lecture and demonstrate Mk 5 AI. At Tangmere Danny and I had been assigned to its inventor, a boffin called Mr Taylor, and we had taken him on test flights whilst it was still at the development stage. He had taught me how to use it, asked for my reactions when I did practice interceptions for him and explained what he was trying to achieve.

I was enjoying life on 4 Squadron, making new friends and revelling in my duties when a bombshell came from out of the blue. On the morning of 4 December I was cycling round the perimeter track on my way to 4 Squadron Flight Hut and I watched an Anson coming in to land. 'Ah,' I thought, 'I bet I am going to be called upon to do my stuff for another VIP' so I was not surprised when half an hour later the CO called out from his office. 'Gosling, report to the Adjutant straight away.' I got there to find a stern faced Adjutant waiting for me 'The Station Commander wants to see you *now*,' he said and his tone was ominous. 'God,' I thought 'what have I done wrong?' I was ushered straight in to face the Group Captain and he did not mince his words. 'Why has an Anson come to take you to Usworth? And what makes you think you can arrange your own posting?' I was gobsmacked. I had heard nothing from Jack Dye since I had phoned him and clearly I had ruffled the feathers of my Squadron Commander who had been so taken aback he had phoned the Station Commander to register his displeasure. He obviously did not want to lose his 'star turn' and no doubt felt I had abused the goodwill and even affection I had been shown by everyone on the Flight. It must have seemed to him that I was a total ingrate and I understood why he was so upset. Stuttering, I tried to explain to the Station Commander that I had been as completely surprised as everyone else, and I told him the whole sorry story. I abjectly apologised, nay, I grovelled for I knew I was deep in the mire. I had never studied King's Rules and Regulations (the RAF bible) but I felt certain that those who specialised in it would throw the book at me. I said I did not expect to be allowed to leave, that I had been well treated here and would be quite happy to stay. Jack Dye was an old mate so I had not only chatted about the difficulties of my journey home but lots of other trivial things. He was still not a happy bunny but he was somewhat mollified and to my surprise he said 'All right, get your clearance from the Adjutant and get out of here before I change my mind.' I thanked him profusely, saluted (I ought not to have done for he was not wearing his hat) and beat a hasty retreat back to the Adjutant's office. He noted my broad smile and pushed some papers to one side, which I suspect he had prepared for charging me, and when I told him that I was going to leave *now* his face was a picture of disbelief. I rushed round the camp handing in my blankets, parachute and the like, and dashed to the waiting Anson as the Group Captain had advised. Arriving at Usworth Jack met me off the plane and roared with laughter when I recounted my ordeal. 'No worries,' he said, 'I'll take care of everything. Welcome aboard.' And he must have for I heard no more of the episode.

At No. 62 Operational Training Unit Usworth, unlike Expansion Scheme Cranfield, I did not have a room and toilet facilities of my own in the Sergeants' Mess but a very basic partioned off bunk at the end of a wooden hut full of trainees. In fact the whole camp was just a collection of WWI wooden huts near Sunderland and I was allotted to Jack's 'B' Flight. I soon settled in and became familiar with the blackened beaches where coal was mined far out under the sea and a bleaker landscape than the rolling pasture lands of Bedfordshire. I flew daily with three pupils in the trusty old Anson with its twin 350 hp Cheetah engines and before long I was doing my instructing from the pilot's seat for it was very docile and easy to fly. It had been intended as a communications hack but we were so short of aircraft that it had been pressed into service for anti-submarine patrols early in the war. Now it was used to train pilots to handle twin-engined aircraft before going on to fly Blenheims, then Beaus and eventually going to a squadron. It was great fun for me to fly them and my pleasure was unbounded when on the first day of 1943 I was awarded a 'Mention in Despatches'. It was too soon after my transfer for Jack to be responsible and in any case he did not have the 'clout' as a mere Flight Lieutenant. No, I knew that I had to thank the powers that be at Cranfield for the honour – no wonder they had felt so aggrieved at my departure. It most probably resulted from the Wing Commanders of No. 3 and 4 Squadrons telling the Group Captain about me not getting any decoration for my five 'kills' and his intervention on my behalf. Perhaps when he gave me permission to leave he had thought 'Well the poor so-and-so deserves a break' but Station Commanders were not renowned for their compassion and however it came about I was truly grateful.

The nearest watering hole was the ancient pit village of Washington with its American associations and I soon became a habitué of the 'Cabbage' (the Allotment Holders' Club) and the local pub 'The Bird in Hand'. Its landlord had lost a son over the North Sea returning from a Bomber Command raid on Germany. All the natives greeted me like one of their own and I cycled there nightly spending many a happy hour in their company rather than taking the bus to Sunderland. Funny what you remember – I still recall how off-putting it was when the rather fetching, heavily made up WAAF waitress in the Sergeants' Mess served my greasy breakfast with Vaseline – based blue eye shadow after a heavy night at 'The Bird in Hand'. Despite the twenty-five years or more difference in their ages the grumpy old Station Warrant Officer had exercised his prerogative by appointing himself her protector from lascivious suitors – other than himself. As the senior aircrew NCO I became his prime suspect and this fuelled the already simmering conflict between the two factions. The basis of the feud was that they had taken years to achieve their status whilst aircrew took relatively little time to gain their rank. At the Xmas Dinner he sat at the top table flanked by his sidekick, the Flight

Sergeant Discipline and the Physical Training Sergeant Raich Carter, the footballer. Suddenly all hell broke loose as the SWO and his chair crashed backwards on to the floor. The Flight Sergeant Discip took off his tunic, rolled up his shirt sleeve and knelt to thrust his brawny arm down the SWO's throat to dislodge a turkey bone the glutton had swallowed. We were convulsed with laughter and when the medics arrived to stretcher him away with a torn gullet a cheer went up from the aircrew lads. When he returned to duty he did his best to exact revenge by coming down hard on any aircrew alleged misdemeanour but fortunately we had a former solicitor among our pupils who knew King's Rules and Regulations better than him. The SWO lost so many cases the CO told him not to waste his time any more and for a while we breathed more easily but the tension was still there.

Meanwhile I continued instructing a succession of courses until in April the unit went over to the training of US Army Air Corps entrants, which reduced us to hysterical laughter and later to tears. We laughed because the Americans' idea of night flying was to follow a radio beam between major destinations, but without it they were hopelessly lost. We cried when we discovered that the most junior ranks with no flying experience were paid five times as much as we were. We scarcely knew where to start for we had to go back beyond even basics but fortunately for them at the end of the course they apparently did not have to pass RAF scrutiny. On Saturday nights in the past I had ventured on to the dance floor at the village hall to do the odd slow waltz (my version was really very odd) but after the Yanks found the place I gave up. The gyrations and gymnastics of their jitter-bugging when the band played nothing but Glen Miller hits were as clearly beyond me as were some of their names like Kirshenbaum, Cusenvity, Veslany and Speierman. To simplify matters we called them all 'buddy' but they kept on saluting me despite being told 'We do not salute NCOs in our Air Force'.

I was so happy when my old mate Johnny Walsh arrived but devastated when he told me his story. After seeing my condition the medics in Valletta had tested the whole 1435 Flight and failed the lot on the spot! Ten days after I left they too were put on a transport plane and returned to Egypt where they later embarked on a ship called the *Laconia* to return to England. Off the coast of North West Africa it was torpedoed and sunk and they had drifted in a lifeboat with little food or water and his pilot, dear Peter Oakes, had gone berserk and jumped overboard. Flight Lieutenant Hayton the New Zealander who had commanded our Malta detachment and suffered from dysentery not quite as bad as mine, had succumbed to its debilitating effects and had been buried at sea. Fourteen days, later just as they lost hope, they were picked up by the Vichy French and sent to an internment camp where conditions were atrocious and they were treated brutally. The Vichy French hated us for in 1940 we had shelled the French fleet at anchor in Oran to prevent the Germans taking the ships over, which would have tipped the balance against our already fragile tenure of the Med. Only after Operation *Torch* (the invasion of Algeria) were they rescued and repatriated to England. On arrival they were sent to a large house in North London where for a week they were 'brainwashed' lest they said anything derogatory about the (Free) French who were our Allies. As officers and NCOs had been sent to different prison camps he had no news of their fate but I detected a subtle change in him.

As long as I had known Johnny he had been detached, almost enigmatic, but now I could sense he had changed and was struggling to hold his emotions in check. He was seething inside, lashing out at all discipline. Yet deep down he was ineffably sad and I wondered if the awful death of timid, lovable Peter was the cause. He had always seemed to be able to insulate himself from such tragedies but was he now regretting that he had not been more supportive of his oppo? Johnny was always a heavy drinker and for days we had been on a massive bender until we were hauled out of bed one morning by the Flight Sergeant Discip when we should have been on the weekly Friday Station Parade. He was so pleased we almost expected him to say 'Gotcha' but he roared 'You should be on parade'. For a moment we were speechless but then we had a flash of inspiration. 'Yes,' we replied 'but we are sick.' 'Get to the MO and if you do not get a sick note you will be on a charge,' he said and stormed out to report his coup to the SWO. We hurried to the sick bay and sheepishly told the MO of our plight. Luckily I knew him well and he said 'Give me a sample of your water.' He took the samples away and returned shortly creased in laughter. 'You should get this bottled,' he said, 'it's about 90% proof. I will send you to Dock for three or four days to dry out.' We ended up in a pre-war maternity home in Low Fell where the WAAF nurses spoiled us rotten including bringing us bottles of Newcastle Brown Ale daily lest we exhibited withdrawal symptoms I suppose. We returned to camp and in the Mess we received so many queries about our health in front of the glowering SWO it even embarrassed us for some of the lads got too enthusiastic and enquired with deep concern three times in an hour.

His discomfort increased for he found there was a defector in his camp who was exposed one night when there was an air raid on Sunderland. When the Ack-Ack opened up the lads in my hut knocked on my bunk door enquiring if they should go to the shelter. 'You can if you wish,' I told them 'but I am staying put, it's too cold outside.' The words were scarcely out of my mouth when the hut door was hurled open and in the beams of their flashlights we saw a man crash on to the floor. Someone switched on the lights and I shouted to him to close the door as it might attract the raiders for in the blackout it would be visible for miles. The man was face down, his shoulders were heaving and he was naked except for his shirt. When we turned him over we saw it was one of our trainee pilots laughing his head off and it took a while to get the whole story out of him. He had been in bed with the WAAF Sergeant PT Instructor and when the guns went off the girls in the hut had knocked on her door to make the same enquiries as my lads had done. Before she dared to open her door he had hastily gathered up his clothes, she helped him out of the window and he ran across the football pitch back to our billet where he fell exhausted on the floor. She was a hefty girl and not the best looking lass on the camp but when the news inevitably spread she certainly became the most popular. In the SWO's presence, enquiries about my health were replaced with 'You going out with Gertie tonight?' and we all giggled delightedly.

I knew how it felt to be so exposed for on returning from my last leave my train had been caught in another air raid and had stopped right in the middle of the high-level bridge over the river outside Newcastle. All trains had no heating in those days for that consumed extra coal and the lights only came on in the stations so I did not notice when the fire in the boilers were put out lest a spark betrayed our position. There I sat looking out in the pale moonlight knowing one bomb on the bridge would land me in the Tyne far below. I felt nakedly exposed and after the raid I sat for two hours in the dark while the engine relit its furnace and raised sufficient steam to crawl into the station. Tired by the stress, frozen and hoping I would never again feel so utterly helpless, I would have given anything to be back in my Beau that night.

The following week I received more bad news – the old school chum I had met in Canada and with whom I had a tacit understanding that we would 'crew up' when he qualified had been killed. He was flying a Miles Master trainer when his single radial engine received a bird strike, his aircraft caught fire, and he was killed in the ensuing crash.

When the word spread around the camp that Goz now had no pilot for his return to ops every trainee pilot suddenly wanted the job and I had my pick. One nice fatherly Pilot Instructor, Flt/Lt Fitzrandolph, asked me outright if I would consider him as he hoped my experience might outweigh the objections he had encountered due to his advanced age – he was thirty-seven! When he sounded out the Unit CO he was turned down again. 'I so envy you young chaps,' he told me, 'I would give anything to get on ops.' I had got on particularly well with one young Sergeant called Woodland when I flew with him and he jumped at my offer to 'crew up' when he had qualified. He left shortly afterwards to go to an OTU at Grantham where he would fly Blenheims before qualifying on Beaus and meet up with me, probably at Cranfield, and together we would go on ops. Just after Jack Dye left to return to ops we instructors were introduced to a new electronic wonder – 'Gee' was a system based on three ground stations and the circular pulses of their transmissions were shown as a grid on a radar screen. Using special maps navigators could pinpoint their position and were thus assisted to plot their courses. It was ingenious but complicated and though its range covered the Ruhr, Northern Germany and the occupied Low Countries unfortunately it did not extend as far as Berlin. Never the less it was badly needed for it was the first navigational aid available to us on the other side of the Channel and it appeared we were being trained to teach Bomber Command navigators in its use.

One evening I had a surprise visitor. I had gone to bed early recuperating from a drinking session the previous night (I could never keep up with Johnny) when the door of my bunk was flung open and in bounced – Danny! 'Come on Goz,' out of bed, let's get p—d like old times.' But I adamantly refused for after the pain he had caused me I would rather have supped with the devil. I had heard he was back in England at Ford and that with his expanded girth he was now universally known as 'Tubby' Daniels. I could not believe he would have the audacity to seek me out and the first thing that came to my mind was 'It's getting near time to go back on ops. He wants me to crew up with him again – no chance!' He tried hard to coax me out of bed, even offering to pay if I was broke, but I would have none of it and he finally slammed my door cursing me as he went. I never had chance to ask him why he had left me out of his combat report and he made no mention of it. I did not even have the satisfaction of telling him I was already fixed up with a pilot for my next tour and that he had a cheek to ask me to fly with him again after the way he had betrayed me. I lay abed for a long time pondering what could have been so important that he had flown the length of England to see me and I concluded that my intuition was right – he had hoped to go back on ops with me. He was probably expecting I would not welcome him with open arms but thought that after a few beers all would be forgiven and he would be able to persuade me. A year ago he might have succeeded but now he could see that he was not going to sway me so he lost his temper and flounced off. I was somehow relieved that he had finally forced a clean break for it freed me to get on with my life without any baggage from the past.

My six-month rest period had but a week to run and I was prepared to leave Usworth for Cranfield to crew up with 'Woody' when shock news came – 'Woody' was dead! He was taking off in a Blenheim at Grantham and had just got airborne when an engine fell off and the plane rolled over to smash into the ground killing him instantly.The aircraft was freshly out of a major inspection and it seemed that the four main bolts that attached the engine to the wing had been only finger tightened. The vibration of the take-off had shaken them loose and when they fell off so did the engine. The aircraft was irrevocably doomed – no pilot in the world could have averted the catastrophe. The poor lad never had a chance. He had no time to bale out and was too low anyway and even if the ejector seat then being perfected by Martin-Baker had been fitted it would have still been a close call. Johnny was having better luck for at the time I had chosen 'Woody' he had 'crewed up' with a Sergeant Pilot who haled from Preston called Les Wignell who had been my second choice and we were so close that I had been the best man at his wedding in Preston and Johnny was his groomsman. I had a difficult journey from Doncaster where I was on leave and did not arrive until it was too late to go for a drink with Johnny who went home as he lived nearby. The great day went well, I made my speech at the reception and the bride and groom left for their honeymoon. Throughout the day it was obvious that Les had told all his family that we were both Malta veterans and we were treated royally.

That night Johnny went home while I stayed over as they said they had a treat for me the next day. After a late breakfast I was told that they had booked seats for the chief bridesmaid and me to see the great tenor Richard Tauber. He was at the height of his popularity and appearing in Blackpool in the musical 'Lilac Time' whose lilting songs were currently all the rage. We had good seats in the dress circle and the star so enchanted us with his superb voice we overlooked that his eighteen-stone frame made him an unlikely romantic male lead. We caught the last bus back to Preston after a memorable musical treat I shall always remember – how

144

kind my hosts had been!

In that last week at Usworth I took stock of my position. 'Woody' was gone, Johnny was 'crewed up' and it was clear that our temporary reunion was nearing its end for it was unlikely we would be posted to the same squadron. Since his arrival I realised that I had been indulging to excess as I lacked his capacity for drink and I had to 'clean up' my act before I went on ops if I wanted to survive. Of course all aircrew were heavy drinkers – they were vibrant young men who knew not what the future held in store – their ethos was 'drink and be merry for tomorrow we die'. I determined that from now on I would be more sensible and only drink in moderation. So my sojourn at Usworth came to an end and I left without bidding the SWO farewell but I bet he was glad to see the back of me.

On 12 June I arrived at 51 OTU gutted, forlorn, without a pilot, and worried about how I would be received. But to my surprise they welcomed me warmly saying 'We have a splendid pilot for you' and introduced me to a certain Flying Officer Hayhurst. I gave him my logbook to read and then left him to make up his mind while I was taken round to my billet, which unlike the other trainees, was in the Sergeants' Mess, and cleared myself with the Adjutant. I met Gordon Hayhurst (for that was his full name) the following day and he told me he had just come out of hospital for he had been flying Hurricanes in Northern Ireland and under Ground Control he had been vectored into the top of a mountain; luckily he had been thrown clear but had broken his back. The shepherd who found him said how unlucky he had been to be hit by the crashing plane whilst walking in the fog and was astounded when he was told 'I wasn't walking, I was piloting the plane!' He said he would be thrilled to get such an experienced navigator, but would I be prepared to take on a pilot with no operational time to his credit? I liked his honesty and we shook hands to seal a deal that lasted beyond the end of the war with never a cross word between us. He was six years older than me, married with a baby son and later I found that he was an accomplished classical pianist. His wife and her sister were lovely singers and broadcast regularly as a duo on the popular dinnertime show 'Workers' Playtime' – and, importantly for me, he was a dog lover (shades of Malta!).

We started flying together at once doing all the exercises I had before taught there but when my presence was not necessary I was used as an instructor. One day there was a heavy overcast at about 2,000 feet, which we were supposed to climb above to do practice interceptions. But at 18,000 feet we were still in thick cloud. Suddenly we juddered and fell into a vertical dive rapidly building up such an airspeed that the weight of 'G' forces pinned us to our seats. I shouted to Gordon 'We have iced up, pull out, pull out.' 'I can't!' he screamed 'I am using all my strength but it isn't enough.' 'Try using your trimmer,' I shouted back and at about 4,000 feet we slowly began to level out. 'Jeeze Goz,' he said 'How did you think of that?' 'Oh I had an experience with a trimmer at Tangmere,' I replied as I gratefully remembered my episode with dear Peter, but I did not elaborate. We were not yet 'out of the wood' for it took us an hour to get the undercart down and when we did we were still in cloud so the Station Commander who was in the

Control Tower offered to guide us in using the Blind Approach equipment. At less than 250 feet we broke through the cloud base to see the camp water tower flash by our port wing, nowhere near the runway. I did not know that in his stress Gordon had forgotten to switch his transmitter off and all the ops room heard me bawling 'Tell him to b—r off, I'll get you down' (or words to that effect). Back came the reply 'Message received and understood.' Appalled by our gaff we went quiet until Gordon said 'Don't worry Goz, I'll apologise to him in the Mess.' I did my stuff with a perfect blind landing and when we got out we walked round the kite for ages for somehow it did not look 'right' and finally we saw why – the port engine was slightly lower than the other. The tremendous 'G' forces that had been put on the aircraft pulling out of the dive had twisted the port wing, jamming the pneumatic arms that lowered the undercart and the aircraft had to be declared a 'write off'. Gordon did apologise to the Group Captain. 'Not to worry old boy,' he said, 'I do understand, it gave the girls in the Tower a good laugh and Gosling's language is so colourful isn't it?' I was glad at the outcome for I had been told he had tried his best to get me a 'gong' and had been told it was now too late to rectify the error but he had managed to get the Mention in Despatches for me and I really rated him.

Johnny and Les arrived and with Gordon and me the four of us had some merry evenings together going to lots of hostelries in Gordon's little Morris 8 car. With Gordon having a wife and child I realised I also had a responsibility to them and so I was glad I had decided never to over indulge. In early July we left Johnny and his oppo behind for a while as the advanced courses were moved to Cranfield's satellite drome, Twinwoods, and I had to exchange my 'en suite' room for a bunk in a 1940s version of a WWI wooden hut. The steel girdered skeleton was filled with a single course of brickwork, and condensation made it so damp that rust was everywhere, even affecting the plumbing. The airfield was built on sand, putting me in mind of Abu Sueir, and the buildings were prime examples of Jerry building at its worst. Gordon got some good news – he had been promoted to Flight Lieutenant and he insisted on taking me for a slap up meal in Bedford but we found the menus had been so restricted by rationing that we eventually decided to settle for a few beers. We were lucky to find a fish and chip shop open on our way home as fat for frying and fish were severely rationed so they had to restrict the days they opened. We continued the curriculum including air-to-ground and air-to-air firing until on 28 August our posting came through and we got a plum, County of Middlesex Squadron No. 604.

So we packed our bags and left unlovely Twinwoods without any regret – it had certainly not been our favourite abode. We said goodbye to friends, phoned Johnny and Les (who told us his wife was pregnant) at Cranfield, collected our logbooks from the Flight Hut and got our clearance from the Adjutant. We set off in Gordon's car (no train warrants, thanks) and as soon as we cleared the camp we stopped for we could not wait any longer to read our assessments from the course. Gordon had done well and was pleased but I was delighted for mine read 'Above Average. Should be an asset to any Squadron', which was praise indeed!

No. 604 was a famous old Auxiliary Squadron formed in 1930 with DH 9As (affectionately known to all in the RAF as Nineacks) and had progressed through Wapitis, Harts, Demons, Gladiators and Blenheims until it received its first Beaus and joined the Night Fighter Force. Many of its original 'weekend' pilots (most of whom had been 'in the city') had so distinguished themselves that their names had become well known. It was presently stationed at Scorton near Catterick, which meant I would be able to get a direct train from Darlington to Donny.

As we drove along I thought what a roller coaster ride the last few months had been for me and chuckled to myself at our feuds with the ground staff. The news of Peter and Hayton had been devastating but it had been good to see Johnny again. After losing two prospective oppos I had been third time lucky for Cranfield had come up with Gordon. Already I was taken with him for although I was the younger he treated me like his older brother and he sang my praises to all and sundry. I thought how good everyone at 51 OTU had been for they had made me so welcome despite my unintended affront and sent me off with the best assessment I had ever seen. I had been so fortunate I began to wonder if the man who dealt the cards had ever existed – he could never have been so benevolent. Could it be that one, or more, of my family who had 'passed on' and had so adored me as a child, was watching over me for I was certainly having more than my fair share of lucky escapes. I did not know – all I knew was that I was really happy, life was good and I burst into song.

CHAPTER TWENTY-THREE

Back in the Old Routine

So we arrived at Scorton, Flight Sergeant Gosling, the much travelled, war scarred veteran at twenty-two, and the ingénue Flight Lieutenant Hayhurst, both of us delighted to be going on ops. He was looking forward to a new experience and I to returning to the camaraderie of life on a squadron, which I had missed more than I would admit. Gordon pulled up at the Guard House and enquired the way to the Adjutant's office where we were told we had been allotted to 'B' Flight. Then Gordon was directed to the Officers' Mess whilst I was told to await transport to my billet. Soon a van arrived and I loaded my gear expecting to be driven to a billet on a dispersed site, and dispersed it certainly was, three miles away in the married quarters on Catterick Airfield. The old grass airfield with no runways was too small for modern aircraft so the hangars were now used as a spares depot and the housing as accommodation. I guessed they were built in the early 1930s and it showed for they were cramped and damp but were situated by the side of the old Great North Road only 100 yards from the Station Hotel. Fifty yards further on was the station and goods yard where Italian prisoners of war unloaded supplies for the massive nearby Army camp. There was also a level crossing where the main Great North road went over the main East Coast railway line. Had the ale been better and the landlord less surly it would have been an ideal watering hole but few of the troops taking the train for a night out in Darlington called at the pub to kick start a riotous evening.

There was a regular RAF transport service to Scorton and I soon got used to the arrangement especially as Gordon picked me up in his car each night to explore the local hostelries. He brought a couple of officers with him to guide us and on the second night I recognised our 'B' Flight Commander, Squadron Leader 'Sandy' Carmichael, a lovely teddy bear of a man, sat in the backseat. This showed Gordon had already made his mark in the Officers' Mess for we were certainly moving in exalted company, but when I saw who was sat beside him I was stunned. It was dear old 'Dusty' Miller, now a Flight Lieutenant and a DFC, with a wide grin on his face. He and I had so much to catch up on from the news of old chums at Tangmere to the fate of the lads from Malta. He too had a new oppo as his old navigator had been declared unfit to fly again and sent on a lecture tour of factories making Beaus to boost the workers' moral. We did not envy the adoration he was getting from dozens of females for we were back on ops and we agreed that was where we were at home. There was much to talk about for Malta had been relieved and 1435 Flight had become a full blown squadron flying Spitfires (we had been right to suspect that something underhand was going on) and Virgil Paul Brennan had been killed in an accident in his native Australia. There were relatively few night fighter squadrons and we talked of the many crews we had met when bad weather made us divert to other aerodromes or they diverted to our base. We considered ourselves to be a select group for we had the fastest twin-engined aircraft and used the most secret up to date equipment. It was my happiest night since I had met Johnny again.

On 10 September I flew with 'Dusty' for my competence on the new Mk 8 AI to be tested, which was a formality for I had instructed on the centimetric system at Cranfield. The arrow type transmitting aerials of the Mk 4 sets were replaced by a parabolic mirror, much like a TV dish, which spun at high speed covering a forty-five-degree cone-shaped area ahead of the plane. This cut out the ground returns, which had previously restricted our range to our height, and we could now 'see' up eight miles with ease. There was only one cathode-ray tube showing distant targets as a 'blip' at its outside rim, which became a full circle in the centre as we got to close range. It was a vast improvement but it came at a price – the aggressive nose of our Beau had sprung an ugly wart (called a 'thimble') housing the parabolic mirror making it look as if it had been stung by a bee!

Having passed this test Gordon and I took our place on the Flight's two days on, two days off roster and at 04.00 hours on 24 September we were scrambled to look for the dinghy of a bomber that had 'ditched' returning from a raid. We were surrounded by bomber aerodromes and were often asked to assist badly shot up or lost aircraft by guiding them home. It was a cold pitch black night and we flew at full speed for we could imagine ourselves in their situation. We crossed the coast near Whitby at 6,000 feet and went over to Seaton Air Sea Rescue Control who directed us to an area some twenty miles out to sea. They explained that the crew's May Day call had been so faint they had been unable to get a 'fix' on their position but said an ASR boat had already put to sea and gave us the R/T channel to contact it directly. This we did asking its Captain to fire a Very light so we could see his position and when he did so we saw the flare was miles away. A little later I thought I spotted a light blinking in the inky darkness and told Gordon to orbit the spot. After a few moments I confirmed my sighting and told Gordon it appeared that someone was trying to send a Morse message but I could not read it. As a wireless operator it would have been no problem for me and I could only assume that the message was being disrupted by the roughness of the sea below. Gordon called the rescue boat who asked us to fire a Very light so that he could steer towards it and this I did every five minutes or so until I ran out of cartridges. We reported this to the boat's Captain and he replied thanking us for our assistance and saying he was near enough to see and we could go home.

We had been airborne over two hours and on our way back we were jubilant that we had saved the crew's lives. When we landed the Station Commander was waiting in the Flight Hut but instead of good news he had a sad tale to tell. The ASR controller had rung to thank him for our cooperation and said 'That navigator must have fantastic eyesight for the light was on a float bobbing about on the water marking the nets of a boat fishing in restricted waters. It was remarkable that he spotted it from over a mile in the air. Please convey my thanks to the crew who managed the "rescue" in such an efficient manner – quite admirable!' He had then invited the squadron to come to see their high-speed boats and be taken for a trip. Our Flight went a week later and we were shown around their boats powered by two Napier aircraft engines and their newest American ones with three big radial engines. Unfortunately there was a heavy fog, which precluded a high-speed run, so our high speed trip had to be cancelled. You would have thought that we would have been feted by 'B' Flight but instead we suffered a backlash as it did not go down well with some for after only three weeks we had already made a name for ourselves. We heard no more about the ditched crew so in official language they would be reported as lost presumed dead.

The trouble was that there were no 'Huns' about ('trade' we called it) and many had been on the squadron for months without making a contact. In the south of England some squadrons had been allowed to go 'intruding' into Northern France (but only with Mk 4 equipment, Mk 8 was too secret to risk losing) to seek out 'trade' that no longer came to them, just as the Germans had done to us at Church Fenton. I had always supposed that the rush to 'crew up' with me was due solely to my expertise but now I began to realise it was also because I was seen as being 'lucky' – I attracted 'trade'! Of course it was no such thing – I had suffered the same way at Tangmere and my 'luck' was getting posted to Malta where 'trade' was plentiful but a repeat was unlikely. There was no hostility towards me but I never made a friendship on 604 Squadron as I had with Johnny but I needed none for I was always out with Gordon and his officer pals.

Every week our clique went to the vaudeville or pantomime in Darlington and we called ourselves 'The Hippodrome Cowboys' but I am sorry to say we were not always as well behaved as befitted officers and gentlemen. I was enjoying life with a splendid pilot who had become my best friend, doing a job I loved, with officer friends who just could not understand the class discrimination I had encountered at Tangmere. They only cared that I had proved I was a damned good navigator and the chip fell from my shoulders. This was what I had always envisaged life in the RAF would be like before I joined up – who could ask for more?

Throughout October and November we did what I had done a year ago at Tangmere, we took off in pairs to practise interceptions only now we were not restricted by the proximity of the Continent and our patrol line was sixty miles off the coast. To and fro we went, frankly bored out of our minds, but without 'trade' there was no option. We had to be prepared 'just in case' – that was the night fighters' lot.

On 1 December 1943 I was promoted to Warrant Officer and proudly strutted around in my new officer-type uniform and though I kept my brevet (wing) I no longer had my hard earned wireless operator badge on my sleeve. The royal badge on my cuff bore the inscription '*Dieu et Mon Droit*', which roughly translated meant 'God and my Right' but every Warrant Officer I ever met swore it really meant 'My God I'm Right'. I also received a pay rise, which if my memory serves me well brought me up to 17 shillings and 6 pence a day (ie 87 new pence) or roughly three times what Dad got. This helped to offset the rising cost of ale and at last I was able to stay almost solvent throughout the week but on the 10th I earned my pay.

The only 'trade' available to us was tantalisingly just out of our reach for daily at 35,000 feet a specially adapted Ju 88 German weather plane flew over just 2,000 feet above our service ceiling. Some crews had struggled up to fire at it but their propellers could not get enough 'bite' on the thin air at that height and the moment they opened fire they stalled and fell a couple of thousand feet. By the time they recovered the intruder was long gone but more worryingly their guns had also jammed. At first the armourers suspected the reason was that the guns were icing up but remembering similar trouble we had in Malta 'Dusty' Miller and I persuaded them to test the ammunition. Gordon and I were sent out to sea to fire a complete operational load of ammo to test our theory. The load consisted of incendiary, explosive, explosive/incendiary and ball shells with not too many tracer rounds for at night they dazzled the pilot and destroyed his night vision. We got down fairly low to the water before Gordon opened up when suddenly there was a bang and I felt a stabbing pain in my shoulder, which spun me round in my seat. The plane shot steeply upwards, filled with smoke and I lost voice contact with Gordon until I saw that my intercom plug had come out. When I plugged it in again he was shouting 'Goz, Goz are you all right? What has happened?' Gingerly I felt for blood on my shoulder before I replied 'Yes, but there's a b—dy great hole in the floor and I can hear crackling like there is something on fire.' We set course for base at full speed and when we landed it was found that a high explosive round had jammed in the breech block and the following round had detonated it. The whole high tensile steel block weighing some 15 or 20 lbs had been blown to bits and it must have been one of the splinters that had hit me. Luckily it did not pierce my Mae West (inflatable vest) and the fire I thought I heard was the noise of the sealing tape from the demolished gun bay doors whipping against the fuselage in the slipstream. All the 20 mm ammo on the station had to be scrapped but again I had been lucky for the explosion had been only a foot below and a yard in front of me and the sliver of steel a mere six inches from my face.

When the new ammo arrived a Norwegian pilot we had on the squadron was sent to test it and he was so low when he opened fire the sudden blast almost forced him into the sea. His propellers touched the waves but he literally heaved the aircraft back into the air with sheer brute force. When he landed incredibly eighteen inches of both props were curled back like a child's windmill – I doubt if anyone else could have done it. He was so strong that when a fifteen stone man teased him about his accent he lifted him into the air and held him against the wall with one hand, his feet inches off the ground. He was usually very placid and a great character who amused us every night by inviting us to accompany him into the 'willage for Viskey and witamins'.

A heavy fall of snow helped to put us in a festive mood for Xmas and to welcome in 1944 and I thought how fortunate I was to have such a cushy life – I should have known it was too good to last. I suppose it began to go wrong from the time the pot bellied stove that provided the only heat in the Flight Hut refused to ignite, leaving us shivering. It defeated all our efforts to kindle it until finally, in desperation, someone devised a sure solution. First we filled the bottom with newspaper to which we added firewood and coke followed by a couple of pints of aviation petrol but we then had to find a safe way to ignite it. Then some genius came up with a brilliant idea – fire a Very pistol round down the cast iron flue pipe. It was so obvious we wondered why we had not thought of it so we trooped outside and summoned the ground crew to find a ladder to get on to the roof. There was much discussion as to who would get on the roof but as we were all basically cowards we detailed the 'erk' who brought the ladder. So up he went, slithering on the snow covered roof, put the pistol down the chimney and fired. There was a sort of a 'whoosh', some window panes flew out, we dived to the ground and when we got to our feet the 'erk' was hanging on to the guttering shouting for help. We helped him down and when we went inside we saw the stove had disintegrated and the flue pipe had shattered, smothering everything in soot. At this point the squadron's Commanding Officer appeared in the doorway staring in disbelief. He asked who was responsible and as no one volunteered he picked the one he thought was the most likely culprit. 'Gosling' he shouted 'into my office.' He clearly thought I was a bit of a live wire and therefore a likely suspect but his interrogation proved futile for how could I explain that it really had been a team effort!

Our CO had a double barrelled name, Constable-Maxwell, and although I respected him for he had a DFC, which proved he was a brave man, and I knew he was very competent pilot, Michael was not a favourite of mine! He was a scion of the aristocracy, said to be about eighty-ninth in succession to the throne – it varied according to the birth or demise of members of the hierarchy. Of course he could never have got the top job for he came from a large Catholic family – two of his much older brothers were Group Captains and Station Commanders. I was very much in favour of our monarchy but I felt he took his standing far too seriously and there was more than a whiff of class distinction about him. I suspect he disliked the company I kept (NCOs should not mix with officers as I did) but I do not know if he had ever voiced his feelings and the happy relationship with my mates continued. His navigator was a jolly nice bloke called Flight Lieutenant Johnny Quinton who had little combat experience and he regularly sought my advice on navigational matters. He clearly relied on my discretion and I was careful not to divulge our discussions to anyone but Gordon, who I knew I could trust implicitly, lest he got a 'wigging from His Eminence'. This was petty for the decisions we arrived at often benefited the whole squadron.

There was now room for us on the camp so we left the married quarters at Catterick and at last met the villagers of Scorton whom we invited into the Mess every Saturday night to play tombola (lotto). It broke the ice and we began to enjoy their company at the local hostelry where we became regulars. It was there that we solved the mystery of the spooky moans and blood curdling yells we heard in the pitch darkness after we had flown and were returning to our billets late at night or early in the morning. At first the locals were reluctant to talk but eventually they confided that they came from a Catholic hospital in the village, which was full of demented and grotesquely malformed boys, run by monks who were dedicated to their care.

On 9 January we were on patrol at 16,000 feet under Seaton Snook GCI control when they directed us to return immediately as the weather was closing down fast at base. Gordon began a swift descent using our height to speed our return and almost at once I felt my eardrums pop with the change in pressure. I tried the old trick of holding my nose and blowing but to no avail and as I was in considerable pain I told him to level out until I had equalised the pressure. I knew that if I failed it could mean permanent deafness and the end of my flying career if the eardrum membrane ruptured but we had to get back before the weather closed in. We slowly began to descend, levelling out when I could no longer stand the pain, and got down just in time. Then I was whisked away in the ambulance Gordon had radioed ahead for. Peter the MO was waiting at the sick bay with kaolin poultices, which he clapped on my ears. They were so hot I let out an almighty yell and shot across the room. 'Don't be such a cissy,' he said and dabbed them on and off his own ear. So admitting I had a low pain threshold I gingerly offered up my ears. I had a reasonably comfortable night but I could hear fluid rushing from side to side each time I turned over. Late the following morning I got up and started to shave but when I raised the pads I got a shock for both my ears were just massive blisters. I went back to the sick bay and roundly cursed a repentant Peter who said 'Sit down and I will cut them off'. 'You BF,' I ranted, 'you did not hold the poultices on long enough to feel the heat' as he applied lashings of vivid Gentian Violet to the open wounds. He said he was terribly sorry and because I would be too sore to put my helmet on he would give me a week's leave. I phoned Gordon who was relieved that my hearing was not at risk and got in a carriage on a train from Darlington to Donny opposite two startled middle-aged ladies. With great purple pads on my ears they assumed I could not hear them debating which sexually transmitted disease I had contracted. I got two more weeks' leave before I could bear to put my helmet on again, which was some consolation, but I was so impatient to fly I had to press him in the end.

Gordon and I resumed our partnership when the squadron was faced with an unexpected crisis. Some of our aircraft had been fitted with a newly developed version of the Hercules engine in which the bottom cylinders 'oiled up' when running at low revs as when taxiing. To avoid taxiing they were parked just twenty yards off the runway but then they started to cough and splutter on the crucial take-off, which was extremely dangerous. When Gordon reported that they even did it when at slow cruising speed our 'chiefy' ('B' Flight's senior engine fitter) refused to believe him. Incensed at this Gordon said 'Right! Get in my aircraft and I'll prove it!' He marched to our plane and with 'chiefy' stood in the well behind him we took off again. At 2,000 feet Gordon throttled back and almost at once there was a bump as the starboard engine cut out, slewing us violently to the right. The 'chiefy' yelled 'Yes, I see sir, I'll fix it!' When he got down he was as white as a sheet. Alas he could not fix it and later that week one of our aircraft was taking off when just as it got airborne an engine cut, swinging it to the right, hitting the top of some trees and crashing in flames into a quarry. The pilot's body was found after two days' digging six feet down under an engine but the navigator was rescued by the crash crew, ablaze, and terribly burned by Perspex melting like treacle as he tried to break through his canopy. He returned after weeks of treatment to collect his gear before going to the famous Dr Archibald McIndoe for plastic surgery. He had been a young Adonis, very popular with the WAAFs, but now he had no nose, ears, eyelids, lips or hair, and his hands were skeletal. He could hardly talk for breathing the scorching heat had even burned down into his windpipe and we were told that only the experimental use of new drugs like penicillin had saved his life. So far as we knew the new engines never came into production; we were just happy to see them disappear.

One day I was playing billiards in the Mess after a night flying test when there was a rumbling explosion and remembering Malta I dived under the table. Emerging cautiously I phoned ops to enquire what was going on only to be told they had no idea but there was a large cloud of dust over Catterick way. The truth soon became known. The evening train to Darlington had been so heavily loaded with troops it had difficulty starting as it tried to leave the station. Its funnel had emitted a shower of sparks, which set fire to the ammunition being unloaded by the Italian prisoners of war in the sidings. The enormous blast had demolished the station, the level crossing and the Station Hotel, killing everyone in the vicinity, but luckily the train itself just got far enough away to escape. I passed that way a couple of days later and it looked as if the whole area had been completely razed to the ground by bulldozers. In the interest of national security the news was completely censored and we never found out how great the death toll had been but it must have been considerable.

There was still no 'trade' but instead of the usual fixed ground stations we started to work with mobile and even shipborne installations. For some time there had been rumours that an invasion was contemplated in 1944 and our new regime certainly seemed to confirm that intention. This change gave us a welcome break from our boring routine but what was to come sent our spirits soaring sky high.

Gordon and I went on leave early in February and when we got back we found the whole place was buzzing with excitement – all our Beaus had gone and the dispersals were full of Mosquitos! They had the same Mk 8 'thimble nose' but with their Merlin engines (as used in the Spitfire) they looked like svelte ladies, sleek and fast, unlike the brutally aggressive Beaus. Amazingly they were made from wood, which had been progressively phased out of use in the RAF over the past twenty years and the old trade of 'Chippy Rigger' had to be revived. There was keen, even cut throat, competition to obtain an early place in the queue to learn how to fly these 'Wooden Wonders'. Apart from the aircraft recognition models we had studied our only previous knowledge of them had come on a visit to Seaton Snook GCI when we had seen a symbol simply haring across the North Sea plotting table. 'What the Devil is that?' we had enquired. 'Oh, that is a Mosquito coming back from Sweden,' they said. 'They are unarmed and bring back ball bearings and sometimes shady anonymous passengers. They are so fast nothing can catch them!' We had no idea then that we would soon be swapping the previously fastest twin-seat aircraft in the world for what had now superseded it as undisputed holder of that coveted title. We could scarcely believe our luck but it confirmed our belief that we were the RAF's elite!

Gordon took his turn to qualify and on 19 February he took me for my first flight in a Mossie and now sat in the cockpit alongside Gordon with the Merlins purring beside me in no time I was totally enchanted and bewitched. You always had to be the master of the Beau or it would bite you but this was a new sensation, like you and the plane were in harmony. It was a revelation, flew like a bird, and did things the Beau could never do like steep diving turns into a dead engine. Best of all I was seated side by side with Gordon not halfway down the fuselage. We spent the rest of the month getting to know our new mounts until on the 29th of the month (it was a leap year) we returned to ops. I was so happy I sang and sang even more than before.

We continued patrolling in our new Mossie and agreed that it was far superior to our Beau even though some deficiencies became apparent. The rear view was not as good even when you faced aft by kneeling on your seat. The Merlin engine was superb but its Achilles heel lay in its glycol cooling system. If the coolant radiator was pierced by even a single bullet that was it – the engine seized up. The radial Hercules of the Beau was more rugged for it was air cooled and would continue to function even if a whole cylinder was shot away. There was, however, one fault that outweighed all the others and really frightened us – the escape hatch was potentially a killer! The Beau had two excellent large exits but the Mossie had only one so small that a large navigator wearing the standard parachute on his bottom could easily become jammed in it. This had already been known to happen and as the pilot could not exit until his oppo got out both had been killed. Not only was the hatch too small it also lacked the Beau's slipstream deflector, which saved you breaking your back or a limb on the tail wheel. The retracting tail wheels were locked down on both aircraft for no one could stop them shimmying (we called it 'Katying' from the line in the Ragtime song 'I wish I could shimmy like my sister Kate'). It could be so severe on landing that the whole tail plane threatened to break off. Practice in diving out of the hatch on to bedding biscuits laid on the ground proved our fears were well founded and small, preferably miniscule, oppos were suddenly in great demand. At 5 feet 5 inches and a mere 7 stone 11 lbs Gordon reckoned me an even greater asset! Our parachutes had to be repacked monthly as the silk generated static electricity, which could cause the canopy to 'candle' (stick together). I recalled that the last time I went to the Parachute Section to collect mine I had seen a Yankee 'back pack' type parachute only 4 inches thick, which would be ideal. So I nipped round there and was in luck for they had just one and as the packer was a Donny lad I 'bagged' it on the spot and I used it ever after.

Smithy was the son of an old workmate, and had married into the Priestnall ice cream family who also had a café only yards from the station. It was on the ground floor of the YMCA hostel next door to the Grand Theatre and it was hit by a bomb, one of the few that had been dropped on the town. On 'Bombers' Moon' nights the moonlight silvered the distinctive shapes of lakes and meandering rivers, the regular outlines of canals and reservoirs and railway tracks polished by constant rail traffic making them invaluable navigational aids. The lines to Leeds and Hull joining the main East Coast track would make Doncaster an easily identifiable target but being smaller than the big conurbations probably saved it from the awful destruction suffered, not once but many times, by every major city in the country.

One night when I was home on leave (from Yatesbury) I remember standing in our back garden watching Sheffield getting blitzed again. Even from twenty miles away we could see the flares, the AA bursts, the flashes of sticks of bombs and the whole sky filled with smoke lit up by raging fires. Throughout there was a drum roll of explosions interspersed with crashing bursts as if gigantic tympani were being assaulted by manic demons – it was a glimpse into hell. Next day petrol buses were commandeered from all the surrounding towns as many bus depots had been destroyed and the city was littered with burnt out trams, but the munitions workers still had to get to their jobs.

The Germans flew down a radio beam from the Continent and when it was intersected by another signal from Norway they dropped their bombs even if the target was obscured by cloud. It was old technology used for years by airlines in America and our scientists had found a way to 'bend' these beams. If they were bent by more than a fraction it would be detected by the Germans gyro compasses and 'give the game away' but a slight deflection would be enough to divert them from their probable target, the Sheaf Valley, a swathe of heavy industry extending as far as Rotherham. It contained Britain's biggest furnaces, rolling mills, lathes, and machine shops producing massive guns for the Navy and goodness knows what else vital to the war effort. There was a downside for if the hoax succeeded it was certain the 'bent' beam would concentrate the bombing on the city centre, wiping it out and causing a heavy loss of life. Many thought that someone made the agonising decision to 'bend' the beam, others averred that 'beam bending' was not used but the Don Valley miraculously escaped major damage and the city centre certainly suffered – we shall never know the truth. Such destruction was now a thing of the past and the only 'trade' was 'tip and run' raids carried out by single-seat day fighter-bombers.

To help relieve the boredom caused by the absence of any 'trade' I began to practise 'blind' landings – a branch of the navigators' art that had interested me even before our experience at Cranfield. Gordon readily agreed when I suggested that we use the system for all our night landings. He arranged with ops that when approaching base he would call in 'Q' code for the barometric pressure at ground level and thereafter he would ask for no further directions except for permission to land. We set this figure on our altimeters and as this gave us our height I had all the information I needed to make a 'blind' landing. You never knew when it might come in handy!

Our preparations for the Second Front continued to gather momentum, and we were informed that we would shortly be housed in tents to increase our mobility. The handful among us who had lived in tents before accepted our perceived superiority with humility knowing that the climate in Africa was no guide to the vagaries of the weather we could expect in Europe. The Assistant Adjutant, a wet behind the ears Pilot Officer, was tasked to find a suitable site in the Wolds behind us for a trial run. 'Not to worry,' he said, 'I have found a lovely little dip in the hills where we shall be nicely sheltered from the wind.' At the weekend, joking but mildly apprehensive, we piled into a couple of lorries and set off in pouring rain to begin our life under canvas. We arrived to find the 'nice little dip' was certainly sheltered but so full of rainwater that only duck boards floating among the tops of tents were visible. Laughing our heads off we piled into the lorries and drank the 'emergency supplies' we had brought on our way back to our comfortable Mess – our initiation into the rigours of mobile operations was temporarily on hold.

On 23 April the squadron moved to Church Fenton, not into tents but the comfort of a front line Night Fighter Aerodrome. Our participation in the invasion of Europe was confirmed when our aircraft were painted with broad black and white stripes near the tail plane and outboard of the engines giving them a piratical look. It was further confirmed when we were taken out of 11 Group and proudly became members of 2nd TAF (2nd Tactical Air Force).

I found the only change since I left Fenton was that the Station Band was now led by a lad from Matlock called Sergeant Jimmy Leach who played the then novel electric organ with his group 'The Organolians'. Monday to Friday he had a regular half hour slot on the BBC and as a result he had become nationally famous. The songs he had written, 'The Little Boy that Santa Claus Forgot' and 'Serenade to a Lonely Star', were all the rage. He was very popular on the camp and on Saturday nights at the Station Dance the top of his piano was filled with pints of free ale. He demolished these at a phenomenal rate with his left hand whilst he kept the tempo going with his right so adroitly that no one noticed, a skill few acquired. The last time I saw him was after the war when he was playing in the bandstand in the gardens of Southport's lovely Lord Street.

I heard some bad news about this time – that gentle man Fitzrandolph who had hoped I might be the ticket to get him on to ops had been killed at Twinwoods. Scuttlebutt had it that he had offered to fly two pupils there from Usworth in his Anson to begin their course but on the landing circuit his wing had been shorn off in a collision with a Beau. All aboard the Anson had been killed but the Beau's crew had survived. How cruel that his innate kindness, which had endeared him to us all, should be his undoing.

Early in May Gordon's broken back started playing him up and he had to go into hospital and to my delight 'Dusty' Miller 'bagged' me as his oppo. With glee we practised 'intruding', revelling in the thrill of our Mossie's speed, which seemed terrific at such a low level. We simulated 'shooting up' goods yards, castles, stations, Army camps, other airfields and everything that came into our view. It was great fun and 'Dusty' said to me 'Wouldn't it be great if this was the real thing?' It was exhilarating and I heartily agreed but somehow I had an uneasy feeling of *déjà vu*, which I pondered in bed that night. The penny dropped when I remembered Danny in his latter days in Malta – 'Dusty' was showing the same over confidence, believing he was indestructible. It was easy to slip into the near euphoric state we called 'gung-ho', imperceptible to you but obvious to others. It lulled 'old timers' who had escaped unscathed from so many close encounters with disaster into a feeling that they were invincible and they began to take chances. We loved our new Mossies so much it was even easier to become careless and make a fatal error of judgement. 'Dusty' was my pal and such a great guy so I fervently hoped I was wrong.

It was the end of May before Gordon returned and though I said nothing of my fears for 'Dusty' I reiterated that gung-ho was not my style – I believed in trying to envisage every possible contingency and being prepared for it in advance. His mother had confided to me that when he was returning from leave and she bade him to take care he used to say 'Don't worry Mum, Goz will look after me!' His faith in me was touching but I knew there was always a chance that something that no one could foresee might still happen and you had to be ready to instantly react.

Meantime on 6 May 'Dusty' and I moved with the squadron to Hurn just outside Bournemouth where we were billeted in a nearby former boys' school. It had been derelict from the start of the war and was very dilapidated and had no electricity but we cared not for it was a move nearer to Occupied Europe. It was the start of a nomadic period when we moved from Station to Station like gypsies, never staying long in one place.

Scuttlebutt came up with some bad news, Jack Dye my old friend from Tangmere and fellow Yorkshireman, who had wangled my transfer to Usworth had been killed. By strange coincidence it was in the same way as Fitzrandolf, only this time the tale was that he had collided with a Sterling bomber over Norwich while on night ops. I was not surprised for several times when Ground Control had directed us to assist lost bombers it had landed us in trouble. Most commonly we tried to guide them out of gun defended zones whilst being shot at by our own Ack-Ack (and on occasion by the bomber itself even after we put our navigation lights on to reassure them). Usually this was because a radar device they carried called IFF (Identification Friend from Foe), which gave out a coded recognition signal, was not switched on so they appeared to be hostiles. Why was it not switched on? Many bomber crews believed that enemy night fighters could 'home in' on IFF transmissions. Whether this was true or not, we forgave them for the poor souls were having a torrid time and their losses were high, but they certainly gave us some torrid moments.

In early June we were restricted to short Night Flying Tests as the Germans might be alerted by increased aerial activity but we had to be prepared in case they made pre-emptive raids to disrupt the build up to the coming onslaught. Every night we waited at full readiness but the possible attack never came. On one of these NFTs Gordon and I heard the most extraordinary R/T conversation we had ever heard or were likely ever to hear again. In a calm, matter of fact, unemotional R/T monotone we heard someone call 'Hello Blue One this is Blue Two going down in flames behind you.' Amazed, Gordon said to me 'Did you hear that?' and before I had time to answer we saw a great spout of flame and smoke shoot up about three miles away. There were several Typhoon and Tempest Squadrons in the area; we had seen them practising low level rocket attacks and we knew they were all having trouble with their Napier Sabre engines. We never found out who it was but we were sure he was too low to bale out and must have been killed.

The whole countryside around us, every wood and coppice, manor house and farmstead, was bursting at the seams with troops and their equipment. There were tanks of all types, including 'funnies' – tanks specially adapted for the forthcoming landing, able to swim, detonate mines, track lay, cross bridges or flame throw. There was transport of every kind from massive tank transporters to Jeeps all hidden or camouflaged and to keep their presence secret civilians were not allowed to enter a 'no go' zone miles deep.

I spent the idle hours of waiting in the dispersal looking back over my time with 604 Squadron. I had come to realise that the class conscious officers I had met who had used the advantages of their rank to exercise their bigotry were not typical of the species. Associating with Gordon, 'Dusty' and others had made me aware that the majority were decent chaps and loyal companions. The 'chip' on my shoulder, which I had carried for so long, had disappeared and my disappointment at not getting my 'gong' had gone with it. My innate good humour had returned and I was a much happier bunny. I also recognised that my relationship with Gordon had changed too – he, and I, had 'come of age'. To his great credit he had assimilated all the 'know how' I had passed on to him and we were now a true partnership, which was how it should be. Even though I was no longer his mentor he continued to laud me for when I flew with other pilots they all wanted me to sing 'like you do with Gordon'. Except old 'Dusty', a staunch Welshman, born and bred in the land of song, who laughingly described my vocal efforts as an 'offence to the ears'. I also considered the future. It looked like I was going to be twice lucky – first to have been in the siege of Malta and now I was going to participate in the greatest invasion the world had ever seen. The great day was clearly imminent, probably in a fortnight we thought, so when we heard the news on the wireless on 6 June we were taken by surprise. It was a sign of our enthusiasm that we expected that we would be sent to France at once but there was a lot of fighting to be done before Landing Fields could be secured and even then close support day fighters with their bombs and rockets would have priority. It was not until the 11th that we became involved doing an uneventful patrol off Cherboug and on the 12th we patrolled from Yvetot to Bernay when we witnessed a naval battle with 'E' Boats. It was frustrating to be sent on leave on the 16th for we felt sure that we should miss some of the action but we need not have worried. When we returned on the 27th the squadron was still at Hurn but had now been designated as part of No. 2 Fighter Pool. At the end of the month Michael Constable-Maxwell left us and in my logbook he had magnanimously written 'Good luck, Goz' despite our differences.

The new CO was Wing Commander Desmond Hughes DSO, DFC, the nicest man you could wish to meet who speedily endeared himself to everyone on the squadron. He was the very antithesis of Michael. He was jolly, sociable, approachable, down to earth and had wide experience – he was just the man we would have chosen ourselves.

On 10 July a grave-faced Gordon drew me on one side and I wondered what I had done wrong. Even though I had sensed that it was something awful I was totally unprepared for what he said. 'Goz I have some bad news for you, Tubby Daniels has been killed.' I literally staggered and he guided me to a chair. 'Sit down old lad, Desmond knew you would be upset so he asked me to break the news to you.' Then he gave me the details. Danny had been flying a Tempest from Ford one night and got too close to a V-1 flying bomb when he shot it down. His engine caught fire, his hood had been jammed by the blast so he could not bale out, he had ditched in the Thames Estuary and his body was recovered at low tide. I said 'Thank you Gordon and thank Desmond for his consideration.' As we were not due to fly that night I made my way directly to my billet where I am not ashamed to say I cried my eyes out.

All night my mind was in a turmoil. My lost award could not have been his fault, Danny had been my friend and we had been through so much together. When he came to Usworth I should have seen he was offering the hand of friendship and I had treated him churlishly like a petulant child. He really had wanted me to 'crew up' with him again to go on ops for at that time the special flight of Tempests with the speed to catch the fast ramjet-engined doodlebugs had not been formed. If I had gone for a beer with him he might have explained everything and now I should never know the truth. I tormented myself imagining his final moments, trapped in a blazing cockpit. How he must have suffered yet with superb skill he had ditched successfully. Getting too close was typical of the gung-ho syndrome I had noticed in Malta but he still might have 'made it', albeit to become another McIndoe guinea pig, if he had been able to open his canopy. He couldn't and he had drowned. My last thought before sleep mercifully claimed me, exhausted and distraught, was of that Church Parade at Goodwood when he had said of the Ford Padre 'That's the man I would like to bury me.' After he had travelled the world it seemed as if Fate had brought him back to Ford so that his wish could be granted. I wondered if he had a premonition? In the morning I reflected that all aircrew had known the risks when they volunteered but never thought their dreams of glory would have such a gruesome ending. I knew I must forget my futile recriminations. Life had to go on – so I began to count my blessings. I was doing a job I loved using state of the art technology, in an aircraft that everyone in the RAF wanted to fly, on a wonderful squadron with a marvellous CO and I had a great rapport with my pilot. It was difficult to imagine what more good fortune anyone could ask for.

On 12 July we moved to Colerne, near Bath, a permanent Station with a pronounced hump in the middle of its runway, which was the cause of us getting into deep trouble. One day we took off and instead of rising into the air we decided it would be fun to do some low flying down the valley at its end, forgetting R/T had only visual range. When we rose up again the R/T was buzzing with frantic calls to the RAF and civil emergency services to look for a crashed Mossie. Shamefacedly we admitted we were all right but we got one hell of a wigging from Desmond, after which he gave us an impish grin and said at least it had been a good exercise for the ground support. (We could not imagine Michael ever saying that.) With Bath being so far from the sea we were surprised that it was full of Navy types until we learned that their Stores Depots had made a strategic move there in 1939. Gordon and I took in the sights, the Roman baths (closed for the duration), the river, the graceful Georgian terraces and we ate in the upstairs drawing room of Beau Nash's house. The staple restaurant fare of Welsh Rarebit seemed strangely incongruous in such stately surroundings.

Since we had moved to 2nd TAF all our movements and operations had been carried out under their direct command. On the night of 17 July Gordon and I were tasked to do an exercise with a mobile control somewhere over the Bridgehead, which did not excite us for they did not have the experience or equipment of the static controllers. Our local control vectored us towards Cherbourg, then handed us over and at once they said 'We have 'trade' for you'. This was amazing for the *Luftwaffe* had been conspicuous by its absence due to the air superiority established by the

Typhoons, Tempests and Tornados whose rocket attacks had forced them to abandon their forward bases and move further inland. We were vectored towards Jersey and soon made contact with an aircraft climbing in circles over the island so I got on its tail and climbed after it, obtaining a 'visual' at 18,000 feet. Although we had been told it was definitely hostile we sat behind still turning and just below trying to identify it before we eventually agreed that it was a Ju 88. We were about to close to make our attack when it suddenly put its nose down and dived towards the east like a bat out of hell. For a moment we thought we had been spotted but we quickly realised it had been gaining height to make a high-speed dive to reach the safety of Occupied France.

Fast as it was going it was no match for the Mossie and I manoeuvred Gordon into position to open fire. We saw our gunfire strike home and bits of debris came hurtling past us so I reminded Gordon not to get too close. It was just as well I did for a moment later its port engine burst into flames and suddenly the whole plane exploded sending dozens of blazing pieces spiralling down.

When Gordon went to report our success on the R/T he found he had been transmitting all the time (again) so he apologised. The controller replied 'Wonderful, wonderful, it was just like being in the plane with you! It's our first! Congratulations!' and we could hear his mates were cheering in the background. On the way home Gordon was in raptures and I was delighted for him and when we landed Desmond was the first to greet us. He rushed to me and said 'They can't deny you now, Goz.' Of course he meant my 'gong' but perversely it did not seem to matter to me that much now. My discontent had never been motivated by false pride but by what I had perceived to be mainly class distinction. After the 'bus driver' episode at Tangmere who could blame me but the root of my belief lay way back in the desperate 1920s and the mean 1930s when the 'them' and 'us' culture had been rife. Now, I was on a squadron where I was well respected and accepted by my peers simply for myself. I had come to realise that my assessment had been wrong and the need for any award disappeared. I knew that Mum and Dad would be delighted and proud so my pleasure was for them at least as much as for myself.

On 25 July we moved to Zeals and back to Colerne just three days later. With all this moving about we were getting dizzy so it was a relief when on 4 August our ground crews got their orders to tranship to France and on the 6th we were to fly to join them. Although it was only a month since D-Day it had seemed a long wait but at long last my second great adventure was about to begin.

CHAPTER TWENTY-FOUR

The Collapse of the Third *Reich*

We nearly missed going to France with the rest of the squadron for on the day our orders came we were scheduled to make our last flight from Colerne to the Cherbourg area where we had our recent 'kill'. We hoped we would have success there again but when we arrived at the western end of our patrol line off Jersey our port engine started to run roughly and the coolant temperature began to rise steadily. We had two options, either cut the engine at once or continue to use it until it threatened to burst into flames. This would get us nearer to home and after talking it over we decided this was what we would do. After ten minutes we did not dare delay any longer so we cut the engine but it kept emitting showers of sparks. The temperature remained the same and the prop, despite being 'feathered' to stop it turning, still did occasional revolutions with a screeching noise. We now had a full blown emergency on our hands and Gordon made a May Day call, which was acknowledged by the Control Tower at Hurn. They instructed us to land there so I tuned to their beacon and we began a slow descent to increase our speed, regularly informing them of our progress. When we got near enough I told Gordon to ask if we could come straight in without doing a landing circuit as the engine was in a critical state. They cleared us to do so and as soon as we landed a truck led us to a safe dispersal where a fire crew and mechanics were waiting. As we were getting out the riggers put up some steps to remove the cowlings and a fitter followed them. There was a piecing scream and the man was hurled to the ground, jerking and rolling about, his arms flailing, fighting off his mates as they vainly tried to grab him. We rushed round from the starboard side. 'What has happened?' we enquired. 'Dunno sir, he got hold of the engine bearers to pull himself up and then this happened,' they replied. We knew at once for we had seen the engine block glowing white hot through the cowlings all the way home. 'He's burned his hands,' we told them. By the time the ambulance came he was lying and moaning, only half conscious, so they gave him an injection, which knocked him out, and rushed him to hospital to become another patient of the burns unit I supposed.

162

In the morning we went to the dispersal and were surprised when they told us they had found the cause of our trouble and the aircraft would be serviceable by noon. We asked if they had news of the fitter and they told us all the flesh had been burned from the inside of his fingers and palm right down to the bones. We took off at 12.20 hours on our way back to Colerne, full of relief for our deliverance from the previous evening. There was only one way to express our delight – a spot of exhilarating low flying. On this glorious summer day we flashed over the fields and woodlands of incomparable old England at nought feet thinking 'this is the life'. After forty minutes of this bliss the damned engine started playing up again and we landed in a sweat wondering if it would be repaired in time for our move abroad. Thereafter HK527 was christened 'The Toaster' by our fitters but, thankfully, they soon found the real fault and we were cleared to go.

We landed in France at a place called Picauville, not far from Bayeaux, to find we had been assigned to the American sector of the bridgehead because they had no night fighters of their own. I was not surprised for the ones I had trained at Usworth had never attained the standard of our RAF pupils and we had advised that they were not ready for further training. However, the Americans, desperate to create a night fighter force of their own quickly had insisted they were capable enough to proceed to Operational Training Units and horror stories of their progress (or rather the lack of it) began to reach us. One was that a Beau, with its notorious tendency to swing on take-off, had crashed into an Airmen's Mess killing a WAAF cook – it would have killed many more had it been mealtime. Now the Yanks had to admit that their attempt to take shortcuts in the making of a night fighter force had failed just as we had warned. It was not the first time they had ignored the freely offered advice that had taken us years of combat experience to acquire.

What happened next? Well, unbelievably, the following day we were sent back to the UK on leave in our clapped out Oxford hack. Impatient to get into the action, we returned to find the squadron had settled down to life in the USAAF and were enthusing about their rations. Every day a Thunderbolt fighter was sent up to 30,000 feet with a long-range belly tank to freeze the special mixture inside it. On landing the tank was opened to reveal luscious ice cream that was served with tinned peaches after our main course of meat with potatoes and sweetcorn. In England such luxuries had disappeared when the war began but operationally things were not so good. The landing strip (known as A8) had been bulldozed out of the middle of a wood, copiously sanded and then great rolls of thick roofing type felt laid on top joined together with tar. It was intended for single-engined fighters so when our heavier Mossies took off the seams came apart with what sounded like a sustained rasping bout of flatulence. Worse still, every night our own aerodrome defence Ack-Ack opened up at us as we were taking off. We soon learned to wait at the end of the 'strip' revving loudly until, after expending thousands of rounds firing at nothing, they calmed down a bit and then we sneaked off as quietly as we could.

The squadron was billeted in a sloping field with our HQ and the Officers'

Quarters in a chateau at the top and our NCOs' tents at the bottom. After I had done my stint I had to walk back in the dark between tapes marking a safe passage through a wood, which had not been cleared of mines, to my tent. One night, using my torch to avoid these hazards, I picked my way home, keeping a sharp look out for German paratroopers reported to be still on the loose in the area. Ready for a good night's kip, I put my revolver under my pillow and tumbled into bed but before I got to sleep I heard someone trying to undo the tent flap. Jerry paratroops I thought as I slipped quietly out of bed, holding my gun in front of me. In one slick movement I flung back the flap and thrust my gun forward straight into the face of – a cow!

The following morning should have been the first of our two rest days but Gordon came to my tent. 'Goz, I've got a job for you.' It did not surprise me for he constantly 'volunteered' his incomparable navigator (in his eyes). 'Yes, you are to fly back to England to take F/O Campbell (not his real name) under close arrest and escort him back here to face a court-martial.' I knew this officer well; he was a nice handsome lad who was always enthusing about his fiancée in Glasgow. He had gone AWOL (absent without leave) before we left England. At Colerne he had become infatuated with a WAAF and just before he went on leave she announced that she was pregnant with his child. He had not returned to the squadron when his leave ended and the Military Police had arrested him at his fiancée's home. They delivered him to Colerne, where I was to meet them and he was to fly us back in an aircraft that we had left there for repairs. I was packed and ready to go when Desmond appeared. 'Sorry Goz,' he said, 'but the Arresting Officer has to be of equal or superior rank to the prisoner so I have to send someone else.' Later that week we heard that the aircraft bringing them to the Continent had crashed and both of them had been killed. That could have, indeed should have, been me! Once again fate, or whatever rules our destiny, had been kind to me. The body was flown back to Scotland where his fiancée said 'I cannot believe Jim is in that coffin.' She was right; there were only scraps of flesh with rocks for makeweight. We debated if the crash was really an accident for there was little high ground on their route. Or was it that Jock realised he could not face the ignominy of his future. It truly did not matter!

On the morning of 12 August the CO called all the squadron aircrew to a meeting in the Mess tent and we wondered what was afoot. He was the last to arrive and looking stern he said 'Warrant Officer Gosling, step forward'. I thought 'Oh my God, what have I done wrong?' He continued:

I have received a cipher from the Air Officer commanding 2nd Tactical Air Force, it reads:
His Majesty the King on the commendation of the Air Commander in Chief has been graciously pleased to award the Distinguished Flying Cross to Warrant Officer D. Gosling 999332, 604 Squadron. Heartiest Congratulations, Steele.

'Goz, I know you cannot get ribbon over here' and then he took a DFC ribbon from his pocket. 'This was the first medal I ever got,' he said and he pinned it on my tunic. 'I can think of no one who deserves it more.' He shook my hand, then laughed out loud. 'You should have seen your face, it was a picture,' he said. What a wonderful gesture from a marvellous man! He was right, I was sweating like a pig, my knees were weak and you could have knocked me down with a feather!

On the first of our next two nights off ops Desmond gathered the officers and NCO aircrew of 'B' Flight to take me out to celebrate, plying me with the finest cognac. Breaking my rule for this auspicious occasion I went through the 'happy' stage, the 'riotous' phase and then like most topers I became maudlin. So soon after his death I wondered if my last 'kill' and now my 'gong', were Danny saying 'Sorry' from beyond the grave. The phase did not last long for I got so drunk I passed out and the lads carried me home and put me to bed. Getting the award as a Warrant Officer had one advantage for unlike the commissioned ranks it carried a gratuity of twenty pounds sterling to 'cover costs'. Outside of medal ribbon I had nothing to buy so I reckoned it would all be profit, not bad for the son of a bus driver!

My joy was brought to an abrupt ending with bad tidings. With the Germans so heavily engaged in the north, the Allies had invaded Southern France on 15 August with an 'uppercut', hoping this would now be their soft under belly. News travelled fast in our close knit community of night fighter squadrons, even of those based abroad (Italy), for it was soon confirmed that Johnny Walsh and his new pilot Les Wignell were posted 'missing, believed dead' on the night of the invasion, thought to have been shot down by a German night fighter. Johnny was the last of the Three Musketeers and Dartagnan as we jokingly called ourselves who had flown from England together. The inscrutable Johnny had been my pal since Tangmere days and I had been best man at Les's wedding. Neither of them were gung-ho so they must have been caught off guard. The last I heard was that his nice little wife was expecting a baby he now would never see. Oh what heartache for his wife with her fatherless child and his kindly parents who had made me feel so at home they had reminded me of my own Mum and Dad – how selfish of me to cause my loved ones such daily anguish. The sad news was a stark reminder that 'Dusty' and I were now the only surviving members of Malta Night Fighter Unit still on ops.

Only days later, by a strange quirk of fate, my private grief was overtaken by a tragedy for the whole squadron. At dinnertime we had been sat outside our tents talking in the sunshine when we heard someone shouting as he came belting down the hill waving a piece of paper. It was one of our Sergeant Navigators waving a telegram. He was ecstatically bawling 'It's a boy! It's a boy! Our first, 8 lbs 7 ozs!' as he dashed from tent to tent. That night we shared the first patrol with him and his pilot, taking off in pairs as usual Gordon and I set course to the British sector in the east while they headed west towards Cherbourg and the Bay of Biscay. We had just gained our operating height of 20,000 feet when we heard Control calling repeatedly 'Hello 29, Hello 29, can you hear me, can you hear me?' Knowing R/T had 'line of sight' limitations we asked Control for permission to try to contact them from our height, which they granted. Twice we called 'Hello 29, this is 26 can we assist you?' After our second call we heard a faint crackly reply 'No... Thank you!' Then silence. We knew at once he was gone, probably 'bounced' by a German night fighter, just like Johnny. But how poignant that it should be on the very day he had received word of his firstborn, leaving another fatherless child. Our radar told us what was in front but we were 'blind' at the rear so Gordon and I did a quick tight circle every now and then to have a look-see if anything was on our tail.

Our appreciation of the gastronomic delights we had enjoyed when we arrived began to wane. American rations were based on calories but because of our customary diet we were lacking carbohydrates and we became ravenously hungry. The Yanks tried to rectify the deficiency by issuing us with a small bag of boiled sweets and two extra slices of bread daily. Bread was in short supply so we supplemented ours by dipping it in locally produced Camembert cheese we had melted in our 'dixies' over a shallow trench with petrol in the bottom. Our BBQ was tasty and became our nightly supper but we yearned for traditional pie and peas or fish and chips.

Some Yanks paid us a courtesy visit to examine the sleek Mossies they had seen flying about, which were a novelty in the American sector. They were from a Transport Maintenance Unit and when we told them that our squadron transport consisted of one 15 cwt Commer truck and the CO's car they were aghast. When we paid them a return visit it was our turn to be aghast for they had fields full of every kind of transport – and a massive pile of scrapped, but mostly repairable, vehicles. It seemed that their title was somewhat of a misnomer for their idea of 'maintenance' was to scrap a broken down vehicle and replace it with a new one. With their innate generosity they presented us with eleven Jeeps and several powerful Harley Davidson motorbikes from their apparently limitless supply. As a special treat they insisted on giving us an open top Mercedes that had belonged to Field Marshal Goering, which had four-wheel drive, four-wheel steering, and a body made of two-inch thick steel. When we left they waved to us and shouted 'So long! Ya got plentya transport na buddies!' The primitive four-wheel steering on the Merc made the car go sideways when attempting to corner and one day it finished upside down in a ditch with a 'B' Flight pilot trapped underneath it. He was hospitalised for a week, which alerted Group who promptly withdrew our 'perks' on the grounds that chronic petrol shortage was restricting the operations of troops on the front line. Goering's Merc was doubtless kept by some Top Brass as his personal 'War Trophy' and, uncharitably, we hoped he would also land in a ditch. By devious means (like an inability to count beyond the fingers on our two hands) we managed to retain one very illicit Jeep for which Desmond devised a rota system so we had it in turn for 'recreational purposes'.

On 9 September the squadron was transferred to a new base at Carpiquet (B17) aerodrome just outside Caen in the British sector. We were told it was a tactical move to support the British Army advances in the east whilst still covering the American sector in the west. We wondered, however, if it was really because the Yanks had got fed up with repairing their roof-felting runway twenty times a day.

166

We were sorry to leave for they had been generous, warm and anxious to make us comfortable – but militarily, well in a word we had found them 'unbelievable'.

Our new base was dreadful, it had been raining for days and our tents were pitched just outside the perimeter track of the aerodrome in a muddy quagmire. The ground crews were struggling to dig a latrine trench in this squelch when a passing American 'Top Kick' (Master Sergeant) stopped to enquire what they were doing and their reply was graphic but unprintable. 'Hold it boys, I'll be back,' he said. Soon he arrived driving a massive bright yellow digger, lowered its revolving buckets into the mud and in no time dug a six foot deep, 100-yard long trench. Turning in his seat he shouted 'There ya are boys, the best goddam bog ya ever had!' and drove off. The lads were delighted but I was not for the 'seating rail' they erected was so high my feet could not touch the ground. Balancing there in the pouring rain I teetered between falling face first into the mud or, horror of horrors, backwards into the trench, making it difficult to concentrate on the job.

On the second morning as I left my tent to go for breakfast an erk (AC2) rushed up asking if I wanted to buy a Nazi souvenir, an offer I quickly refused when I saw he was scraping flesh and bones out of a jackboot with his bare hands. We were told that the Canadians who captured the drome, under orders to keep the pressure on their retreating foes, had no time to bury the dead so they had just bulldozed their slit trenches in on top of them. The continuous rain had made the ground settle properly and grotesquely twisted putrefied arms and legs had begun to appear. We had hated the mud but we were horrified to find it was full of German corpses and we wondered why we had not been billeted in the brick-built barracks captured from the Germans. The answer was simple – everything in them was 'booby trapped' and as it was too dangerous to clear them they were finally blown up. It was the same everywhere. Even a desirable-looking chair at the bottom of a bomb crater could be a mine trap, and 'scrounging', which was so commonplace that it was almost recognised as an RAF trade, became such a deadly hazard it was strictly prohibited.

As there was nothing to do on our days off we decided to walk into Caen itself hoping to find something to relieve our boredom. Once was enough for the devastation caused by numerous bomber raids intended to assist Montgomery's troops to break through the stiff German resistance had left the place in ruins. Old men smoking pipes lolled in doorways with only rubble behind them and stared balefully at us as we walked by. We scrambled over the stonework from the shattered houses blocking the streets until we saw a sign warning us that the debris was also mined made us turn back more depressed than ever – and all the time it rained.

Desmond sometimes released the Commer truck to make an evening visit to the seaside town of Trouville, next door to the well know high class racing resort of Deauville, in an effort to raise morale. With safety in mind I had cultivated 'Smithy' from Donny as he was the only man in the Section qualified to pack my Yankee parachute. Corporal Smith also had an even more prized attribute; he had earned the reputation of being the squadron's best 'scrounger'. I realised I should have known better than to accept his invitation to accompany him on one of these trips when he boarded the truck lugging a large Jerry can. On the way we passed a place that 'Smithy' said was called Troane where British heavy bombers had caught a Panzer Division hiding in a wood. In broad daylight they had left the tanks at all angles, and the few deafened, dazed survivors were still staggering out up to twenty-four hours afterwards. The wood was stripped of every leaf, the earth was a cratered moonscape and the scorched stumps of trees reminded me of the popular pre-war film 'The Petrified Forest'.

When we arrived at our destination 'Smithy' made straight for a nearby café where the owner whisked the can into the back and emerged with a wad of francs that he furtively counted out to 'our boy'. Petrol, cigs and coffee beans were the currency of the thriving *Marché Noir* and profits were so enormous 'Smithy' declared that tonight was his treat. Saying he was going to complete my education he took me to a brothel but was miffed when I refused to go 'Upstairs Air Force' with harlots who had said the same to German troops only days ago.

Gordon's turn came to use the 'recreational' Jeep and we, with another crew, set out to travel through the now open Falais Gap to see the carnage inflicted by our marauding fighter-bombers. As it had been some days since the breakthrough we did not expect that we would see much there but we had studied our maps and we planned to go into the Loire Valley if time permitted. How wrong we were for evidence of the slaughter was plain to see. Miles of bombed and rocketed German lorries, tanks, carts with the bloated bodies of their horses and nameless wooden crosses or upturned rifles with German helmets hanging on them littered the roadsides. We had seen enough and hurried to Le Mans, passing the racing circuit, and then drove over tree-covered hills into lush valleys, each with its own lovely fairy tale chateau until we parked in the town square of Angers. The lads took off hoping to find an open bistro whilst I stayed to guard the Jeep. An inquisitive crowd gathered, and a young girl asked what Army I was in as she was puzzled by the French motto on my sleeve. Replying in my schoolboy French I eventually made her understand and when my pals returned she excitedly insisted that we must meet her *Maman*. We hoisted her into the Jeep and following her directions soon arrived at her home. On hearing her daughter's animated explanation, her bright red haired *Maman* wearing a garish kimono opened the door to us and in perfect English asked if we would do her the honour of dining with her. We had not eaten all day so we accepted gratefully taking care to be as gracious as she. Over the dinner table we learned that she had not heard from her husband since he left to join the *Maquis* (French Underground) months ago and she prayed he was still alive. She described the American soldiers who had liberated the town as crude and brash saying how good it was to be in sophisticated, intelligent company at last, which made us look around to see who she meant – surely not us! We left at 22.00 hours in our open Jeep and when we got back the following morning we were soaked to the skin for all night it had poured with rain. Nevertheless we had enjoyed our jaunt – on reflection it was the only thing I ever enjoyed at Carpiquet.

Operating conditions were appalling, the perimeter track was lit by paraffin lamps that we could hardly see through our windscreens in the rain and if an aircraft landing wheel strayed off the taxiway it sank axle deep in mud. Trying to use its engines to free it was not an option for it made it sink deeper and risked bending the ends of the props. The tractor that came to its aid would be unable to pull it out so it stayed there until first light when they began digging it out literally inch by inch. We took off in pairs as usual but then one aircraft went to the west to honour our commitment to the Americans while the other flew east to the expanding British Sector. There was no 'trade' as the day fighters had established daylight air superiority over the bridgehead and German night fighters were busy defending their homeland. Our only diversion was watching Le Havre being heavily shelled by off shore naval units, which was a spectacular sight. It was said that Desmond had protested vigorously that the conditions on the aerodrome were unacceptable and after twenty miserable days at Carpiquet on 24 September wc moved to Predannack in lovely Cornwall.

Gordon and I were sent off an hour ahead of the main party to arrange for their impending arrival. When we were nearing our new base we called their Tower, giving them our Estimated Time of Arrival (ETA) and they responded by telling us the bearing of the runway in use. It was only when we got within visual distance that we saw there was a massive weather front rushing in from the north. In minutes it would reach the drome making landing impossible so I directed Gordon to get right down on the 'deck' and turn to port out to sea. Using the runway bearing and their AI beacon I then brought him round in a tight starboard turn and as we pulled up over the low cliffs we saw the runway ahead with the 'front' just seventy-five yards from its end. 'Bl—dy marvellous Goz,' Gordon enthused and then called the Control Tower. 'This is Two Six landed and clear,' he said rather smugly. There was a delay before a clearly confused Controller replied 'Hello 26, where are you?' and Gordon could scarcely control his giggle as he answered 'Just parking on your visitors' apron.' He was beside himself with delight. What a priceless story this would be – the Controller who lost an aircraft on his own aerodrome! By now the whole aerodrome was blanked out by the front and the rest of the squadron was diverted to Hurn. When they arrived the following day Gordon was in sparkling form as he recounted the episode in the Mess to gusts of riotous laughter. He probably embroidered my feat for my prowess in 'blind' landings became legendary throughout the squadron and Desmond called me into his office. 'Goz, I am recommending you for a commission, any objections?' he said. Objections? There was nothing I would not do for that man and I heard myself saying 'No objections and, er, thank you sir'.

Desmond got moving with bewildering speed for a day or two later I was interviewed by the Station Commander Group Captain Finucane, a New Zealander, who greeted me warmly. His first question put me in a spin 'Were you the "Gosling" who my cousin sometimes mentioned in his letters from Malta?' 'Would that be Paddy sir?' I enquired and he nodded his assent. 'Oh yes, Paddy was a pal of mine out there.' From then on he talked to me like an old chum. 'I see from your record you are well qualified, air gunner, wireless operator, radar operator, navigator – why not a pilot? I can arrange it for you.' I thanked him for his kind offer but going to some Commonwealth Training Scheme Course on a parched prairie in Canada with new entrants to the Service was not my idea of fun. I explained that having served on operational squadrons for so long I did not want to leave my pals at this late stage in the war. I thought it wiser not to disclose that I had done hours of illegal piloting on Ansons during my rest period. As I left he shook my hand and with a twinkle in his eye he said 'I understand you specialise in blind landing techniques.' I guessed he had overheard Gordon joking in the Mess or maybe Desmond had ribbed him about having a 'blind' aerodrome Controller. Either way I was genuinely pleased for since my 'rehabilitation' my prejudices against commissioning were long gone and I knew the officers in 604 Squadron were smashing chaps.

Predannack was a great place only a field or two away from what is now the Earth Station at Goonhilly Downs and close to Helston, made famous in song by its Annual 'Floral' Dance (it is really their 'Furry' Dance). Cycling there I was surprised to see a new aerodrome being built, which I learned was for planes being delivered from America to land if they were short of fuel. Its altitude made it free from the mists that regularly enveloped the tin chimneys of our billets and now it has become HMS Culdrose, the main base of the RNAS. These mists came off the sea and from the surrounding bogs immortalised by Sherlock Holmes in his novels. On the two days I was not on ops I cycled to The Lizard (the 'heel' of Cornwall – Land's End is its toe) and tiny smugglers' coves like Cadgwith. In the pub I got to know the local fishermen and an Agriculture and Fisheries Officer who lived there with his 'popsie'. He was none other than the son of Sir Arthur Conan Doyle, the author of the Sherlock Holmes novels – nice work if you can get it!

Earlier in the war Mum had seen an airman gazing at the houses as he walked by. Hoping that someone might assist 'Our Dennis' in like manner she went outside and asked if she could help him find what he was looking for. He worked at Doncaster Airport as an engine fitter on the civilian passenger aircraft impressed into RAF service when the war began and a right motley lot they were. There were DH Flamingos, Albatrosses, Ensigns, Monospars, Scions and even old HP 42s, which were a nightmare to keep serviceable as there were virtually no spares for them. He said his name was Bob and he was was seeking a place to bring his wife. She remembered an old friend who had recently lost his wife and got her lodgings with him and a job as his housekeeper. Every night the pair came to Mum's for a game of cards and a bite of supper and when I met them on my return from Malta Sylvia was calling Mum her second mother. She came from the nearby little Cornish village of Porthallow and I cycled through St Keverne where testament to the sacrifices of the rowed lifeboat crews was evidenced in the church and its graveyard. I then took a road so unfrequented there was grass growing in the middle to her home 'Roskorwell', a farm tucked almost into the hillside to shield it from the bitter winter gales that had wrecked hundreds of vessels on the coastline and on the rocks hidden offshore over the centuries.

I was greeted by her mother and her pregnant elder sister who was going to call her child 'Grace' after Mum. When her father came home from the farm he proved to be one of the most remarkable men I have ever met. Herbert Peter Allen was a dyed-in-the-wool Cornish man, a former Methodist lay preacher who had ridden round his parish on horseback, and knew all the folklore of what he called 'the hundred square miles' – the area from The Lizard to Nare Point. Cornwall is a superstitious county and I was fascinated by his knowledge of the frightening myths and dark fables of the countryside as we walked together. One bright but rainy morning as we walked to Gillan Creek we got so close to a rainbow that I could see the spectrum of colours between my face and my outstretched hand. Yes, I stood at the bottom of a rainbow but I have yet to find the pot of gold. Despite his religion he did not demur when I went to the 'Five Pilchards' in the village for a couple of pints at night to meet the locals. When they heard that Sylvia was with my mother up north and I was at Herbert's I was immediately accepted. I cycled to Porthallow as often as I could for walking and talking with Herbert had convinced me that Cornwall was the place I loved best in all England – after Yorkshire of course.

When Carpiquet became untenable the invasion planners had no option but to send us to Predannack for there was simply no room elsewhere. When we were on ops we had to fly to our forward base at Ford in the afternoon to top up our fuel so that we could operate under 2nd TAF control. Ford held unhappy memories for me as it was the place that Danny had operated from the night he got killed. On the other hand my knowledge of the area was useful especially when we were landing in dirty weather when I was careful to keep Gordon well away from the high ground of the South Downs just to the north. Flying back to Predannack every morning was tiring but it was worth the hassle to be able to spend our two days off there. Desmond knew our feelings and was pleased that it kept his aircrew happy, which was always his prime concern. October came and 2nd TAF decided to give us a couple of weeks' rest so I did not fly until the 14th of the month. On the 25th I became Pilot Officer D. Gosling 190344 and now I could associate with my erstwhile friends, a practice that had so troubled Michael but Desmond had openly encouraged. The appointment was 'probationary' for six months so for that time I had to be a good boy if I did not want to embarrass the admirable Desmond and I certainly did not want to do that.

We continued our shuttle service until 4 December when the squadron was moved to Odiham, where the Intelligence Officer was the well known jazzman Syd Phillips. With Gordon vamping at the piano he delighted us nightly in the Mess by playing all the standards and many of his own compositions. We now patrolled further east to Walcheren where the Germans had blown the dykes on the island reclaimed from the sea to slow the Allied drive along the coast. The Mulberry Harbour had been partially destroyed by gales and was too far behind the front line so Montgomery urgently needed to secure a major port nearer to the front lines.

On 17 December we set off for our new patrol line that we had to approach from the west to enter the Brussels gun corridor. Halfway through a brilliant white light suddenly appeared, which held station in front and slightly to port although our airspeed was over 300 mph. We had never before seen a light of such an intensity yet it did not illuminate our aircraft or the clouds around us. We excitedly asked each other what it could be as puzzled and wary we followed it for about five minutes when it disappeared. Gordon rocked our plane from side to side to see if it was below but it had simply vanished. We were still saying 'What the hell was that?' when it reappeared off our starboard wing tip though we could not tell how far away it was and there it stayed for several minutes. We peered at it intently but we could see nothing but this strange light that emitted no light until without warning it shot off at tremendous speed and in a second it was gone. We completed our patrol and reported this amazing phenomenon to the Intelligence Officer but no one ever mentioned it again. It was definitely not a Meteor for it was too fast and there was no jet trail. Nobody could explain the lightless light and the way our report was hushed up leaves me believing it was an Unidentified Flying Object – a UFO!

We had worked out that our present posting was a stepping stone on our return to 2nd TAF somewhere in France and sure enough we were posted to Lille Vendeville (B51) on 1 January 1945. We were billeted in a nice hotel with a balcony above a band that played to the drinkers in the large hall that fronted the city's main square.

Nightly we listened to the music of the band and the singers, including one of our own navigators. It was an affront to my ego that his efforts were considered superior to mine so I consoled myself with excellent cognac from the bar. Lille was not a pretty place but there were plenty of bistros to explore and occasional diversions like seeing the ladies who had their hair shaved off for consorting with the German troops. We were bussed out to the aerodrome where the mine-infested German barrack blocks had been blown up. The runways, taxi tracks and hardstandings were in good condition as was a substantial Flight Office but it still had that distinctive smell the Germans always left behind. We first noticed this pong in captured aircraft and attributed it to the ersatz oil and fuel they used. It clung to everything they touched and we could tell at once that Jerry had been there but we never found out what it was. We patrolled the Ruhr on 3 and 16 January without any 'contacts' and on the 18th, the very day Gordon became a Squadron Leader, we took off for a new patrol line over Nijmegen where we hoped to have better luck.

It was a dark night with no moon. We had been airborne about twenty minutes when we flew into torrential rain and violent turbulence and with a crackle the R/T and intercom packed up. We were enveloped in static electricity that created swathes of blue light round the arcs of the props. It was called St Elmo's Fire and I had seen it before but never like this. Great lightening-like flashes leapt from the inboard fuel tanks to the radio mast behind our heads and the noise was terrific so we had to shout to each other. Gordon was fighting to control the madly bucking aircraft, which was tossed about as if it was weightless. But there was one glimmer of hope – my radar was still on. 'Turn back,' I yelled, 'I'll try to get in at base!' As he yanked on the controls the aircraft almost inverted. I tuned to our base beacon, began a steady descent from 5,000 feet and despite being tossed about even in our harnesses we battled our way to base at 500 feet from where I hoped to make a 'blind' approach. The storm still raged and we had not broken cloud so I told Gordon we dare not go any lower for the barometric pressure at base would have changed since we took off so I had no idea of our height. We could not call to ask what the pressure was now so I bawled at him to 'go through the gate' and climb away. The 'gate' was the wire stop on the throttles you had to be break through to get emergency boost that the engines could only maintain for three minutes.

He shouted 'I did that ten minutes ago but I still cannot climb. Goz, do you want to bale out?' 'No, no!' I bawled at the top of my voice. 'We may not be high enough and even if I made it I don't think you would. Go straight ahead and we'll take our chances.' The rain was now cyclonic, we could not even see the engines, but a couple of minutes later there was a swooshing noise, a bang, an almighty flash and I thought 'this is the end'. Instead to our disbelief we saw our altimeter showed that we had been literally been sucked up to 3,000 feet. I yelled 'Come out of the gate and rest the engines!' Then the intercom and the R/T came on and the static flashes and St Elmo's Fire ceased. We were far from being out of the woods so I made a decision to turn to port from our westerly course to try to get out of the storm. That way I knew there was no high ground and I figured that if we had to bale out at least we would be over the land, not in the Channel. Gordon called base who said they were still 'clamped down' and advised us to go to Brussels Melsbroek, which was open. I tuned to their AI beacon and the weather started to clear so we landed without difficulty and when we got out of the aircraft a trembling Gordon hugged me saying 'Good old Goz, you've done it again'. I said 'No, it wasn't me, that was divine intervention! You nearly broke a record – Squadron Leader for just one day!' and I laughed. We were taken to the Officers' Mess in the city square of Brussels, fed and led to a dormitory where Gordon went out like a light as soon as he hit his bed. No wonder, the poor lad was exhausted by wrestling to control the aircraft in the storm.

Over breakfast I told him that I reckoned the sudden uplift was due to a raging thermal inside the cumulus cloud and the static had been earthed to ground via the dense rain thus restoring the R/T. When we saw our aircraft next morning we were taken aback for all the roundels and squadron markings had been burnt off, every metal panel was burnished like silver and on the way home the engines ran a bit roughly. Desmond came out to look at it and said 'My God, you have been lucky, I went through it at 20,000 and it was bad enough up there but you were at the bottom where it would be many times worse.' It was the nearest I had been to disaster since losing a prop in Malta and reminded me that however prepared I tried to be Fate could still deal a fatal hand.

For the rest of January we were grounded by the heaviest snowfalls in decades. It was still deep on 5 February when we were due to go on leave. Bright and early we went to board our venerable Oxford but the engine fitters said they hoped it would be serviceable later in the day. The last time we went on leave in it the engines began to fail over the Channel and only by throwing out everything moveable, including the seats, did we lighten it enough to coax it over the English coast. Ever the optimist I was the first back after dinner when one of the fitters told me they were waiting for spares and the kite would not be ready until tomorrow. I was rueing my misfortune when I saw an American pilot looking at our Mossies so I strolled over and took him inside 'W', our aircraft. He was very impressed and when I told about losing a day of my leave he said 'No problem, I'll take you, we are almost refuelled.' Pausing only to ask our fitters to let my mates know I was soon beside Lieutenant Jacobsen winging my way to dear old England. Nearing his base at Great Ashwell we saw a lot of towering cumulus ahead. 'Gee', I hope we don't get into that,' he said. 'One of our boys did last week and they all had to bale out, one of the guys got killed.' I thought 'Uh, oh, the Yanks again.' But all was well except that I was now stranded in the wilds of deepest Suffolk. The kindly Jacobsen Jeeped me to the nearest railway station and after changing several times I eventually managed to get to London. I arrived home at midnight tired but triumphant. I had only lost half a day of my leave and had a unique experience to boot.

Our tour of duty was nearing its end so Gordon spoke to the CO to see if we could stay together on our rest. Desmond began looking for, as he put it, 'a good home' for us and had found Gordon and me an exciting posting to Defford in Worcestershire at the Telecommunications Flying Unit. Sir Watson-Watt, the inventor of radar, had taken over the colleges at nearby Malvern to house the boffins of his Telecommunications Research Establishment bringing their inventions to be calibrated and assessed at TFU. Gordon said 'Desmond has been looking for a posting where your skills would be useful and he says this will be "right up your street" as we shall be testing experimental equipment.' Dear old Desmond, he must have given our posting a lot of thought, which was kind of him.

We had to wait a month until the posts at Defford became vacant but Desmond arranged for us to be kept on squadron strength for that time, most of which we spent on leave. When we finally had to go we were really sad for we would dearly have loved to stay with 604 Squadron to the end of the war. At our farewell party we got exceedingly drunk to drown the sorrow of our parting from such jolly fine chaps – especially Desmond!

The challenge of Defford awaited me and I wondered what whoever ruled my fate had in store – but I no longer feared for I knew they would take care of me.

CHAPTER TWENTY-FIVE

The Ultimate Question

During our month's extension Desmond had twice let Gordon and I 'borrow' the Oxford to take a 'look-see' at our new home at Defford and it behaved impeccably as if to say 'Thank goodness they are going'. We liked what we saw for the officers' billets were set in an apple orchard near Pershore, not far from the cathedral city of Worcester. The aerodrome was sited in the middle of the beautiful Vale of Evesham, bounded on the west by the Malvern Hills and to the east by the Cotswolds. All around there was flat land yet the Air Ministry had built the main runway so that on take-off you were directly in line with Bredon, the only hill in the Vale. Your most vulnerable time was when you were using full boost to take off and we had to use it for longer to clear the hill. It wasn't exactly dangerous but it certainly made life more interesting.

Less appealing was the attitude of some of the Admin staff who were distinctly 'sniffy', questioning how we came to have use of the squadron hack. They were mostly men who were embittered by our swift promotion and the publicity lavished on aircrews (or Brylcreem Boys as we were called). They felt their role was equally as important yet the media never gave them a mention because they had only 'flown a desk'. They tried to make us feel uncomfortable by asking why we were not wearing Volunteer Reserve shoulder flashes – a practice long discontinued on squadrons –implying that they as 'Regulars' were somehow a superior breed. By 1945 the RAF was ten times its pre-war strength and after operational losses had taken such a toll of 'Regular' aircrew remnants like them were now only a tiny minority. This expansion had initially been to their advantage for instead of retiring with NCO rank many had risen to become Squadron Leaders as they assembled their little empires. After demobilisation, which was getting ever nearer, they knew that the post-war Service could not justify present staffing levels so they would soon be declared 'surplus to requirements' and dismissed – their halcyon days were numbered! To be frank we found them obnoxious and we hoped job satisfaction would outweigh such pettiness but we left with some apprehension for it did not bode well.

We arrived, officially, on 1 April (not an auspicious date) and two days later Desmond sent the Oxford to deliver our logbooks, which we had left at Lille to await his signature at the end of March. I was ecstatic when I saw the assessment he had given me. 'Has completed a very satisfactory tour. Well above average' it read and coming from such a peerless man as he it was more than I had ever dared to hope for. Gordon had been made Squadron Leader in charge of 'C' Flight and I became its senior navigator. There were three Flights, each having one of every aircraft currently in use by Bomber, Coastal/Transport and Fighter Command so that experimental equipment could be tested on the type of aircraft it was designed for.

Hearing in the Mess that Bomber Flight needed a 'Gee' operator Gordon boasted that his navigator had instructed pupils how to use the device so I was promptly commandeered by the Bomber Flight. Arriving at the Flight I admitted, red faced, that although he had spoken the truth I had not touched a 'Gee' set for almost three years and I was, to say the least, rusty! Regardless, 'B' Flight kept me so I began my flying at Defford in Warwick and Wellington bombers (the legendary 'Wimpeys'), both designed by Sir Barnes Wallis. He was the first to realise that the immensely strong geodetic system could be adapted for aircraft construction. This brilliant man also invented the 22,000-lb Grand Slam bomb, which was the largest bomb of the War, so big only the Lancaster could carry it. He also invented the 'swing wing', permitting a lower landing speed but greatly increasing the top speed of fighter aircraft, which was copied world wide.

When two weeks later Gordon insisted on my return I found him uncharacteristically short tempered, very much on edge, and I knew what was troubling him. We had been scheduled to make our last patrol from Lille and had gone to our aircraft in the afternoon to do the usual Night Flying Test. The airfield was deep in snow but footpaths had been cleared leaving them so icy we slipped and slithered as we walked to the dispersal. Gordon fired up the engines and we started to taxi out but when we reached the road to the perimeter track it was like glass. When he gently opened the throttles the aircraft skidded sideways into the piled up snow and the starboard wheel sank up to its axle. He tried to free us by using full throttle but from my side I could see we were sinking deeper so I yelled to him to cut the engines. I do not know what he was thinking about for he ignored me, gave the engines another blast and as had happened so often at Carpiquet, over a foot of the prop ends smashed into the concrete of the approach track. Since then Gordon had been on tenterhooks waiting to hear if the Board of Inquiry had held him responsible for the damage to the prop and maybe the starboard engine. One day I was in the Mess when a telephone call came for him and in his absence I said I would take it. It was Desmond phoning from Lille. 'Tell Gordon he has been cleared, mainly because you testified that he did everything by the book.' Then he roared with laughter and said 'You little fibber Goz!'

A relieved Gordon and I began testing equipment for fighter aircraft, which was our introduction to a curious species called 'Boffin'. They were younger than I had imagined and deep in a world of their own. They seemed not to notice anything around them – when we called to them they sort of awoke with a start. All were geniuses in their own field but they had no idea of more mundane matters and sartorially they defied description. Dishevelled, unwashed and unshaven they were frequently thrown out of the Mess by outraged members of the Old Guard incoherently babbling about 'standards in the service' and the like. We were vastly amused but understanding for at times they flew with us and I was closeted with them for up to three hours in the back of a Beau as they taught me how to operate their prototype equipment. It was an ordeal that made us profoundly grateful that a Mossie cockpit was only big enough for the crew of two. One was caught on a stepladder using a brace and bit to bore a hole through the main spar of a Mossie to install an aerial. Alas he had done too much damage before he was spotted and a new wing had to be fitted.

The largest part of our duties was calibrating the new gadgets they brought us, which was boring, particularly for the pilot who had to fly very precise courses in a pattern similar to an electric heating element. Back and forth we went, always keeping the exact height and turning at the predetermined rate even in cloud. It demanded total concentration from both of us for navigators were charged to watch the instruments too and draw the pilot's attention to any deviation. After three hours of this sophisticated torture we were completely whacked and if we were flying aircraft used by the Navy it was worse for their Air Speed Indicators were calibrated in knots, which I had to convert to MPH. When the series of tests were completed we were supposed to give an honest assessment but Gordon considered some of my comments were too forthright and regularly restrained me from using abbreviations such as 'BF'.

May 1945 was a momentous month for me. I was promoted to Flying Officer having kept my nose clean, albeit sometimes with difficulty, for the required six months. I saw less of Gordon as he began 'living out' with his wife and baby son in a local house he had rented and I celebrated my twenty-fourth birthday on the 13th. I went on leave and I recall standing outside Doncaster's unique Mansion House when the Mayor declared that the war in Europe was over. The crowds around me were delirious with delight and I tried to look as happy as they were, but I had tears in my eyes thinking of all the fine men I had known who had not lived to see this moment. Walking home my mind was in turmoil. Their names and faces flashed through my head. There were so many, they were so young and full of life, why did they have to suffer such terrible tragic deaths? Every night I slept fitfully for each time I closed my eyes their images came back, laughing, joking, drinking, singing as we had done in the past.

When I returned from my leave bad news awaited me – 'Dusty' Miller had been killed less than two weeks before the end of the war. Years later I was reading the Mosquito Aircrew Association's journal *Mossie* when I came across an article by his navigator, F/O Barclay, telling the full story of his last mission. Late in the war the Night Fighter Development Unit where 'Dusty' (now sporting a bar to his DFC) was posted for his 'rest period' was freed to do intruder patrols over Germany. Flares dropped by other aircraft had shown that the airfield that was their primary target had no aircraft on it so the leader to whom 'Dusty' was flying No. 2 decided to attack Horshing Airfield only three miles away. This was not a wise decision for the defenders would have been alerted when they saw the flares nearby. Nevertheless the leader decided to attack so 'Dusty' dropped his flares and followed the lead plane in. The flak was always worse for the second attacker yet he still destroyed a Ju 188 and then he made a fatal mistake – he came round for another pass. It had been drummed into us that we must never go round again because the gunners would be ready and waiting if we did. They were. They raked the fuselage, one engine stopped, the other was hit and 'Dusty' told his oppo to bale out. Now the escape hatch problem we had identified long ago showed up as we knew it would. Halfway out his navigator's parachute got stuck in the narrow exit hatch. 'Dusty' leaned over, pushed him out, and seconds later the aircraft exploded, with him inside it. It was typical of the man that he had sacrificed his own life to save his oppo. Oh 'Dusty', 'Dusty', I remember what you said as we 'beat up' Church Fenton goods yard. 'Wouldn't it be great if this was for real?' Did you think this might be your last chance to realise your ambition? I remembered too my fears that 'Dusty' was becoming gung-ho but I knew if I had mentioned them to him he would only have laughed. Like a swashbuckling cavalier he scorned danger and rebelled against authority as I did. He was great company and the best friend a man could wish for. I was now the sole survivor of the Malta Flight and I marvelled at my good fortune. There was solace for me in knowing he died fulfilling his dream and as a Man of War, if he had lived, he would have been unhappy and ill suited to the humdrum of civilian life.

The variety of aircraft we flew provided some relief from the monotony of endless calibrating. Some we had never flown before and we had great fun learning to handle them but the ones that nearly were our undoing were those we knew well – they were the 'Mossies'! The first had been reported to have a vicious vibration at the base of the windscreen but the riggers could find no explanation. It occurred when 290 IAS (Indicated Air Speed) was exceeded or in a turn and it was Gordon's responsibility as Flight Commander to discover the cause. Full of confidence we boarded the aircraft thinking we would soon sort the problem out so we climbed to 12,000 feet and at 280 IAS Gordon threw it into a steep turn. Tremendous vibration started at once, so severe we thought the whole canopy would come off and the windscreen would smash into our faces but when he levelled out the vibrations ceased. Then he accelerated beyond the critical level speed and they began again, increasing in intensity. I left my seat to feel if I could pinpoint the source of the trouble but all I could determine was that it seemed to be all along the base of the windscreen. At 320 IAS he decided that to go faster was too dangerous so he reduced speed until the vibrations stopped and we discussed what to do next. For an hour we racked our brains but try as we might nothing made any difference. We put in our report and after further ground inspection proved fruitless the aircraft was scrapped.

On another day we took off and after thirty minutes or so I noticed a wisp of smoke in the cockpit and an acrid smell of rubber burning. At first Gordon did not get a whiff of it (his nose was not as big as mine) and when he did I told him I suspected a fuse had blown somewhere. I examined every fuse in the electrical panel on my side of the cockpit but finding nothing amiss I told him to land immediately. He needed no prompting for by now the smoke was making us cough, gasp for breath and our eyes were smarting – even so we were only just in time. It was found that the generator on the port engine was somehow shorting onto the dinghy release wire above our heads; it became red hot and began to burn through the rubber of the dinghy behind us. By the time we landed it had scorched the top of the flare and Very light cartridges stowed there and they were about to ignite. I had heard of 'going out in a blaze of glory' but we had (only just) escaped a spectacular pyrotechnic end that would have given the phrase a whole new dimension. Instead, I could still wake up each morning, lie contented in my bed and feast my eyes on the apple blossom outside my bunk window that was now in full bloom.

The Station Commander, Group Captain McDonald, knew that since the end of the war in Europe everyone in the Mess had but one thought in their heads – what shall I do in the future? There were options: volunteer for the war in the Pacific, try to get a regular commission or be demobbed. He called the officers to a meeting where he gave his assessment of our chances. He started by saying the RAF would not be recruiting aircrew as rockets would replace aircraft except in Transport Command who would need a few, presumably because a way to strap troops and stores to a rocket had not yet been invented. Only officers with university degrees need apply for the few vacancies in Logistics, Engineering and Education Branches, which ruled out practically all of us. We did not know then how ludicrously wrong his judgement was. He came up with a suggestion, a ship would shortly transport half of TRE to a place we had never heard of called Woomera in Australia where the space for rocket firing was limitless. If we joined them we would have the advantage of being in at the inception of this new technology. He turned smartly on his heel and left satisfied that he had been most helpful and informative. He had indeed – he had almost made up my mind for me. I would get back to Civvy Street as soon as I could before all the plum jobs were taken. As for Australia, 'limitless space for rockets to be fired' could only mean somewhere in the snake-infested Outback miles from civilisation and with Boffins boring holes in the bottom to install aerials the boat would probably sink before it got there. I hate snakes so it was 'Thank you Mr M, but not on your Nellie!'

McDonald was a mysterious man, unlike any Station Commander I had ever met for they were usually highly decorated officers, aristocrats, the well connected, or even academics. So far as I knew he fell into none of these categories. He was fiftyish, built like a prop forward and I wondered if he owed his exalted rank to being the star of an RAF rugger team long ago. His manner was blunt, almost bullying, and some of his edicts bordered on the unbelievable for he was certainly a loose cannon. He had a very pretty trophy wife, several years his junior, who made Lucille Ball (the original dumb blonde) appear quite intellectual. When he played squash to control his expanding girth she would invite sycophantic young officers to take coffee with her and I christened them the 'dahling brigade' so you may reasonably assume I was never one of the favoured few. I suspected that

Gordon had been singing my praises again for I was ordered to accompany 'his nibs' when he decided to learn how to fly a Mossie. He asked me questions that convinced me Gordon had told him he often let me pilot the dual control Mossie we had on our Flight. On one occasion I navigated him to Wyton when he was summoned to meet Air Vice Marshal Donald Bennett, the Australian former airline pilot who founded the Pathfinder Force. In 1943 the 'Oboe' equipment invented by Defford Boffins had transformed the accuracy of night bombing when it was installed in Pathfinder Mossies as it enabled them to drop their markers over any city even if it was obscured by cloud. It was ideal for area bombing but Bennett may have wanted to know if development had yet made it so precise that single buildings could be targeted

I was still undecided whether or not to leave the Service as Civvie Street was not at all attractive for job prospects were as bad as in the worst of the depression. Food, furniture, clothing, in fact everything was rationed, most of all petrol. Paradoxically, it was the petrol rationing that clinched my decision for when it spread to the RAF our flying was limited to no more than 20 hours a month. My logbook tells me that in May I flew for just 4 hours 50 minutes, August 5 hours, September 3 hours 35 minutes, October 5 hours and November 1 hour 55 minutes and so on, none of it at night. I had joined up to fly and now my *raison d'être* was gone, the answer to the ultimate question was clear. Reluctantly, I would return to Civvy Street. The consolation was that we had loads of free time and I went boating at Tewksbury on the Severn with Gordon and his family and in my newly acquired MG I went home every weekend (from Friday teatime to Monday morning) taking my friend, Flight Lieutenant Dan Maskell, who came from Sheffield. The aircrews had plenty of petrol for their cars for when a Beau was refuelled there was an overflow and standing under the wings we collected gallons each time. The ground crews were very cooperative and overfilled until our drums were full.

My MG was nothing like Peter Oakes' immaculate 'Hoover' but it was the best I could afford and after I scrounged the brake cables off the Station Magister to replace its non-existent brakes, at only £95 it was a snip. It was allegedly a four-seater and could be described as a family car if your two children were under six years of age. Every night Dan and I sought out a different pub going as far afield as the curiously named 'Copp Cut Elm' in Bromsgrove but mostly we drank and played darts locally. A couple of nights a week we visited one of the hostelries in Worcester, including the smallest pub in England, to play skittles or bowls. That glorious summer we travelled far and wide to Broadway in the Cotswolds, went boating at Evesham, Ross on Wye and Tewkesbury, visited Gloucester and Cheltenham, Malvern and into the Brecon Beacons beyond, living the life of Riley and enjoying every minute. But all good things come to an end and the mobility of the aircrew made the Station Provost Marshal (Service Police Chief) begin to suspect we had a fiddle going. One day his tiny mind came up with the only possible explanation – the beggars must be using aircraft fuel. As a dedicated Old Guard member he saw a way of ingratiating himself with their leader, the Adjutant, and together they hatched a plan to catch us red handed. One Monday morning when they thought we would be least expecting it he would descend on the camp with all his SPs (Service Policemen) and in a spectacular *coup de grâce* swoop on our cars. It was so beautifully simple they must have purred. Unfortunately for them and providentially for us his assistant was an ex-navigator who had been certified medically unfit to fly. For months he had been bullied by his boss but now he scented the heady aroma of revenge and he tipped us off. From the Mess windows we watched delightedly as posses swept up to the car park and the dispersal huts but not one aircrew car was in sight for they were all in lay-bys outside the camp beyond his jurisdiction. They had only looked at aircrew cars but they might have had better success with a certain Wing Commander's Lanchester parked outside the Officers' Mess, which he had adapted to run on Tractor Vaporising Oil. He started it on petrol and by closing its radiator louvres he soon had the engine hot enough to switch over to TVO, which he used until he was nearly home when he went back to petrol to clean the plugs. This worked well until one day he had to stop at traffic lights in the middle of Birmingham on his way home and when he accelerated away he left a policeman standing nearby enveloped in a cloud of soot. Looking like a sweep with soot in his eyes he could not even see to take down the cars number. At dinner we sat looking angelic while they glowered at us but our benefactor went without his food for he feared the 'cat that supped the milk' expression on his face might be his undoing.

Dan and I had discussed our prospects in Civvy Street and we agreed they were not good. Gordon had already made his decision for he was old enough to have established himself in his job before he left. Our first choice was Imperial Airways but so many pilots and navigators were on the market that there were probably no vacancies by now. It was the only British airline at that time and there was no tourist industry until years later when some farsighted entrepreneurs like Freddy Laker tried to create a market using war surplus Dakotas. We were totally unqualified for anything but flying, so it looked as if we would have to return to the pre-war jobs we had left as callow youths but would there be vacancies for us now we were men? I still hankered after the medical profession but I was told that as a 'mature student' I should have to pay for my six-year training course myself, and I simply did not have that kind of money.

Gordon had been demobbed so Dan and I were detailed to take a Boffin in an Anson to the Royal Aircraft Establishment at Farnborough. While he went about his business we wandered around the airfield and found a collection of German planes.

There were dozens, one or more of every type, and it was obvious they were being flown, tested and assessed. One experimental aircraft had a propeller in front of the pilot and another behind him, which would have minced him if he tried to bale out. It was called the 'Ascender' but we thought of a different pronunciation, which would have been more appropriate. We went inside the ubiquitous Ju 52 transport plane and a monster eight-engined, twin-boomed job, and looked into the cockpits of various fighters, including the latest rocket-powered Me 163. I asked Dan which of them he would have liked to fly and he replied emphatically 'None' but I fancied trying the Ju 88 I had so often encountered to compare it with a Beau. They had one thing in common; they all reeked of that awful distinctive Jerry smell.

Meanwhile, Dan and I continued our nightly jaunts, choosing places to which there was no public transport and were outside cycle range from the camp. This was because demobilisation was taking so long that some drunken airmen became impatient and tried to vent their frustration on officers out on the town in Worcester. Some of those who had narrowly escaped being drawn into a fight reported the aggressors to the Station Commander who called us all to a meeting. He said he would not discipline any airman who insulted or attacked an officer. We should accept their challenge and give them a good thrashing. We looked at each other aghast. Was he serious? Indeed he was. He went on to say that we had come running to him as if he was our mother. We were old enough to fight our own battles and he was not going to molly coddle us; it was high time we stood on our own two feet. He stormed out leaving us speechless. We did not even have time to ask him if he would support us when some crafty airman reported us for GBH as was inevitable. I wanted to seek assurance he had arranged that Lonsdale rules and the usual weight categories would be adhered to in these bouts. I also wished to know if there was an undernourished featherweight division to accommodate me. Talk about stupidity, he must be stark staring bonkers for his brainwave meant that all but fifteen stone, six footers would run the risk of getting beaten up if they ventured out. His outburst showed he had given no thought to its consequences and now he faced a dilemma.

Ever resourceful he thought up a solution, he would resurrect pre war 'Dining In' nights to keep us on camp and thus out of trouble. They were so dreary we would do anything to avoid them, even volunteering for duty as Station Orderly Officer. One memorable night his wife called loudly to a blushing Adonis seated at a distant table. 'Oh Dahling, why didn't you come for coffee today? I missed you.' The Mess went quiet, her spouse looked apoplectic, and the meal ended in embarrassed silence but there were no more coffee mornings. My theories about his past were strengthened when after 23.00 hours the tables were cleared and he suddenly became animated. 'Let's play rugger,' he chortled as he helped to move the furniture. A waiter brought a piece of chalk, he selected his team and threw himself enthusiastically into the game. There were no rules; you just had to put a cross on the wall if you got to 'their' end. When he was exhausted he encouraged the lads to pile tables precariously on top of each other so that some drunken fool could climb up and write his name on the ceiling. It was infantile and stupid but he was in his element. 'Well done!' he shouted if someone succeeded and he roared with laughter when the tables collapsed bringing a man crashing to the ground.

A steady stream (well more of a trickle) of officers was getting demobbed and one Pilot Officer had spoken openly in the Mess that he regretted he had never baled out. In his final week he was flying a Beau over South Wales when he called base to report he had engine trouble and was going to bale out. They enquired what was wrong but received no reply. They were still wondering what had happened when the police rang up to say he had baled out and having seen his parachute land had rushed to his rescue. He was now in their custody and could we please come and fetch him. When asked what had happened to the aircraft they said they knew not but they had last seen it flying north. Later that day a report came that it had crashed in marshy ground west of Shrewsbury and crash investigators were sent to examine the wreck. Considering the plane had flown nearly 100 miles on its own, not surprisingly they confirmed the suspicion that the engines were in good condition. At his trial he said he had set the plane on a course out to sea before he jumped so that it would not kill anyone when it crashed but somehow it had turned round and flown north. The officer did not get his demob; instead he was sentenced to three years in the glasshouse, which gave him ample time to ponder if he had been the victim of the Beau's revenge. Determined to exonerate itself and to point an accusing finger at him it had changed course and chose to crash on soft ground to preserve the evidence.

We were given Xmas leave and when we returned in January 1946 we found that half the TRE Boffins had left for the Antipodes and we saw only a few who wandered around looking more lost than ever. At last we could understand why, for all flying had ceased and rumours abounded that the camp was to close. I was given the job of Link Trainer Instructor and I had a busy time helping dozens of pilots (including McDonald) to keep their hand in. Football matches were arranged, bingo nights, shoots with the local farmers, anything to relieve the tedium. We went home at weekends but some were too far away and we pitied them. As you can well imagine Defford was not a happy place and everyone longed for their release.

In a way I was sorry when Dan's turn came for he would miss seeing the Vale at its glorious best with the fruit trees bursting into blossom yet I was happy he was escaping the crushing boredom. We promised to meet when I got home but even my promotion to Flight Lieutenant did not compensate for the loss of his company on our jaunts. So the days dragged by until at long, long last my discharge paper came too.

For some minutes I sat staring at it, almost not believing that such an insignificant slip of paper could mean the end of my dreams. Oh, I had loved the RAF so much, after the joy of flying, pitting my skills against the elements in the blackness of the night and the incomparable comradeship of squadron life, this was like a death sentence. I sighed deeply and put the paper aside. For months I had agonised before taking the ultimate decision that Service life would never be the same without the danger and excitement of operational flying. I thought of those dear departed pals who had been like brothers and I realised how fortunate I was to be alive. Yes, I had made the right decision and there was no going back.

The day before my discharge I was stowing my gear when I noticed I was entitled to four new towels and I went to the Adjutant's to get him to sign the chit enabling me to draw them from the Stores. Vindictively he flung the paper back at me. 'No way,' he said, 'you are being discharged.' This was a moment the Old Guarder was savouring. I pointed out that I would have got them earlier had I remembered but he was adamant. I went back to my billet and considered what to do. It may seem petty now but those towels were on coupons and of a quality not available in Civvy Street, so back I went determined to have what I was legally entitled to. I marched into the Adjutant's office and declared loudly that I wished to see the Station Commander. 'For what reason?' he snottily asked. I stuck my nose in his face and growled 'To get my towels'. He visibly wilted, turned on his heel and said to a WAAF 'Give him the chit'. When she brought it to me she whispered 'He said, "What can you expect from these Temporaries?"' Grabbing the chit I called out loudly so that he could not fail to hear 'These desk wallahs would have [well, shall I say evacuated their bowels] on ops' and left her trying to conceal her glee. It was childish and perhaps not strictly true but he was lucky for only the possibility that it might delay my demob had saved him from a smack in the teeth – I must have been maturing!

Next day on the train I met a civilian chap who told me he was an explosives expert who specialised in blowing things up on film sets. If he was too heavy handed and demolished too much it could cost thousands. At the station he gave me a lift in the chauffeured Rolls-Royce waiting for him asking the driver to detour to the Demob Centre, which was not far from Pinewood Studios where he was going. I compared this to my arrival at Padgate. How long ago was it? It was going on seven of the best years of my life yet in terms of experiences a lifetime. When I got out he shook my hand, wished me luck and I almost asked if he knew of any vacancies in the film industry. Unwittingly, he had already done much for me as during the journey he had taken my mind off the end of an era for me. In a warehouse reminiscent of a train terminal bursting with piles of hats, shirts, underwear, socks, shoes and racks of suits and overcoats I was told to make my choice. It was a well organised, slickly efficient, impersonal sausage machine, an automaton that knew not the dangers and tribulations the men passing through had experienced. Some wore the ribbons of medals awarded them by a once grateful nation that now no longer needed them; they looked bewildered and lost. I was so sorry, for years they had been numbers but now their numbers were being taken away and they were, somehow, just nothing. I wondered if this was to be the fate of us all. There were dressed dummies and mirrors to assist all ranks of the Army, Navy and Air Force but the selection was limited to only a few designs so easily recognisable that folks said 'Wearing your demob suit I see'. I took my pick and got away as fast as I could, I was so depressed, tired and dispirited that all I wanted was to get home. When I arrived in my beloved Donny I hardly recognised the place, feeling that I did not belong here. I stood outside the station looking round and saw *it* had not changed; the change was in *me*.

It was the 4th of June and my Great Adventure was over.

CHAPTER TWENTY-SIX

The Aftermath

After my return Mum took me with her to the Old Cemetery on her regular visit to the four graves of my maternal and paternal grandparents and two aunts. Nothing could have reminded me more that I was indeed back home for I had accompanied her on her Saturday pilgrimage since I was a tot. As Mum arranged her flowers I stood looking at their graves wondering which one had been my Guardian Angel; it could have been any one of them for they had all adored me as a child. It might have been dear Auntie Polly or Grandma Ogley but it could even have been all of them, and irreverently I wondered if they had a roster. 'Don't forget it's your turn to look after "Our Dennis" tomorrow.' We wandered around town; the buildings were the same but I did not see a single familiar face and the feeling that I no longer belonged here came rushing back. My beloved Donny had become a stranger to me.

I tried hard to settle down and make a life for myself in Civvy Street but I was like a rudderless boat without an anchor drifting aimlessly to I knew not where. Peter, who had been brought up like my brother, came home from Italy but he left to live with his wife in Halifax. I went back to my old job at the Co-op thinking most of the lads would have returned from the fray and we would be pals as we had been before. Not so, they were uncomfortable knowing I had been an officer and thought I was no longer of their class. I really did give it a go – I stuck it out for three weeks before deciding it was not going to work. It was just as well for when the whole Department, Outfitting, Ready Mades, Bespoke and the Workshop, moved into the new Emporium across the road it was downgraded to one counter with two female assistants.

Most of the Yanks had gone home taking the wives they had met here (known as GI Brides) with them leaving many an aching heart, and sometimes a more personal reminder than a drawer full of silk stockings. The girls they left behind were roundly condemned by those who often had little justification for they too had strayed from the straight and narrow but their philanderings had been with British Forces. Human nature being what it is it was only to be expected, especially in such uncertain times, for they were in the flush of youth and wanting to be loved. Some had not heard from their husbands for months and could only assume they were still alive if they had not received the dreaded 'regret to inform you' letter. Others claimed that they had been released from their commitment by enlightened spouses who realised that marital abstinence for up to three years was unnatural and put their wives under stress. Whatever the reason, infidelity had become a national disease.

A couple of atom bombs brought the Pacific War to an abrupt ending and then former prisoners of Japanese war camps returned home looking emaciated and ill, so undernourished they were just like the bags of bones we had seen at the cinema in the Nazi extermination camps. They caused a wave of outrage and indignation but when the veterans of the Burma campaign began to arrive after three years abroad without leave there was an even greater outcry. Those infamous Astor sisters who had been Hitler's biggest admirers wanted them to be kept out of the country, calling them the 'Syphilitic Army of the East'. Poor blighters, they had been fighting in the jungle at unheard of places like Imphal and Kohima and with Wingate's Chindits behind enemy lines where mail, when it eventually caught up with them, came in bundles at a time for each man. No wonder their wives had not heard from them! Arriving home many found offspring that could not possibly be theirs or children who did not recognise the fathers they had not seen for so long. The nation showed them they were not the 'Forgotten Army' (as they called themselves) and vented their fury on the despicable Astors who should have been locked up when war broke out.

We were under no illusion that our war was to be the 'War to end all Wars' as was the hope in 1918 but when relations with Russia deteriorated to near breaking point many believed that we should soon be at war again. We felt the first chill of the Cold War when the Berlin Airlift began and for a while I had hopes that I might be recalled to the RAF. I was out of luck for time passed and although there was still tension in the air it became clear that the prospect of nuclear war was too awful to contemplate. Strange that the ultimate weapon should also be the ultimate deterrent.

I regularly picked up Dan from his parents' general shop in Darnall, Sheffield. We went out for a drink and I found he was also unsettled and jobless. Mum had always fancied running a shop and I liked the idea of being my own boss so we viewed several before settling on one in Harworth, a pit village seven miles from Donny. It was owned by an ex-steeplejack who had fallen from a high chimney and married the woman who had nursed him back to fragile health. As she was much younger than him, he had bought the shop as an interest for her and now the war was over they were retiring to the coast. We arranged to rent the premises for an initial term of three years by which time we hoped we could afford to buy them. They would sell us the 'Goodwill', fixtures and fittings so it suited me nicely for my gratuity was under £250 and Mum and Dad were going to loan me the rest. Only after I moved in did I discover the snag – 'Goodwill' included a points system based on pre-war sales that now governed the supply of stock to the shop. The allocation for a business that had been no more than a sideline was so small that the profit on it was not enough to live on. It was a challenge I enthusiastically accepted and I threw myself into building up the business. I had one attribute that I learned in the Service that might stand me in good stead – scrounging! My old parachute packer 'Smithy' had been an excellent tutor, but having parted from his wife he had left Donny and was probably now in London. I imagined him as King of the Spivs with a toothbrush moustache, a kipper tie and zoot suit but I remembered what he had taught me. I scrounged, wheedled, cajoled and pleaded. I tried new lines, obtained franchises from the major toy and tobacco firms, and scoured the country for supplies until I turned a potential disaster into a thriving concern. I worked my socks off until my shop became known by men as *the* tobacconist for cigs, pipe and chewing tobacco, by ladies as *the* confectioner and children far beyond the village itself knew it as 'Gosling's, *the* Toyshop'. No wonder as every Friday after lunch I had queues of men waiting for an ounce of light shag and twenty proper cigs (not those horrid half Turkish Pashas) out of the 20 lbs I got weekly – a deal I had negotiated with a local wholesaler. For the ladies I had the best chocolates, biscuits, Lyons cakes, Walls ice cream and discreetly sold dozens of hair dyes. For the boys I had Meccano, Hornby windup and electric trains, Triang toys, bikes, pedal cars and scooters and for the girls lovely dolls, prams and teddy bears. When we went to buy the property at the end of the three-year lease its price had tripled. 'You're doing well,' I was told. 'It's worth that and more.' So we settled before he demanded a further increase.

All this I achieved without trading on my DFC for no civilian, only officers still in uniform, was allowed to make mention of it until recently. It was unfair, petty and bureaucracy at its silly worst for no one would wear a medal ribbon on a civilian suit.

However, I had not made this transformation alone for halfway through the process I had acquired my greatest asset, a blonde beauty called Irene eight years younger than me who became my wife. She came from a Sheffield working class family and instead of being an only child I suddenly inherited a whole new family of her mum and dad and eight siblings whom I found delightful. Mum took to her immediately and loved her dearly; she became the daughter Mum might have bore but dare not because of her displaced hip. Moreover, as Mum was now in failing health, she instinctively knew that this twenty-one-year-old slip of a girl would look after 'Our Dennis' with the same love and care she had lavished on me. I had always been a 'Ladies' Man' but not in the usual context for I had been born into a predominantly female family of Mum, Grandma Ogley and Mum's two sisters, Polly and Elsie, who had no children of their own. I spent so much time with them that Dad put his foot down complaining that he did not see enough of me. No wonder I have always felt at ease among women and all my life I have thanked them for instilling in me a sensitivity so often lacking in my male friends. I soon found that Irene's female intuition (but I believe it was her sensitivity) made her a better judge of character than me and she was so rarely mistaken I came to rely on her judgement. She was warm, beautiful, clever and charismatic with the common touch yet she was always the lady. We regularly sat on the 'top table' at functions large and small, informal and official, where she was as much at ease conversing with the high and mighty as making the humble feel at home. She was the perfect hostess and I was a lucky, lucky man for we were so close we were as one and for forty-eight years she gave me her love and constant support. I adored her, she was *special*! Now I am only half a man, lost without her guidance and lonely without having her by my side for we always were together.

I still missed the Service so much I tried to enrol with the South Yorkshire Auxiliary Squadron but they were converting to single-seat fighters. In desperation I joined 2008 Squadron ATC based at No. 1 Bomber Group HQ at Bawtry Hall, commanded their Detachment at Maltby Grammar School and taught gliding at Doncaster Airport. Irene and I went to their yearly training camp at Locking (Weston Super Mare) where I instructed the cadets how to use their parachutes before loading them into an old Anson. At the end of the day the pilot asked the officers if they would like a flight and guess who was first inside? Seated beside him I was soon at the controls beating up a destroyer at anchor in the bay. Most of the officers were civilians who had never been in the RAF and thinking that I was putting their lives at risk they reported me and I got a telling off from the CO who had never been a Serviceman either (he was the Managing Director of Barnsley Brewery, which I suppose could be loosely classified as war work). To hell with him, I could not have cared less, I had flown again and for a short while I had felt the same old thrill.

The highlight of our week was a visit to Danny's parents who lived nearby and being so close gave me an opportunity I could not miss. We could see little of Curry Rivel for there was a thick fog and I was glad to find the local pub where I asked for directions to his home. I explained the purpose of my foray into the wilds of Somerset and the landlord said 'I used to be in the RAF, come back after you have seen them and have a drink.' In the dusk we followed his directions, up a driveway lined with dense bushes to a large Victorian house. It had a heavily studded front door and when we rapped with the large iron knocker it resounded eerily as if the house was empty. Then we heard the echo of dogs barking and bolts being drawn until the door creaked open slightly and a woman's head peered round it. I told her who I was and opening the door wide she asked us in. Ushering two spaniel dogs away she took us down a hallway dimly lit by a single naked bulb to a room where her husband sat in a winged armchair. What a room it was! The walls were covered in mounted foxes' heads, brushes, hunting regalia and unusual potted plants littered the heavy ornate furniture. The room was so cluttered that she had to hurriedly clear a seat for us before she could tell him who we were. He jumped up, shook my hand heartily, thanked me profusely for seeking them out, and asked what we would have to drink. Clearing papers from the table she put huge gin and tonics before us and when they pressed another on us, had they not been such nice people, we might have suspected they were trying to drug us. It was all so Transylvanian – the fog, the dripping driveway, the echoing building, the creaking door and this room were straight out of a Dracula film. We talked for an hour or so, he mostly about the Hunt of which he was Master, and I understood for he clearly found it difficult to talk of Danny. When we made our apologies and prepared to leave he disappeared for a moment and came back with a small packet in his hand. 'Of all his mates you are the only one who has come to see us,' he said. 'These negatives were in his top pocket when they recovered his …' and his voice trailed away. 'They are pictures he took in Malta. Would you like them?' As touched as him I took them and we left them with their grief. Some of these photos are in this book; the film was blue with seawater and you can see the marks made by the cleaning. The question was 'Why were they in his pocket?' Did he keep them there as a talisman or did he have a premonition?

We made our way to the pub where the landlord greeted us like old friends. He brought out 1934 photos of him as a gunner in an old Wapiti, with no half wing and just the rank of Leading Aircraftsman typical of those days. The aircraft had crashed on landing, he lost a leg and was invalided out, but he felt that all aircrew were special and he was still one of them. He and his wife were ex-Charleston champions and his party piece was to swing his wooden leg over her head. After closing time we went into the kitchen and continued drinking his excellent ale until there was a knock on the door. Quick as a flash he gathered up our glasses and put them in the oven beside the fireplace before he opened the door. When he saw it was the local bobby he said 'Why didn't you give us "I tiddly iti pom pom" you clot?'Out came the beer from the oven and we all sat drinking till dawn. What a night – we supped gallons of ale, and we discovered what wonderful people they were.

From time to time news of old friends filtered through to me. First I heard that lovely man Sandy Carmichael, my former 604 Squadron Flight Commander, had been killed in a car crash in Germany. It did not surprise me for he never stopped at crossroads; he reckoned that way he got across so quickly there was less chance of being hit. He would never ask me to sing for him again when we flew together. That quiet man Johnnie Quinton, another of my 604 Squadron pals, had won a posthumous George Medal for giving his parachute to an ATC cadet who was having a ride in his Wellington. Hastily he had shown the cadet how to work the parachute and pushed him out before the plane had crashed and Johnnie had been killed. Scuttlebutt also had it that the odious Adjutant from Defford had been 'dismissed the Service' having been seen engaged in sexual activity with a WAAF officer through the steamed up windows of his car parked outside the Officers' Mess. After my confrontation with him over my towels I sincerely hoped the rumour was true and that our benefactor in the petrol fiasco had made the arrest. Both Michael Constable-Maxwell and Desmond Hughes had desk jobs in London and the last I heard were taking pot shots at each other with their revolvers in the corridors of the Air Ministry.

Many, many years later some friends brought a Maltese couple to my home and I fished out a number of souvenirs I had kept of my time on the island. Amongst them I found John Gatt's last letter to me, which I had never answered as I was invalided out to Egypt. I expressed my regret for my oversight and noting the address on the letterhead they said they lived quite near there and would try to contact him. They eventually wrote to say they had been unsuccessful for Gatt is as common as Smith is here so I wrote to *The Times of Malta* to explain my quest. Immediately I got three replies. One was from John's little brother Joe and one from the little girl who had been shown such deference by my gang. She was now the Noble Mrs Mavina Portelli who said she remembered me from when I was billeted with her uncle, the Baron Testaferrata. The last was from John who was coming that week to Barts Hospital in London for a heart operation. So I went to see him there, learnt that he was a Jesuit Priest who had spent his life as a missionary in India and I had the pleasure of his company often in the succeeding years.

To show off my new wife I sought Gordon at his old address in Oldham but he had left and after many enquiries we were told he had moved to a large house on a new estate on the outskirts. He was pleased to see us and he told us he regularly went abroad for his firm as was evidenced by the Eastern rugs and artefacts that adorned his home. I asked where his wife was and he said 'In hospital, she has got terminal cancer and my lad is at Manchester Grammar School. He wants to be a doctor.' Where had I heard that before? Oh yes, that had been my ambition and what was I now? A shop keeper! I hoped he would have better fortune than me. Crossing the Pennines in the dark on our way home I was quiet and Irene, sensing my mood, did not break into my thoughts. I was recalling the lovely times I had boating on the river at Tewkesbury when his 'lad' was a baby and his wife a radiant mother. I was shocked by his dreadful news and I wondered if there was any justice in this world. It led me to think of the cruel fate that had befallen so many I had known in the RAF and eventually to ponder on my own career. What had my time in the Service done for me – or to me?

It was not easy but how could I regret the years I had spent in the Service when I would have been learning a trade that had now virtually ceased to exist. Just before the war I had passed the entry requirements for the London School of Economics and by now I might well have become an MP for I had been sounded out by the local Labour Party. A bus driver's son who became a war hero and had now made his way as a successful business man was manna from heaven for them. I was not really interested in politics but think of it, I could have spent years as a member of the Opposition. The RAF had taken the best years of my life but in return they had made a callow hick from the sticks into a worldly wise man. True, the process had been brutal at times, heart breaking at others, but it had taught me how to face almost anything with aplomb. I had spent years learning skills that were of no benefit to me but I had become resolute and self reliant where before I would have been overwhelmed. The pros and cons were endless but I felt it had made a better man of me the hard way and in the main I was happy with what I had become. Best of all to my Mum, Dad and Irene I was still 'Our Dennis' and that was all I had ever really wanted to be.

Slowly I came to accept that my flying days were over and I applied myself to making my mark in a new life. We left Harworth and I became the Sub Postmaster of Eckington, near Sheffield, and joined the National Federation of Sub Postmasters where I found an outlet for my combative talents. The RAF had given me confidence to face the future with a smile and I took to this new environment like a duck (or a Gosling) takes to water. There we met many nice people who over a period of time paid me the compliment I most treasured – they called me 'Our Dennis'!

I had known the indescribable joys of flying, swooping and wheeling free as a bird, racing low over the sea, soaring above the highest mountains, but for me the nights had always been the best. Wondrous nights when a full moon lit up the towering cumulus like fairy castles or made a fluffy quilt of the stratus below me, the glittering stars with no smog to dull their brilliance, seeing the timeless mystical battlements of Malta. It was another world, a world of my own, for when the weather was foul the RAF had taught me how to become its master. I had lived in places I would never have visited, and known the comradeship of men I would remember for as long as I lived. Oh yes, the RAF had done me proud. I thanked whoever it was taking care of me for letting me enjoy my Great Adventure – well, most of it!

Epilogue

Dear Reader,

Historians write of great battles of the past with the benefit of hindsight and all the details known only to the High Command at the time. The men taking part in these conflicts knew nothing of the overall picture and sometimes precious little of even the bit they were involved in. The men on the ground and in the air were so fully occupied struggling for survival that they had no time to wonder about the grand scenario – that was for the Generals. So it was with me, and I decided to tell you the story of we underlings that was just as compelling yet more personal and to my mind more interesting than any war book. I wanted you, my readers, to relive my experiences as they happened to me. I wanted to take you by the hand and have you walk beside me through the joy and the pain, share the laughs and the heartache, take pleasure in the triumphs and agonise with me when things went wrong. I wanted you to understand what life was like for working class people before the war and how it influenced so much of my Service life. I knew it was foolish to think that a literary novice like me could achieve this ambitious aim and that I had set myself a tough task but throughout I have tried. To this end I steadfastly refused to consult any reference books and as I am not on the internet I would have to rely solely on my logbook. I need not have worried for therein I found entries with exact dates and comments, everything I needed to bring the memories flooding back. For almost a year working on my PC with one finger I have tried so hard to make you realise that every word I have written is a true account of how, when or why it all happened. If I have made you feel it happened not just to *me* but to *us* my cup would overflow with joy. I truly hope I have!

Dennis Gosling

Postscript

I looked at the Foreword in my book. That's it I thought, I've done it, my story for all to see. Then, sixty-four years after the event my friend Joe Pickin, a former RAF Adjutant, now ninety and an accomplished artist, brought me the citation for my award. It was the first time I had seen it because the *London Gazette* was not available in France. It read:

> GOSLING, Dennis, W.O. 999332, 604 Sqd. This Officer has participated in many sorties. He is an extremely efficient Observer and has assisted in the destruction of 6 enemy aircraft. His keenness and devotion to duty have been unfailing.

I do not know if a book is supposed to have a Postscript but I have always strived to have the last word. Wing Commander Desmond Hughes had moved swiftly to get me the award I had long awaited and I strongly suspect he had a hand in the wording of the text so I am not only glad but proud to concede *this* last word to the lovely gallant man!

Index